CONSUMER
A͟ͅVSM

Sara Miller McCune founded SAGE Publishing in 1965 to support the dissemination of usable knowledge and educate a global community. SAGE publishes more than 1000 journals and over 800 new books each year, spanning a wide range of subject areas. Our growing selection of library products includes archives, data, case studies and video. SAGE remains majority owned by our founder and after her lifetime will become owned by a charitable trust that secures the company's continued independence.

Los Angeles | London | New Delhi | Singapore | Washington DC | Melbourne

Eleftheria J. Lekakis

CONSUMER ACTIVISM

PROMOTIONAL Culture

& RESISTANCE

$SAGE

Los Angeles | London | New Delhi
Singapore | Washington DC | Melbourne

SAGE Publications Ltd
1 Oliver's Yard
55 City Road
London EC1Y 1SP

SAGE Publications Inc.
2455 Teller Road
Thousand Oaks, California 91320

SAGE Publications India Pvt Ltd
B 1/I 1 Mohan Cooperative Industrial Area
Mathura Road
New Delhi 110 044

SAGE Publications Asia-Pacific Pte Ltd
3 Church Street
#10-04 Samsung Hub
Singapore 049483

Editor: Michael Ainsley
Editorial assistant: Rhoda Ola-Said
Production editor: Sarah Sewell
Copyeditor: William Baginsky
Proofreader: Bryan Campbell
Marketing manager: Lucia Sweet
Cover design: Francis Kenney
Typeset by: C&M Digitals (P) Ltd, Chennai, India

© Eleftheria J. Lekakis 2022

Apart from any fair dealing for the purposes of research, private study, or criticism or review, as permitted under the Copyright, Designs and Patents Act, 1988, this publication may not be reproduced, stored or transmitted in any form, or by any means, without the prior permission in writing of the publisher, or in the case of reprographic reproduction, in accordance with the terms of licences issued by the Copyright Licensing Agency. Enquiries concerning reproduction outside those terms should be sent to the publisher.

Library of Congress Control Number: 2022932491

British Library Cataloguing in Publication data

A catalogue record for this book is available from the British Library

ISBN 978-1-5297-2310-6
ISBN 978-1-5297-2309-0 (pbk)

CONTENTS

Endorsements ix
About the Author xi
Acknowledgements xiii

1 Consumer Activism: An Introduction 1

    The End of Consumerism as We Know It? 1
    Promotional Cultures and Resistance: Activism against and
        through Consumerism and Advertising 4
    What This Book Does 8
    Structure of the Book 11
    Conclusion 14

2 Conceptualizing Consumer Activism 17

    Introduction: Can Individuals Save the Planet or Ourselves? 17
    Approaches to Consumer Activism 19
        Political Science 20
        International Development 21
        Sociology 21
        Cultural and Communication Studies 23
        Critical Marketing Studies 24
        Summarizing Approaches to Consumer Activism 24
    Agencies of Consumer Activism 26
        Citizens: Reduce, Reuse, Recycle 26
        Market Actors: From Brand Activism to Green/Pink/Woke/Carewashing 28
        Celebrities: From Promoting Change to Promoting
            Consumption and Vice Versa 30
        Subvertisers: From Lone Jammers to Collective Movements 31
    Media and Consumer Activism: Methods and Approaches 33
        Ecologies 35
        Publicities 37
        Responsibilities 38
    Conclusion 40

3 Nationalism, Race, Ethnicity, and Consumer Activism — 45

- Introduction: Can a Consumer Save the National Economy? — 45
- Key Concepts — 46
  - Race and Ethnicity — 47
  - Nations and Nationalism — 48
- Nationalism and Consumption: Key Theories — 50
  - Banal Nationalism and Everyday Nationhood — 52
  - Economic Nationalism — 54
  - Consumer Nationalism — 56
  - Nationalism, 'Backlash Politics', and Consumer Activism — 57
  - There is Nothing Post-Racial about Consumer Activism — 58
- Critical Issues — 60
  - The importance of history, especially social history, in relation to race and ethnicity — 60
  - The importance of nationalism as banal ideology — 61
  - The importance of agency — 61
  - The importance of justice — 62
- Researching Consumer Activism and Nationalism: Methodologies — 62
- Case Study: Consumer Activism in Hong Kong's Yellow Economic Circle — 64
  - Some Context about the Dispute between Hong Kong and China — 64
  - Yellow Economic Circle — 65
  - Analysing the Yellow Economic Circle through Consumer Activism and Nationalism — 66
  - The Hong Kong economy and the impact of the Yellow Economic Circle — 67
- Questions for Future Case Studies — 67
- Conclusion — 68

4 Gender, Feminism and Consumer Activism — 73

- Introduction: Can Gender Justice Be Progressed through Consumer Activism? — 73
- Key Concepts — 74
  - Gender — 74
  - From Feminism to Postfeminism? — 76
- Feminism and Consumption: Key Theories — 78
  - Gender and Political Consumerism — 79
  - Feminism and the Politics of Consumption — 80
- Critical Issues — 85
- Researching Consumer Activism and Feminism: Methodologies — 87
- Case Study: When a Chocolate Brand Sells Love and Diversity — 89
  - Some Context about Feminism and LGBTQ Justice in Greece — 89
  - Background on the Lacta Brand and Its Advertising History — 90

The #ActForLove Campaign	91
Analysing #ActForLove as Commodity Activism	92
Questions for Future Case Studies	93
Conclusion	94

5 Consumer Activism in the Environment — 97

Introduction: Can We Consume Ourselves out of the Climate Crisis?	97
Key Concepts	98
Climate Change, Sustainable Development and Alternatives	98
Sustainable Consumption, Green Consumerism and Alternatives	99
Theory: Environmentally Conscious Consumption as Consuming Less and Differently	101
The Politics of Green Consumerism and Sustainable Consumption	102
Media Discourses, Technologies, and the Environmental Paradox	106
Critical Issues	108
Researching Consumer Activism and Environmentalism: Methodologies	110
Case Study: The Environmental Politics of Smartphone Consumption	112
What's Behind the Screen? The Environmental Cost of Smartphones and Obsolescence Injustice	112
What Can consumers Do? Environmental Consumer Activism and Smartphones	114
Questions for Future Case Studies	116
Conclusion	117

6 Celebrity Advocacy and Consumer Activism — 121

Introduction: Who Wants to be an… 'Activist'?	121
Key Concepts	123
Celebrity	123
Media, Celebrity, and Ordinary People	123
Celebrity Advocacy and Celebrity Humanitarianism: 'Charitainment' and Beyond	125
Key Theories: Celebrities, Causes, and Consumption	126
From Band Aid to Brand Aid	126
Celebrity Authenticity vs Accountability	128
Simplified Causes and Consumer-Friendly Solutions	131
North/South Relations	133
Celebrity Advocacy in the South	135
Critical Issues	137
Researching Celebrity Advocacy and Consumer Activism: Methodologies	139
Case Study: Celebrity Chef Jamie Oliver and Youth-Led Advocacy for Healthy Eating in the UK	140

	Celebrity Chef Jamie Oliver and Health Advocacy in the UK	140
	Appraising Jamie Oliver's Celebrity Advocacy	142
	Bite Back 2030: Celebrity-Backed, Youth-Led, and Health-Related Advocacy Organization	143
	Celebrity Chef and Bite Back 2030 Campaign for Advertising Regulation and against Obesity	144
	Campaign Impact	144
	Questions for Future Case Studies	146
	Conclusion	146

7 Subvertising as Anti-Consumerism — 151

Introduction: Can We Protest Consumerism through Advertising? — 151
Key Concepts — 153
    Culture Jamming — 154
    Subvertising — 155
Key Theories — 155
    Anti-Consumerism and Ideology — 155
    Society of the Spectacle Past and Present: Ethical, Fascist, Commercial Spectacles — 156
    Culture Jamming: Incorporation, Play, Participation and Pedagogy, Law — 158
Critical Issues — 167
Researching Anti-Consumerism and Subvertising: Methodologies — 169
Case Study: Resistance is Female — 171
    Analysing Resistance is Female through Anti-Consumerism and Culture Jamming — 174
    The Impact of Resistance is Female — 176
Questions for Future Case Studies — 178
Conclusion — 178

8 Conclusion — 183

So What? — 183
Summary of Debates: Markets, Consumers, and Media Technologies — 185
Consumer Activism and Beyond: Resistance Practices in Promotional Culture — 188
Activism and Consumption: Possibilities, Limitations, and Ambiguities — 191

Appendix — 195
References — 197
Index — 227

ENDORSEMENTS

Consumer Activism discusses in an interesting way the complexities of and dilemmas involved in using the market as an arena for politics. Eleftheria Lekakis argues for putting more scholarly emphasis on the global South and considering more systematically the role of nationalism, race, ethnicity, gender, feminism, and environmentalism in this form of activism. Thought-provoking examples on these topics are included in the book. Importantly, the book focuses on the role of celebrity and corporate promotion, and even anti-consumerist activism. The term 'consumer solutionism' is coined to emphasize the limitations of consumer activism as a central means of contemporary resistance today. This book adds additional perspectives to the study of political consumerism.

    Michele Micheletti, Professor Emerita in Political Science, Stockholm University

Consumers of the world, unite! *Consumer Activism* is both an excellent intellectual reference and a savvy guide for educators and students. Eleftheria Lekakis reminds us that as consumers, we can do much more than just buy our way out of social or political problems. Through creative and collective efforts, consumers can work to end unfair and inequitable market practices and can promote concerted action on such major issues as climate change, racial justice or women's rights. Rich with key concepts, contemporary themes, and provocative case studies, this book will foster necessary conversations about power and politics in consumer culture.

    Melissa Aronczyk, Associate Professor of Media Studies, Rutgers University

This book offers a crucial intervention to both critical studies of consumption and action research into activism. It authoritatively explores the complex and multiplying links between branding and neoliberal culture, consumer practices and social justice, and calls for an urgent renegotiation of ethics in response. *Consumer Activism* will be an indispensable resource for research and pedagogy in the urgent years ahead, as humanity reckons with the effects of climate change, deepening inequality, and increasingly feverish consumption.

    Mehita Iqani, South African Research Chair in Science Communication, Stellenbosch University

An interesting, well written, and thoughtful book that by posing particular emphasis on advertising and promotional communication addresses the complex question of why consumers, especially in wealthy nations, keep overconsuming by virtually ignoring the consequences on other people and our planet. Eleftheria Lekakis critically explores alternatives and opportunities for resistance by focusing on practices of consumer activism aimed at raising awareness and promoting more just and sustainable uses of the marketplace.

      Francesca Forno, Associate Professor of Sociology, University of Trento

ABOUT THE AUTHOR

Eleftheria Lekakis is Senior Lecturer/Associate Professor in Media and Communications at the School of Media, Arts and Humanities at the University of Sussex. Her research focuses on communication, consumer culture, and politics. Her first book, *Coffee Activism and the Politics of Fair trade and Ethical Consumption in the Global North*, explored the relationship between fair trade consumption and political participation. She has also co-edited *Art, Law, Power*, a volume on the intersections of artistic practice and resistance in relation to the law. Her published work has appeared in journals such as the *Journal of Consumer Culture, Popular Communication, Social Movement Studies*, as well as edited collections such as the *Sage Handbook of Consumer Culture*, the *Oxford Handbook of Political Consumerism*, and the *Routledge Handbook of Advertising and Promotional Culture*. Eleftheria teaches on topics related to advertising and promotional culture, as well as media and social change. Eleftheria has been a visiting scholar at the University of Pennsylvania, University of Bergamo, and Universitat Pompeu Fabra.

ACKNOWLEDGEMENTS

It takes a community to write a book. This one is the culmination of fifteen years of research on the topic and plentiful conversations with colleagues, students, and friends throughout this period. That being said, any mistakes or misreadings in this book are obviously mine and mine alone.

Warm thanks to my commissioning editor Michael Ainsley for the long meeting in Leicester that helped note the brushstrokes of the book, and for his stable, snappy, and supportive comments throughout the process.

Gracious thank you to José Fernández-Cavia and the Department of Communication at the Universidad Pompeu Fabra for their hospitality during the summer of 2019, which provided a most fruitful ground for setting the book in motion. It takes time and space to plan and plot a book, and I was generously granted that.

I have genuinely appreciated vivid discussions with students on the MA Media Practice for Development and Social Change at the University of Sussex from 2013 to 2019. Thank you for thought-provoking conversations about the urgency, challenges, and operations of social change across the world. Particular thanks to former student Júlia Dotras for alerting me to the near-reality programme *The Activist* that opens Chapter 6. It has also been truly exciting to run the postgraduate module Promotional Culture, where students have shared so many experiences and examples from around the world.

Grateful thanks to colleagues who have provided feedback on various versions of this work: Caroline Bassett, Alexandra Cosima Budabin, Stefania Charitou, Andreas Chatzidakis, Marina Dekavalla, Simidele Dosekun, Flor Enghel, Katherine Farrimond, Lambros Fatsis, Ben Highmore, Kim Humphery, Mehita Iqani, César Jiménez-Martínez, Tim Jordan, Tanya Kant, Kate Lacey, Sara Liao, Jo Littler, Kate O'Riordan, Pollyanna Ruiz, Fidèle A. Vlavo, and last but never least, Photini Vrikki.

I will always extend deep gratitude to my parents and siblings who remain a source of love and support in ever-changing ways. Finally, devoted thank you to Nikos for pushing me to think outside the comfort of disciplines, for warming up everyday life, and for raising our family with me. The journey continues.

ONE
CONSUMER ACTIVISM: AN INTRODUCTION

The End of Consumerism as We Know It?

It seems we are massively entering a quarantine of consumption.
(Li Edelkoort, trend forecaster)[1]

March 2020 marks the end of consumerism as we've come to know it.
(Lyndsey Fox, VP of strategy at Allen & Gerritsen)[2]

How did you shop during the 2020–21 lockdowns? Since the emergence of the COVID-19 pandemic, strange things have been happening in the world of consumption and consumer culture. Concurrent trends of mass consumerism in the form of panic buying or pandemic-therapy buying existed alongside anti-consumerism in the form of thrifting or overall abstaining. Politicians, as they do in times of crisis, urged us to consume, but this time responsibly. Thinking of others, some consumers followed calls to 'buy local', as lists with independent businesses in their locales circulated. Some people followed Extinction Rebellion's (XR) call to Boycott Fashion for a year. State and market actors heralded frontline workers (inclusive of supermarket and store cashiers and delivery workers) as the 'heroes' of the pandemic. At the same time, fast fashion online retailers saw sales soar, while the world started shopping on the Chinese e-commerce platform Alibaba. Online shopping skyrocketed and brands increased their investment in social media to provide entertainment content and 'authentic' experiences to consumers. Marketers became inclined to come even closer to (financially) pressed and (politically) pressurizing consumers and embrace 'consumer activism', especially in terms of how brands treat people within their workforce and in the community. The extent to which COVID-19 influenced individual and corporate behaviour and responsibility in the marketplace remains a crucial question.

Rather than considering such impacts of the pandemic as sudden changes, it is best to consider them as amplifications of what was already there: the urgency of climate change, the invisibility of increasing injustice, the polarizing effect of a failed neoliberal politics, the interdependence of the global South and global North, and the questionable role of consumers as agents of social and environmental change. In Bangladesh, the garment industry was exempt from the national lockdown. Workers in fast fashion supply chains were the invisible and unsung 'heroes' of consumption under COVID-19. In spring 2020, seven years after the Rana Plaza disaster,[3] UK fast fashion retailers severed their orders from the Bangladeshi garment industry, leaving over a million workers without pay or job security. Ongoing campaigns from organizations such as Fashion Revolution, Clean Clothes, and Labour behind the Label have been raising attention to the hazardous and precarious conditions under which garment workers (mostly women) have been operating during the pandemic.[4] Despite the state and corporate rhetoric of care, and the salutations to frontline workers, their own position as precarious subjects prevails. In the United Kingdom, millions of people have experienced severe food insecurity during COVID 19, according to a report by the country's Food Standards Agency (2021), but food shortages were prevalent long before the pandemic. Meanwhile, throughout the 20th century, the average income of the global 10 per cent has remained at least 38 times higher than that of the bottom 50 per cent,[5] while billionaires' wealth rose by a third during the pandemic.[6] Across the global South and global North, there is at least a third of food wasted at the post-harvest or processing stages and the retail or consumer stages respectively (UNEP, 2021). Overall, research suggested that by 2020, the mass of stuff we have made (concrete, metal, plastic, bricks, and asphalt) is greater than the mass of living matter on the planet.[7]

Why does mass consumerism persist? In China, Alibaba has transformed Singles' Day from a celebration of singlehood to the world's largest shopping event that celebrates togetherness through consumption (Sun and Creech, 2019). In the United States, since 2015, Amazon has created its own consumer 'holiday' (Prime Day) which by 2021 was observed in 20 countries and accompanied by shows featuring celebrity musicians. According to Amazon, US sales during Prime Day 2019 surpassed the previous Black Friday and Cyber Monday combined[8] (though Singles' Day had already surpassed them in 2021).[9] Black Friday (traditionally also a US consumer 'holiday' that has also expanded in several countries), and Cyber Monday (the online equivalent that follows) raise serious concerns as to their environmental impact. In 2020, Cyber Monday was expected to be 'the biggest digital sales day in history in the United States'.[10] Mass consumerism, amplified by online shopping and subsequent shipping has significant carbon footprints. According to The Dirty Delivery Report, UK deliveries for Black Friday in 2020 produced the equivalent carbon of 435 return flights between London and New York, or the weight of 61,308 elephants (Haqqi, 2020). There are, on the other hand, anti-consumer holidays such as Buy Nothing Day and Buy Nothing Christmas in North America, while environmental organizations have created programmes for more sustainable consumption such as Simplify the Holidays by the Center for Biological Diversity. Alternatives to mass consumerism in the form of anti-consumerism, responsible, or reduced consumerism exist. Yet the state of the planet suggests that these might not be enough. So, why do we keep consuming? This complex question cannot be answered by addressing a universal 'we'. Consumers in the global North and in highly industrialized countries such as China have heavier environmental footprints than those in the global South. What is wrong with mass consumerism? What are its alternatives? What opportunities exist for resistance? These are the key concerns that animate this book.

Connecting consumerism with advertising and contesting their dominance is one way of addressing the politics of consumption, which is at the heart of this book. A report commissioned by the UK grassroots network AdFree Cities and entitled *At What Cost?* (Harrop, 2021) reviews the impact of advertising and consumerism on human, community, and planetary wellbeing. This revealing report includes a series of important facts such as, for instance, that in 2020 advertisers globally spent 14 times the money needed to support record levels of humanitarian assistance (Harrop, 2021). It identifies key direct and indirect negative impacts of advertising and connects the unruly threads of mass consumerism to the politics of promotion: from gender stereotyping sexualization of children, greenhouse gas emissions, and promotion of materialistic values, advertising is strategic communication that we can and should protect ourselves against through international human rights treaties (ibid.). Across the world, collectives and networks are connecting advertising and promotional communication with routine mass consumerism to articulate a critique that merges with race, gender, and environmental justice. What challenges does activism targeting advertising pose on mass consumerism?

Overworked garment workers, exhausted delivery workers, visible heroes, invisible injustices, heightened carbon footprints, and e-waste (the discard of electronics that are consistently among the most popular purchases during Prime Day), which is the fastest growing form of domestic waste. Yet there is more and more information enabling consumers to use the marketplace to pursue political ends. Where does this all leave us? This book builds on work that questions what constitutes activism through consumption and the extent to which it can be mobilized for social and environmental change. It shows how important it is to study consumer activism as a set of practices through interdisciplinary perspectives that reveal a politics of nationalism, race, gender, and the environment, as well as to explore intermediaries of consumerism (celebrities) and anti-consumerism (subvertisers). Consumer activism ranges from practising politics in the marketplace (through boycotting or 'buycotting') to alternative economic practices, lobbying businesses or governments, practising minimal or mindful consumption, or addressing the complicity of advertising in climate change. This book aims to provide a critical interrogation of how citizens, collectives, and corporations use the marketplace for political purposes, and to shed light on what political possibilities can exist within promotional cultures. It identifies affordances and limitations, as well as trends and tensions, and offers a nuanced perspective of the possibilities we are presented with in addressing global social and environmental challenges.

Promotional Cultures and Resistance: Activism against and through Consumerism and Advertising

Consumer activism includes a variety of forms of resistance in contemporary culture, that is conditioned by consumer culture, media culture, and, more broadly, promotional culture. I call it 'consumer' activism not because I want to centre or privilege 'the consumer', but to acknowledge and appraise the centrality and impact of consumer practices in contemporary culture. Promotional culture, for Andrew Wernick (1991) is the result of the increasing and pervasive influence of advertising on all forms of communication, which has spearheaded the centrality of the market in all aspects of social life. Promotional culture is a portmanteau term for the exploration of processes, practices, agents, technologies, and ethics involved in consumption. In other words, promotional culture is contemporary culture to the extent that promotional industries (advertising, PR, marketing, and branding) define the way individuals, states, and civil society organizations communicate and engage with one another in relationships mediated by promotionalism (Cronin, 2018; Edwards, 2018). In the words of Alison Hearn, 'promotionalism is the dominant symbolic language and mode of expression of advanced corporate commodity capitalism, and branding practices and consumer campaigns are the places where the dominant mode of production, transnational corporate capitalism, literally and figuratively *becomes* culture' (2012: 28). There are numerous reasons to remain critical towards promotional culture: the meshing of journalism and advertising (how can we be critical citizens when news is sponsored by advertising?), advertising as entertainment (how can we enjoy leisurely time and expand our imagination without being sold something?), labour in the gig economy (how can we ensure safe and secure labour rights and conditions for workers?), surveillance (how can we understand and uphold our right to privacy?), and the corporatization of higher education (how can we teach and learn without the financial pressures of privatized universities?). Particularly, the role promotional industries play within struggles for social and environmental justice needs to be critically appraised. Are promotional industries and intermediaries performing rather than practising politics? How can we make sense of 'woke' ('alert to injustice and discrimination in society, especially racism'[11]) advertising such as Nike's 'Dream Crazy' ad or Gillette's 'The Best Men Can Be' ad in their strategic communication of racial and gender justice and in light of the backlash they receive by ideological opponents (often consumers). The prevalence of promotional culture, then, also conditions all possibilities for advocating and acting on the grounds of social and environmental justice. Perhaps attempts to address injustice through the marketplace fall short in the noise of promotionalism (communication geared to sell products or promote brands), the algorithmic control of programmatic advertising (the automated buying and selling of online advertising), or the inaccurate, vague, or irrelevant communication of racial justice ('wokewashing') or gender equality ('pinkwashing')? Perhaps there are also opportunities for subversion and redirection of attention to social and environmental justice? The book offers outlines for such answers.

The nature of contemporary promotional cultures is complex, hybrid, and liminal, as Ian Somerville and Lee Edwards argue, adding that 'promotional culture is a continually emergent manifestation of the struggle between agency and structure, a hybrid form of power where the outcome is never certain' (2021: 98). As Melissa Aronczyk also suggests, it is best to avoid deterministic arguments and to examine advertising '*as* communication rather than merely as a fetter upon it' (2021: 115, italics in original). As Aronczyk continues, '[i]t is simply not possible to dismiss promotion when it forms the basis of so much of our sociality: online communication, digital platforms, labour patterns, home and work environments, the gig economy—we are all promotional selves now' (ibid.: 116). How can the powers of promotion be harnessed for progressive social change? A key tension posed by promotional culture is that action within the marketplace is bound to the logics of the marketplace. Indeed, individualized consumer activism is no panacea. I am in agreement with Melissa Aronczyk, Lee Edwards, and Anu Kantola who suggest that it 'cannot replace collective action outside the market; on the contrary, it places the market at the centre of politics and civil society, rather than serving to protect the political sphere from the influence of commerce and private interests' (2017: 142). However, a key argument of this book is that consumer activism does not merely include individualized action. The field of consumer activism as activism against and through consumerism and advertising remains open to progressive and productive possibilities for our shared global futures, and yet it also contains concerns and dangers for progressive consumer politics. Why?

First, consumer activism includes but goes beyond individual habits. Yes, this can include alternative forms of consumption such as preference of ethical (e.g. fair trade, cruelty-free), green (e.g. recycled, upcycled, sustainable), or political (e.g. supporting specific communities) commodities or abstaining from flying or owning a car or from supporting businesses that have questionable environmental policies or records of human rights violations. These (non)consumption choices can present arenas for potential political change in that they can extend beyond individual habits into collective behaviour and community-building (Lekakis, 2013; Stolle and Micheletti, 2015). We also cannot ignore challenges such as individualization through discreet individual practices, commodification through practices of even more consumption, and depoliticization through a focus on promotional market gains. As several scholars have argued, individualized consumer action in the form of ethical consumption can designate citizenship as market agency (Horton and Street, 2021; Humphery and Jordan, 2018), but also, importantly, it ignores income inequalities and is 'structured as economic privilege' (Salonen, 2021: 14). Tad Skotnicki argues that the construction of contemporary activism is linked to the emergence of today's 'sympathetic consumer', a figure that 'harbors a seductive, twofold danger' (2021: 186): the perpetuation of consumerism and a potential nihilism. The question, then, becomes whether consumer activism 'can promote systemic thinking and channel these consumer-centered intuitions toward other types of collective political action or struggle' (ibid.). However, consumer activism also includes practices such as petitioning the government, lobbying for corporate accountability, or organizing public workshops or interest groups. From websites and Change.org petitions to digital apps, the toolkit of consumer activists is broad in scope and intersects with larger historical and contemporary causes. It is important to consider how consumer advocacy also shapes consumer activism.

Second, the centrality of advertising as a means of communication presents fruitful opportunities for advocacy and activism. In terms of advocacy, there is a long history of consumer groups working to safeguard consumer interests and consumer advocacy organizations concerned with consumer safety and product reliability (Lang and Gabriel, 2005). An example of resistance towards promotional culture is US-based Fair Play (previously Campaign for a Commercial-Free Childhood) that advocates for childhood without brands. One of Fair Play's wins has been (temporarily) stopping Facebook from launching 'Instagram Kids' (under 13 years old).[12] Fair Play is not a consumer organization, but a 'nonprofit organization committed to helping children thrive in an increasingly commercialized, screen-obsessed culture, and the only organization dedicated to ending marketing to children'.[13] I want to suggest that such examples of formally or informally organized collectives that challenge brands and consumerism highlight the necessity of conceptualizing 'consumer' rights alternatively; not just from centring consumers, but also asking how promotional culture impacts citizens and how their human rights need to be protected in this context.

Consumer activism also includes creative tactical practices such as culture jamming and subvertising. These are practices of subverting promotional communication to hold brands responsible or proclaim activist causes. Considering anti-consumerist movements is key in understanding resistance in promotional culture. For example, grassroots networks that challenge the negative effects of advertising, as mentioned earlier in the chapter, are in operation from Argentina (Proyecto Squatters) to the UK (AdFree Cities), while individuals and collectives have coalesced into a transnational social movement (Subvertisers International)

(Lekakis, 2021). Additionally, consumer activist practices targeting advertising are increasingly used by social movements. For example, Labour behind the Label, the UK platform of Clean Clothes,[14] has been campaigning for labour justice by supporting workers' demands, holding brands and governments to account behind the scenes and in the streets since 2001. During the COVID-19 pandemic, they have been lobbying retailers to protect workers in their supply chains; their research suggests that workers are owed between £2-4 billion for the first three months of the pandemic, as major brands cancelled or stalled their orders.[15] Furthermore, they exposed irresponsible practices (allegedly operating their Leicester factory in full capacity during lockdown, paying workers £3 per hour, and subjecting them to intimidation) by Boohoo, an e-retailer that has thrived during the pandemic (Labour behind the Label, 2020). The organization ran a subvertising campaign on Instagram during Black Friday 2020;[16] the subverted advertising used Boohoo advertising as the base image adding speech bubbles commenting on illegal labour practices and #payyourworkers (Figure 1.1).

Figure 1.1
Source: www.instagram.com/p/CH-XLgBDhMY (22 November 2021)

A year later, Boohoo published a list of factories it uses around the world in a pledge to transparency.[17] A significant previous win was the organization's instrumental role in getting UK retailers to sign the Bangladesh Accord on Fire and Building Safety,[18] and ensuring that Rana Plaza victims receive long-term compensation. Consumer activism can bring change, through it does not instantly solve the complex issues and injustices that continue to characterize global supply chains.

Bringing these together, my definition of consumer activism is more inclusive than ethical consumption or boycotting. It includes discreet or connected practices of and related to consumption and advertising that range from buying ('buycotting') or not buying (boycotting) products and services to petitioning, campaigning, practising veganism, minimalism or freeganism,[19] targeting advertising, and resisting mass consumerism and the permeation of promotional culture. Thinking about consumption as a set of practices is important to avoid its celebration or condemnation (Sassatelli, 2007). The same goes for consumer activism. To do so, Marlyne Sahakian and Harold Wilhite argue we need to recognize:

> the distributed nature of agency across three pillars: people and the knowledge they embody, both physically and mentally; things or the objects and infrastructures that influence and are influenced by everyday life; and socially grounded contexts, a wide category that includes everything from social norms and values to institutions and legal frameworks. (2014: 39)

In addition, they argue that space and time are important dimensions to social practice theory. The location of practices within localized global spaces and times are key to breaking away from a Northern approach to consumer activism as a phenomenon that is happening 'here' to deal with problems 'there'.

What This Book Does

Scholars have pursued critical questioning of conscious or contentious consumption practices (for a comprehensive review of relevant research see Chapter 2). Yet despite the important interventions, the literature suffers from some fragmentation. This book responds to these, first, by promoting an understanding of agency beyond the problematic citizen–consumer hybrid. The debate has passed from active versus passive consumers to individual versus collective consumer action, and arguments amass concerning the neoliberal demise of the lone consumer activist who self-regulates, and the absence of collective action. Yet the work of collectives around the world focusing on alternative practices and futures suggests otherwise (Ariztia et al., 2016; Lekakis and Forno, 2019). While this book does not provide a global picture, it invites research on this front. Consumer activism agents have proliferated, as promotional culture has expanded to unequivocally engage with social and environmental change. From celebrities to corporations, promotional intermediaries and industries expand their advocacy and activism and bring about persistent questions as to the location and contestation of power within promotional culture. Can, for instance, gender justice be progressed through corporate rhetoric and femvertising (advertising with feminist messaging)? What are the political consequences of celebrities advocating against HIV/AIDS, fast fashion or climate change? Chapters 4 and 6 tackle such questions.

Second, this book provides a comprehensive approach to consumer activism beyond buying (buycotting) or not buying (boycotting) things to express or impact politics through the marketplace. For the most part, the literature has tended to focus on analyses of ethical consumption (e.g. fair trade, cruelty-free) or green consumerism (e.g. toxic-free, recycled commodities). However, as political consumerism theory has progressed, it has uncovered additional practices, such as lifestyle politics (longer investment in ethical lifestyles, such as veganism and voluntary simplicity), and discursive political consumerism (discursive practices addressing consumerism or brands) (Stolle and Micheletti, 2015). This opening up of practices in consumer activism allows us to connect with increasing initiatives focused on curbing, contesting or correcting advertising as dominant culture both in the form of grassroots networks and in the form of digital networks (Braun et al., 2019). Chapters 2 and 7 expand on this enhanced approach.

Third, this book highlights the ambivalence of ideology across different practices of consumer activism. The majority of relevant research tends to focus on consumer activism vis-à-vis progressive social change, though recognizing its entanglement with neoliberal culture. Within the social sciences and the humanities, research on consumption for regressive purposes remains limited. Here, by regressive politics I refer to various brands of conservative politics, typically rejecting progress on social and environmental justice goals. Regressive goals are continuously pursued through the marketplace. For example, consumers rebel against the presence of commodities such as halal meat that remind them of or recognize minority groups in the marketplace (Johnson et al., 2017; Lekakis, 2019; Pecot et al., 2021). There is scope for a critical analysis of racialized manifestations of consumer activism, within struggles for both progressive and regressive politics. Chapter 3 focuses on nationalism, as well as race and ethnicity in the marketplace.

Fourth, the book connects consumer activism to media technologies and activism. The role of information and communication has been key in the formation of consumer activists. Despite the increasing centrality of digital technologies, there is currently limited research on the relationship between consumer activism and media activism (Kampf, 2018; Minocher, 2019; Treré and Yu, 2021). Through online petition sites, hashtag campaigns, apps, and social media platforms, consumer activism finds ground to develop or disappear. To avoid determinist approaches to digital media technologies in the mobilization of consumer activism, this book offers a framework based on practice theory (Chapter 2). In addition, every chapter offers critical issues drawn from theoretical frameworks presented and a reflection on corresponding methodological approaches. Yet it goes even further in questioning the environmental costs of the very technologies that inform, connect, and mobilize. Chapter 5 explores smartphone consumption specifically, reflecting on the device through the lens of environmental consumer activism.

Finally, this book brings attention to the imbalance of studies of consumer activism between the global North and South. It attempts to go beyond a study of consumer activism in the global North. I follow Lisa Ann Richey's perspective in that 'there is no "North" as an empirical place, but rather "North" as a position in a hierarchy between North and South, across levels and geographies' (2016a: 10). Hierarchies of attention in the study of mass consumerism in the global North for instance have tended to exclude its effects in the form of waste across the global South (Iqani, 2020). Like the majority of academic research, studies of activism and consumption are skewed towards the global North, while distorted narratives of consumer culture about the global South prevail (Iqani, 2016). What can we learn from exploring consumer video activism in China (Yu, 2021)? This book is an attempt to address asymmetries of North/South by foregrounding relevant research on the topic and inviting work on this field by offering comprehensive conceptual, theoretical, and methodological guidelines. Its case studies are not global but transnational and refer to contexts that I am more familiar with that are original and animate the frameworks constructed.

The book you have at hand or on your screen contributes to related debates through an innovative approach on consumer activism. First, it connects it to contemporary struggles as they appear in relation to nationalism and ethnic/racial justice, gender in relation to feminism, and the environment in relation to sustainability and environmental justice. Second, it presents a contextual approach to the agents of consumer activism, and a critical appraisal of the increasing politicization of promotional agents (corporations and celebrities). Third, it offers a cautionary tale regarding the ideological goals of consumer activists, not all of whom are fighting for progressive social change. Fourth, it illustrates consumer activism as connected to advertising resistance and promotional culture. Finally, it offers a theoretical and methodological mapping of knowledge produced and original transnational case studies to illustrate how this can be operationalized. This comprehensive exploration of consumer activism has various aims: to place it in historical context; to identify its political potential through its use by different agents and media technologies; to interrogate its relationship with promotional industries, especially advertising; to explore its role within activist toolkits; and to question the extent of its influence. In doing so, I contribute to critical consumption studies (Humphery, 2010; Littler, 2009; Mukherjee and Banet-Weiser, 2012), media activism (Barassi, 2015; Mattoni, 2017; Treré, 2019) and promotional culture (Aronczyk and Powers, 2010; Cronin, 2018; Edwards, 2018). By enhancing and connecting debates within these fields, I propose a comprehensive approach to consumer activism.

Structure of the Book

The next chapter conceptualizes consumer activism within interdisciplinary debates. It highlights how different methodological approaches can yield different perspectives and argues for a practice approach to consumer activism as a holistic approach that accounts for technological affordances, agentic practices, and contingent impact. Through a survey of political science, sociology, development and international relations, critical marketing studies, communication, and cultural studies, I identify key arguments, tensions, and gaps. To illustrate how consumer activism can go beyond an individualistic politics, I then focus on the multiple agents of consumer activism (citizens, corporations, celebrities, subvertisers), while noting how agents connected to promotional industries (corporations and celebrities) can still enjoy privileged visibility. The chapter then explores consumer activism in relation to media technologies by reviewing relevant research regarding digitally enabled or digitally native examples and offers a series of questions for future case studies. It concludes by arguing for the importance of applying a (media) practice perspective (Barassi, 2015; Couldry, 2012; Treré, 2019) to analyses of consumer activism by focusing on ecologies, publicities, and responsibilities.

Each chapter thereafter follows the same format to deliver a comprehensive perspective into consumer activism. They open with a vivid illustration of one or more examples to highlight the operations of consumer activism, and then present relevant key concepts, before moving on to discuss key theories and identify critical issues. Following on, they shed light on different methodological approaches within the literature and appraise an original case study in relation to the topics and themes raised. The discussion and insights are presented in the conclusion. Chapter 3 opens with the question of shopping to support one's national economy, a narrative that tends to be promulgated in times of crisis. It aims to deconstruct the myth of nationalism within the marketplace by questioning 'nations', 'race', and 'ethnicity', and appraises relevant theories (banal nationalism, everyday nationhood, economic nationalism, and consumer nationalism). Overall, it argues that we need to construct a historical framework in relation to the propagation of nationalism (in relation to race and ethnicity) through the marketplace, that there is nothing post-racial (suggestive that race is no longer a significant social issue) about consumer activism, that religion underscores consumer activism, and that history, ideology, agency, and justice matter in conceptualizations of the phenomenon. Its case study is the Yellow Economic Circle, a pro-democracy consumer campaign in Hong Kong, where protesters employed economic resistance in the form of 'buycotting' businesses friendly to their movement, and boycotting businesses that were not, tracing their allegiances through crowd-sourcing information on apps.

Chapter 4 questions whether gender justice can be achieved through consumer activism. Through key concepts (gender, feminism, postfeminism) and theories, it challenges the idea that feminism can be advanced through the market and discusses the issues involved in its marketization (e.g. neo-colonial articulations of feminism that produce binaries between women in the global North and women in the global South, or the simplification of social change through femvertising). The chapter suggests approaches to evaluate the possibilities of consumer activism for gender justice. First, we need to 'gender' consumer activism (to understand how consumption is a field of socioeconomic disparities, gendered divisions of labour, an embodied and affective experience and one which is ridden with meaning through representations prior, during, and after shopping). Second, we need to conceptualize the feminist movement as a collective movement. Third, we need to contextualize gender historically, to think of this beyond the Global North and in relation to post-colonialism, and finally, to identify an intersectional feminist politics. The case study discussed here is one of the first socially conscious advertising campaigns in Greece that celebrated diversity, which was commissioned by a chocolate brand (Lacta).

Chapter 5 questions whether we can consume ourselves out of the climate crisis. Conceptualizing climate change, sustainable development, sustainable consumption and green consumerism, this chapter presents arguments and analysis on environmentally conscious consumption. It revisits the question of an individualized politics of consumption and reappraises the role of media and communications technologies in enabling social change. The chapter highlights an ongoing yet under-researched area of media and communication studies that concerns a paradox: while media technologies are appraised as harbingers of social change, their environmental footprint is impossible to ignore, especially as they contribute to the fastest growing form of domestic waste (e-waste). Critical issues concern, first, the connection of environmentalism to a politics of justice. This is inseparable from movements for labour justice (think of labour conditions in the electronics industries), environmental justice (think of how garbage is shipped to the global South or how within the global North communities of colour are routinely targeted to host facilities such as landfills), and gender justice (think of how households are presented as key sites for sustainable consumption, and how domestic labour remains gendered). Second, green consumerism is a limited option in environmentalism, typically exacerbated by promotional narratives and contingent to the socio-economic positions of consumers. Third, media technologies hold potential for promoting causes, but have significant carbon footprints. Fourth, consuming less is important, as are cultures and politics of repair. The case study presented in this chapter is the smartphone and the limits of consumer activism in relation to its consumption.

Chapter 6 questions how consumer activism has become common practice among promotional intermediaries such as celebrities and influencers. After appraising the concepts of celebrity, ordinary people turned celebrities through media culture, as well as celebrity advocacy and celebrity humanitarianism, this chapter evaluates key theories pertaining to celebrities, causes, and consumption spanning from Band Aid and Brand Aid to question authenticity and accountability, promotion of simplified causes and solutions, and uneven North/South relations. It maps out critical issues relating to the importance of political economy, consumer-friendly simplifications, celebrity in North/South relations, and celebrity as gendered and racialized. The case study discussed is celebrity chef Jamie Oliver and the youth-led advocacy organization Bite Back 2030 that he co-founded, and their campaigning to ban junk food advertising in the UK.

Chapter 7 asks whether and how we can protest consumerism through advertising. It introduces key concepts (anti-consumerism, culture jamming, subvertising) and appraises key theories in relation to activism through and against advertising related to ideology, society of the spectacle, as well as culture jamming. It highlights the importance of history to resist incorporation of advertising resistance to the promotional fold, the importance of ideology in identifying what subvertisers resist and how, the importance of agency in fostering connections and collaborations between multiple constituents, and, again, the importance of justice in understanding human rights in relation to resistance to the ubiquity and consequences of advertising. This chapter explores the case of the US-based subvertising collective Resistance is Female, through anti-consumerism approaches and interviews with its members.

Chapter 8 reflects on key arguments and situates resistance practices within promotional culture. Importantly, as previous chapters do, it highlights key issues and methodological paths for the analysis of consumer activism. Overall, *Consumer Activism* is concerned with the following questions: Under what conditions can it be an effective tool of protest? What ideological ambiguities might there be? To what extent can media technologies be mobilized for social or environmental change? What is the role of consumers in progressing causes through the marketplace? What can we do as critical individuals, collectives, neighbourhoods, organizations, cities, countries? How are media being used by campaigners, citizens, and market actors to communicate consumer activism? What potential can consumer activism demonstrate in challenging or exacerbating inequalities?

Conclusion

What is the common strand linking ethical fashion trends and movements, the targeting of pro-China brands by Hong Kong protesters, the burning of New Balance shoes during Donald Trump's inauguration, the market of recycled goods, the Extinction Rebellion year-long fashion boycott, the anti-consumerist stance of Instagrammers saying that they will not buy certain products, femvertising campaigns, and campaigns against advertising in public spaces? They are all part of contemporary consumer activism. Consumer activism includes highly or loosely organized, collective, or individual actions that employ the market as an area of contestation, broadening the field of consumption by using the marketplace and the media for political contention. The variance of consumer activism can range from regressive (e.g. social hate such as sexism and racism) to progressive political goals (e.g. fights against repression and for representation). Technological developments have enabled as well as disabled struggles centred on inequality and injustice. By highlighting and nuancing consumer activism, this book illuminates struggles for ethical and sustainable futures through the marketplace and the media and offers guidelines for social sciences and humanities research on contemporary manifestations of consumer activism.

In these politically uncertain times, one thing is certain: buying things has never been easier, faster, or more varied in terms of aesthetic or ethical choices. Buying at the supermarket comes with a host of offers, buying through online consumer platforms comes with personalized suggestions and buying in social media style 'marketplaces' further reinforces the idea that consumer purchases (and politics) can be forwarded at the click of a button. This is 'consumer solutionism', and the book presents arguments and evidence as to why it will not save the world. We cannot dismiss the way that consumer advocacy can be a force for advancing socially progressive goals, but also we cannot celebrate the power of consumers, as if social and environmental change depended on them. Avoiding a deterministic approach to the richness of practices that comprise contemporary consumer activism, this book also offers a constructive approach to examining and analysing the phenomenon. It provides key conceptual, theoretical, and methodological tools and illustrative case studies to expand an analysis of resistance within promotional culture. Within promotional culture, consumer activism can either be stalled or accelerated. There is a hierarchy of promotionalism whereby elites, celebrities and corporations enjoy privileged attention by ushering in particular brands of activism.

This book analyses consumer activism through its mobilization for nationalistic (racial/ethnic), gender (feminist/queer) and environmental (green/sustainable) causes, as well as its propagation by intermediaries such as celebrities and subvertisers. Consumer activism deserves serious analysis across time and space, and in terms of its agents, technologies, and narratives of change. It can re-animate historical accounts, reappraise contemporary phenomena, and reconfigure the power we hold as individuals and communities in addressing or responding to specific or shared concerns. One-dimensional analyses of the phenomenon through one-medium approaches produce deterministic (either positive or negative) conclusions which fall short of the complexity of practices, the ecology of media technologies, and the conditions of everyday life. This book offers key considerations for a holistic examination of case studies through a media practice approach, and probes questions on their implication for a global post-pandemic politics.

Notes

1. www.dezeen.com/2020/03/09/li-edelkoort-coronavirus-reset/ (8 November 2021).
2. https://adage.com/article/opinion/opinion-covid-19-will-change-consumerism-forever/2246736 (8 August 2021).
3. The Rana Plaza factory collapsed in 2013, killing over 1,000 workers, injuring over 2,000 of them, and bringing global attention to the supply chains of fast fashion, and efforts to raise safety standards and labour rights.
4. www.fashionrevolution.org/the-impact-of-covid-19-on-the-people-who-make-our-clothes/ (8 November 2021); https://labourbehindthelabel.org/report-brands-are-pushing-garment-workers-to-breaking-point-during-the-pandemic/ (8 November 2021); https://labourbehindthelabel.org/report-boohoo-covid-19-the-people-behind-the-profit/ (8 November 2021).
5. https://wid.world/news-article/global-income-inequality-1820-2020/ (8 November 2021).
6. www.bbc.com/news/business-54446285#:~:text=Billionaires%20have%20seen%20their%20fortunes,and%20industry%20earning%20the%20most.&text=It%20also%20said%20the%20number,up%20from%202%2C158%20in%202017 (30 August 2021).
7. www.theguardian.com/environment/2020/dec/09/human-made-materials-now-outweigh-earths-entire-biomass-study (23 September 2021).
8. www.aboutamazon.com/news/retail/the-history-of-prime-day (8 November 2021).
9. www.techinasia.com/china-singles-day-versus-black-friday-cyber-monday-sales (8 November 2021).
10. www.cnbc.com/2020/11/28/black-friday-2020-online-shopping-surges-22percent-to-record-9-billion-adobe-says.html (8 November 2021).
11. www.lexico.com/definition/woke (8 November 2021).
12. www.bbc.com/news/technology-58707753 (20 October 2021).
13. https://fairplayforkids.org/mission-impact/ (20 October 2021).
14. Clean Clothes is a transnational civil society campaign and alliance of the garment industry's largest alliance of labour unions and non-governmental organizations.
15. https://labourbehindthelabel.org/covid-19-brand-tracker/ (25 October 2021).

16. www.instagram.com/boowho.org_/ (9 November 2021).
17. www.bbc.com/news/uk-england-leicestershire-58705346 (25 October 2021).
18. www.industriall-union.org/signatories-to-the-2018-accord (25 October 2021).
19. Freeganism is an ideology and invested lifestyle in which individuals practice minimal consumption and participation in the economy, and resort to practices such as recovery of wasted food.

TWO
CONCEPTUALIZING CONSUMER ACTIVISM

Introduction: Can Individuals Save the Planet or Ourselves?

Teen actor Ella Gross is inviting me (and you) to join her in support of #ActNow, a United Nations (UN) campaign for individual action on climate change.[1] The children's model – who has appeared in GAP, H&M, and Zara advertising – is reminding me that 'living more sustainably doesn't have to be a huge effort, and now is a great time to start!' 'How is that possible?' you might ask, through 'this super cool app' that helps 'build sustainable habits and make more conscious choices' in order to 'do our part to make things better'.[2] I download the app *A World (in support of Act Now)*. Am I ready to do my part? I am invited to participate in the one Million Actions Challenge (e.g. clothes swaps, food donation, beach cleans, talks, and workshops), as '2021 must be the year where we turn it around and take bold, transformative action for the planet'. As I enter the app, I see my 'level' as 'the spark', and I am given my pathway to action, where I can log my preferred choices and track my progress to see how much of a difference I am making individually and in relation to other people. Through watching short informative videos about the campaign and logging habits (such as trying three deep breaths as an act of kindness or embracing a reusable water bottle), I get more points and my level rises to 'the awakening'. As I graduate to the next level, 'the pivot' (where I am now officially considered 'part of the solution'), I find out that part of the journey of a change-maker is 'becoming a mindful consumer'. The first step, I am told, is 'realizing your power' (Figure 2.1).

Consumer power has been celebrated and contested, applauded and deplored by popular commentators, journalists and Instagrammers, public intellectuals and TikTokers (the latter two being personalities that sometimes converge),[3] and scholars of many persuasions. Drawing on interdisciplinary research, this chapter highlights the importance of a media practice approach and argues against what I call 'consumer solutionism', the unruffled celebration of consumer activism as the primary means of contemporary resistance in promotional culture. Exploring ecologies (changes in

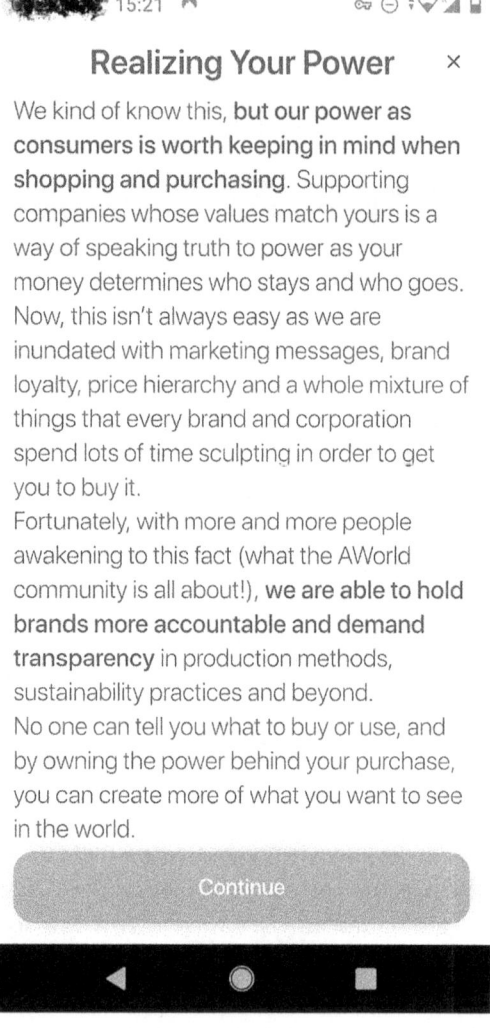

Figure 2.1 Screenshot from app (13 October 2021)

the media and communications environment), publicities (ideological information and communication), and responsibilities (appeals to individual, collective, or corporate action), this chapter contributes to constructive approaches to technological or consumer agency.

According to the app, the final step towards becoming a mindful consumer is asking myself a set of questions: 'Do I really need this? Can I buy it secondhand? Where is this purchase coming from? Who made it? Was the product made locally or sustainably? What is it made of? Is this brand transparent? How long will this last?' Indeed, if I can offer a shorthand definition of consumer activism, it would be that it is questioning justice in the processes of production and distribution of consumer goods in terms of both the labour involved as well as the environmental costs of sourcing, making, and shipping the product, and then translating that questioning into action. It would also be relevant to add to this definition the question of how consumer goods fit within contemporary consumer culture in terms of the values and identifications they promote, and the cultural histories they draw from. It is important, then, to consider consumer activism both in relation to critical political economy concerns, such as social and environmental justice, as well as critical cultural analyses in relation to representations, consumers, and aspirations.

A key debate within consumer activism is individualization, and the way in which agents are constructed and action is coordinated. In another video in support of the Act Now campaign, influencer and author Connor Franta is urging me to take individual action, offering his own choice of a plant-based diet, which is 'near and dear' to his heart.[4] And pop star Ronnie Jones' original song 'The Future Is in Our Hands' proclaimed that 'mother nature's beauty can only be saved by a miracle and that miracle all depends on you'. Of course, the Act Now campaign is exactly that, a campaign for individual action on climate change, but it is also exemplary of many attempts to invite conscientious citizens into the marketplace.

This chapter explores relevant debates, highlights the importance of methodology, and illustrates the multiplicity of agents and hybridity of technologies in the making of consumer activism in a post-pandemic context. It asks, how can we critically understand the conditions of the evolution of the phenomenon and identify issues for its contemporary manifestations? What opportunities for furthering progressive social change and what critical issues must we be aware of? In what follows, I offer a comprehensive review of interdisciplinary research on the topic, and then proceed to illustrate the agents and technologies of consumer activism. Finally, I review key issues pertaining to the significance of consumer activism and the methods and approaches used to study it. Overall, this chapter argues that we need to pay attention to the historical, agentic, and technological context, as well as the complexity of everyday practices, in order to understand consumer activism. To do so is to realize that, at the end of the day, individual consumption alone will not save the planet or us, though it has its role to play in the changes that are happening or will be happening.

Approaches to Consumer Activism

We can find many scholarly responses to what constitutes a politics borne of consumption. Consumer activism comes in many shapes and forms: buying or not buying products for ethical, environmental, or religious reasons, participating in alternative economic practices, holding businesses accountable, advocating for justice or sustainability, or practising minimal or mindful consumption, or anti-consumerism. As such, it has been explored by political science, sociology, development and international relations, critical marketing studies, communication, and cultural studies. Below, I identify key themes and debates arising from this interdisciplinary research.

Political Science

Political science has approached the politics of consumption through the forms and practices of citizens within marketplaces in an attempt to reclaim political agency beyond the sphere of parliamentary and civil society politics. Since the early 2000s, pioneering work by Michele Micheletti and colleagues has resulted in a field of study of political participation under the umbrella of 'political consumerism'. The term is defined as 'individualized collective action' which puts citizens' identity at the heart of their political pursuits, identifying their own departure points and drawing on their own networks to create their own narratives and take personal and joint responsibility towards urgent causes through 'everyday activism in variety of settings' (Micheletti, 2003: 27). Importantly, political consumerism manifests in and through the marketplace; originally, this was conceptualized as supporting or rejecting businesses through consumption ('buycott') or non-consumption (boycott), while it slowly grew to include culture jamming or 'discursive political consumerism' and, finally, lifestyle politics (Stolle and Micheletti, 2015). Its study has been extended to numerous industries, even prohibited or obscured, such as the cannabis market (Bennett, 2021). For the most part, political scientists still tend to consider political consumerism as either participation in boycotts or 'buycotts' (Copeland and Boulianne, 2022; Zorell, 2019), although the phenomenon has significantly expanded to include the study of the responsibilities and practices of both individuals and industries (Boström et al., 2019). Another intervention of political science is Caroline Heldman's *Protest in the Marketplace*, which argues that this practice generally strengthens US democracy. Heldman defines consumer activism as 'citizen actions directed towards business entities to explicitly influence the distribution of social goods or social values' (2017: 4). Heldman also expands its typology beyond boycotting and boycotting ('(non)consumption') to investment actions (socially responsible investing, shareholder resolutions, and divestment), social media actions (social media and activist blogs that raise attention to, for instance, sexist marketing practices, but also social action petition sites, such as Change.org) and direct action (e.g. protests, sit-ins, teach-ins, and culture jamming).

International Development

International relations and development studies scholars have also explored consumer agency in relation to civil society and the marketplace, particularly questioning how it is mobilized through advocacy and humanitarian communication. The case of the RED phenomenon (a brand in itself that implored consumers to shop for change by connecting popular brands with the cause of the HIV/AIDS crisis in Africa), as Lisa Ann Richey and Stefano Ponte have extensively analysed, 'reconfigures international development around aid celebrities and consumer-citizens united to do good by dressing well' (2011: 5). They also identify the centrality of the market arena for causes, as advocated by political scientists, which they call 'the emerging realm of "causumerism"' (ibid.: 9) and posit that a significant shift is happening from '"conscious consumption" to "compassionate consumption" [that] deflects attention from addressing the causes of problems to solving their manifestations' (ibid.). Ponte and Richey (2014) further formalize their conceptual model of Brand Aid at the intersection of cause-related marketing (CRM), branded products, and celebrities. Celebrities, in particular, have been explored as harbingers of brand aid, such as actor Ben Affleck mediating social change in Congo through partnership with a chocolate brand (Richey and Budabin, 2016) and a coffee brand, like actor George Clooney (Budabin, 2020), or former reality TV participant Blake Mycoskie and TOMS shoes (Richey and Ponte, 2021). Coming from a critical political economy perspective, these scholars argue that '"[b]uying" is "buying into" an imaginary of development in which consumers can make a difference' (ibid.: 82) and that although 'whether business is good for development is an ongoing debate ... "buying into development", at least in some form, is good for business' (Ponte and Richey, 2014: 83). Scholars argue that the market-friendly communication of Brand Aid likens systemic problems to solvable issues (Kipp and Hawkins, 2019), commodifying not only causes, but also bodies of distant Others (Daley, 2013).

Sociology

Sociological approaches to consumer activism engage with its identities, values, ideologies, and impact. Sociologists have analysed ethical consumption as an everyday practice, arguing that this is a 'situated' phenomenon within confounded realities (Adams and Raisborough, 2008, 2010). In *The Sociology of Consumption*, Joel Stillerman focuses on the rise of mass consumerism and the margins of consumer culture, as well as consumer citizenship (boycotts, ethical consumption and culture jamming), arguing that through consumption, 'we recognize ourselves and the world around us, construct meaningful relationships, reproduce inequalities, and engage with politics' (2015: 165). These contradictions of consumption (identity and community building alongside inequality reproduction) characterize sociological debates on consumer activism.

Josée Johnston (2008) questions ideological tensions and contradictions in the way in which a business advocating for ethical consumption (Whole Foods Market) frames the hybrid citizen-consumer, warning against premature celebrations of a balanced hybrid, especially in the way it manifests in a corporate market setting. The argument here is that there is 'superficial attention to citizenship goals in order to serve three consumerist interests better: consumer choice, status distinction, and ecological cornucopianism' (Johnston 2008: 229). In other words, Johnston regards the expression of politics through consumption as a mirage for the reproduction of market logic, inequality and technological solutionism for the environment. In *Foodies*,[5] through discourse analysis (magazine food writing, restaurant reviews, and blogs) and interviews, Johnston and Baumann argue that the discourse of 'foodie politics' is 'characterized by a tension between ideologies of consumerism (that maximize individual choice and pleasure) and citizenship (that emphasize responsibility to a larger social and ecological collective)' (2015: 113). Drawing on qualitative methods (focus groups, participant observation, and interviews), in *Fair Trade and the Citizen-Consumer*, Kathryn Wheeler argues that 'a moral hierarchy of value is created in which the fair-trade choice is defended as the only course of action that a concerned and ethical consumer ought to make' (2012: 178).

Drawing on US survey data, Margaret Willis and Juliet Schor analyse 'conscious consumption' as 'any choice about products or services made as a way to express values of sustainability, social justice, corporate responsibility, or workers' rights and that takes into account the larger context of production, distribution, or impacts of goods and services' (2012: 162). In accordance with wider research on political consumerism, they suggest that conscious consumption does not threaten other forms of collective political involvement, and might even have a positive relationship with these, although 'it is neither obvious nor straightforward that a society can consume its way into social justice or environmental sustainability' (2012: 161). During the Trump administration, Amanda Dewey and Dana Fisher suggest that 'consumption is likely to be integrated further into civic engagement and political behavior for those involved' (2019: 12). What is useful here is Keith Brown's (2019) suggestion that we cannot abandon the idea that markets are potential arenas for change, and that we should pay attention to the supply chains of markets for ethically labelled goods and to the emotional processes that connect consumers to these ethical markets. Overall, debates within sociology have tended to question the extent to which consumer activism can foster broader social change or reproduce existing structures, ideologies, and inequalities.

Cultural and Communication Studies

Similarly, cultural studies and communication studies have offered a complex perspective to consumer activism, drawing from 'a hugely inventive array of disciplinary tools from the academic toolbox' (Littler, 2016: 238). Binkley and Littler distinguish between 'anti-consumption (consuming less) and anti-consumerism (consuming differently)' (2008: 525), where the latter involves practices contesting or running counter to consumer capitalism (and are also inevitably about consuming less). In *Radical Consumption*, Littler (2009) unpacks the location of ethics, morality, and responsibility in contemporary ethical consumption, the political potential of 'caring consumption', the imagined role and futures of consumer activism, and the ecological conundrum of 'green consumption'.

In *Excess*, Kim Humphery suggests that anti-consumerism (an umbrella term for questioning mass consumerism) is:

> a field of alternative social and economic practices, a political stance and current, that traverses movements of various kinds – from the strategically oriented to the experientially based – and invokes an array of political perspectives and strategies – from the liberal to the libertarian, and from the planned to the impetuous. (2010: 109)

For Humphery, a typology of anti-consumerism includes cultural politics (e.g. culture jamming), civic politics (e.g. ethical consumption), life politics (e.g. minimalism, veganism), community-oriented politics (e.g. collective practices in the social and solidarity economy) and systemic politics (e.g. struggles related to institutional practices and concerning environmental justice, advertising regulation, economic inequality). Humphery's holistic approach to anti-consumerism allows for a more comprehensive approach to consumer activism as resistance in promotional culture.

Similarly, in their edited collection *Ethical Consumption*, Lewis and Potter highlight the fluidity and consequent challenge of defining the politics of consumption and discuss how 'the emergent scholarship around ethical consumption likewise reflects the inchoate nature of "the field", with work in the area drawing upon and moving between political economy, geography, sociology, cultural studies, business studies and sustainability studies' (2011: 5). Focusing on the rise of brand culture, they depart from political consumerism to present a diverse range of approaches to the politics, commodities, and materiality, as well as practices, sites, and representations of ethical consumerism.

In *Commodity Activism*, Banet-Weiser and Mukherjee work from the assertion that activism in the US has become tied up in neoliberal brand culture and discuss how this 'reshapes and reimagines forms and practices of social (and political) activism into marketable commodities and takes specific form within brand culture' (2012: 16). Their edited collection unpacks commodity activism and how 'symbolic, rhetorical, and discursive means by which historical traditions of social activism are being hollowed out and rearticulated in commodity form' (ibid.: 3). In *Coffee Activism and the Politics of Fair Trade and Ethical Consumption in the Global North*, I appraise political consumerism as a form of cultural citizenship. There, I argue that the histories, agents, and narratives of fair trade have steadily migrated to the marketplace, leaving solidarity approaches in the limelight, despite their continued presence and oppositional readings of promotional narratives by ethically consuming citizens (Lekakis, 2013). Overall, research here has focused on the location and interrogation of ethics within resistance in promotional culture, carving out new territory for the expression and operation of consumer activism.

Critical Marketing Studies

There are also a couple of notable interdisciplinary approaches in the form of edited collections from critical marketing scholars. Edited by co-founder of the *Ethical Consumer* magazine in the UK and two marketing scholars, *Ethical Consumer* (Harrison et al., 2005) is an introduction to the concept, charting the contexts, behaviour, discourses, narratives, and effectiveness of consumer activism. *Ethics and Morality in Consumption: Interdisciplinary Perspectives* (Shaw et al., 2016) also pushes for consideration of different disciplinary approaches in relation to the individual and society. The first book takes a nuanced approach to 'the ethical consumer' yet homes in on histories, campaigns, information sources, and networks of collaboration and contestation for consumer activists. The second book adds a discussion on the permeation of consumption ethics within society, and considers motives and contexts – and the interrelationship between them – as well as contesting notions of ethical consumption.

Summarizing Approaches to Consumer Activism

1. Consumer activism matters
2. Context matters
3. Ideology matters
4. Agency matters
5. Methodology matters

What is clear from the review of this rich literature is that, first, consumer activism matters, though the extent to which it does can only be approached within a comprehensive theoretical and methodological approach, as this book suggests. Consumer activism remains central in theorizations of politics, development, culture, and everyday life. If it is not possible to campaign for local, national, or transnational causes without being offered a chance to buy a memento of your participation and if it is not possible to express your support or disdain of the way a business conducts its operations, then we need to keep the focus on who campaigns for change, why, when, and how. Second, context matters. There is a consistent tendency to commonly locate consumer activism within North America or North Western Europe, although research identifies and problematizes the rise of ethical consumption in the South, as scholars argue that consumer activism can manifest differently through collective structures of care from South America to Southern Europe (Ariztia et al., 2016; Kleine, 2016; Lekakis and Forno, 2019). Third, ideology matters. Research has tended to focus on the progressive politics pursued by citizens through political consumerism, although there is recognition that there are cases where it is used against minorities, and that 'it can also be a tool to support nationalism, intolerance, exclusiveness, or other types of hatred' (Stolle and Micheletti, 2015: 39; see also Chapter 3). There is limited research on the complex ideological tensions of consumer activism. Fourth, agency matters. To reiterate the discussion in the introduction to this chapter, for some, political consumerism is an individualized action that displaces collective action (though this is not how Michele Micheletti regards it), while for others it is a complex set of considerations and practices within evolving and precarious lives.

The discussion on political agencies is central to consumer activism. Natalie Fenton discusses how 'the politics of choice' (2017: 74) repoliticizes citizens at the same time as it limits them to a predetermined array of choices, and I elsewhere offer a grounded account of how this works within the market-driven politics of the UK (Lekakis, 2013). This also resonates with how institutional intermediaries of ethical consumption promote 'consumer choice as a vector of political agency' (Barnett et al., 2011: 201), and contemporary consumer activism is characterized by 'a neoliberal emphasis on the individual consumer' (Banet-Weiser and Mukherjee, 2012: 11). As Léna Pellandini-Simányi argues, 'most of the problems addressed by ethical consumerism are systemic, and therefore require systemic rather than individual solutions. Addressing them within the framework of individual choice assigns the decision and the responsibility to the private level' (2014: 166).

Yet at the same time, consumer activism is connected to social movements and their strategies. Breaking from the definition of consumer activism as restricted in ethical consumption, such research has regarded its connection to social movements whether as part of their strategic repertoire (Balsiger, 2010; Colli, 2020; Forno and Graziano, 2014; Micheletti and Stolle, 2015), or as the coalescence of activists into a social movement against advertising culture and ideology (Lekakis, 2021). Here, finally, it is also important to underscore that methodology influences the formation of knowledge on the topic. We can see, for instance, how a focus on quantitative data can produce arguments for the existence or variation of participation, while a focus on qualitative data can illustrate the perspectives and practices of such participation. A combination of approaches focusing on practices can illuminate the location and dynamics of consumer activism in the context of digitalized and polarized politics, market activism, and continuing economic and environmental injustice in a post-pandemic context.

To summarize, this book puts forward an approach to consumer activism that recognizes that it matters (but apprehends the extent to which it does), that context matters (but avoids simplifications of where, when, and whose actions matter), that ideology matters (but avoids a consideration of consumer activism as explicitly progressive), and that agents matter (but appraises who these are, and how they are informed and form partnerships). Finally, methodologies matter, and this is precisely why each chapter from now on includes a dedicated section on methodological perspectives of the literature presented.

Agencies of Consumer Activism

This section focuses on agencies of consumer activism after the rise of ethical consumption in the 2000s, which as Celia Lury writes, concerns the 'reaffirmation of the moral dimension of ethical choice' (2011: 172). I introduce discourses and debates on agencies of citizens, market actors, celebrities, and subvertisers. In doing so, we can see how within consumer activism, narratives of change tend to highlight individual consumer power, and privilege agents connected to promotional industries (corporations, celebrities), while there are also counter-narratives of collectivity, and alternative visions beyond mass consumerism.

Citizens: Reduce, Reuse, Recycle

Whether or not individual citizens influence social and environmental change through their consumption is a key question within the literature. This section takes on the 'reduce, reuse, recycle' narratives of individual action through consumption practices to question the extent to which consumer activism is exclusively about individual action or whether it can also appear as collective action. For the most part, academics have argued that these narratives regulate the individual and delegate responsibility to them for the problem of mass consumerism (see also Chapter 5). In *Garbage in Popular Culture*, Mehita Iqani (2020) offers three case studies to explore themes of (individual and collective) agency and hope in the 'reduce-reuse-recycle' narratives. Iqani argues that waste has come to define humanity and argues for the significance of 'waste-work' (how it maps onto existing structures of privilege) and the way in which 'trashscapes' are increasingly defining the world around us.

Regarding reduced consumption, Iqani discusses the case of the luxury of waste-free consumption of influencer 'Zero Trash Girl', and how class, race, and gender typically condition such consumer practices born out of environmentalism and are exemplary of the usual (middle-class, educated) suspects. While reduced consumption promotes consumer activism that regulates the individual, and presents questionable outcomes for broader change, and the choice of being an ethical consumer reproduces the self as a neoliberal subject, reuse narratives, by contrast, hold the potential for collaborative engagement.

Reuse narratives are more complex and while they demand individual action, they offer opportunities for collective engagements. Iqani (2020) analyses the community art project iThemba Tower that was made with over 7,000 recycled plastic drinks bottles decorating a decommissioned 20-metre-high cellular tower. The project included workshops aimed to teach children about plastic waste and responsibility and infuse the message of hope. Similar cases of this are happening locally, sometimes in schools (e.g. The Trash Art Museum in Chios, Greece[6]), because of art teachers. Artists are also part of larger movements against consumerism and commodification, such as the case of subvertising activism as I discuss later in this chapter, and in Chapter 7. Thus, through such cases, there is potential for public pedagogies beyond mass and individual consumerism.

Recycling is connected to green consumerism, but it is also a form of labour (Littler, 2009; Wheeler and Glucksmann, 2013). In addition to the importance of the macro-level of global recycling (e.g. China's 'National Sword' Policy banning the import of plastics since 2018), it is also important to make visible the micro-level of human recycling labour. Centring on the work of the SWaCH collective, a cooperative of women recyclers in India, Iqani notes how it can provide 'an inspirational model for thinking about how human innovation, passion, and creativity, as well as collectively organized action can deal cleverly with both systemic economic oppression and waste in ways that support humans to reach their full potential' (2020: 62).

Citizens thus mobilize through different narratives and practices that can either confirm or contest the constant calls for individual action; through examples of collaborative forms of labour such as the above, it is possible to see the economic and cultural viabilities of life within consumerism. As Rob Harrison states, 'an individual consumer's purchases in a mass market won't make much impact on its own' (2022: 37). But a collective response can. Beyond 'reduce-reuse-recycle' narratives, there are collective responses to mass consumerism, such as consumer–producer cooperatives, community-supported agriculture, solidarity purchasing groups, ecovillages, barter groups, urban gardening, municipal zero waste strategies, and transition town networks. Beyond individual or collective action, however, a host of organizational agents have also embarked on crusades for change.

Market Actors: From Brand Activism to Green/Pink/Woke/Carewashing

Market actors have stepped into the arena of global social change willingly or unwillingly, yet definitely and decisively. As Sarah Banet-Weiser (2012a) argues in *Authentic™*, branding is now a context for contemporary culture and attempts to save the world, though branding can only be understood as ambivalent in that it can be experienced in different ways. In 2019, Ogilvy published a report called 'Making Brands Matter for the Generations to Come',[7] arguing that there has been a significant shift from the 'environmental and philanthropic consumers' of the late 20th century to the 'conscious' consumers of the late 2000s onwards, and, acknowledging increasing income inequalities, said to anticipate a shift towards affordable and attainable 'conscious' consumption. Indeed, as Susie Khamis argues, 'brands do not just "play" politics for short-term market gain; rather, they do politics – addressing both consumers with cash, as well as (and at the same time) citizens with agency and choice' (2020: 3). There are even brands that present themselves as anti-corporate and sustainable, such as Oatly, a milk alternative whose key promotional narrative is that buying the product is not ethical shopping, but actual political activism (Ledin and Machin, 2020). Social science and humanities scholars who study how market actors promote and practice activism notice how this can weaken activism by non-business actors and offer decontextualized and consumerist understandings of social change (Aronczyk, 2013; Montez de Oca et al., 2020; Polynczuk-Alenius and Pantti, 2017; Richey and Ponte, 2011). Corporations draw lessons from social movements and address citizens who want to be critical in their consumption through corporate social responsibility (CSR) communication (e.g. United Colors of Benetton's GREEN B project[8]), cause-related marketing (CRM) campaigns (e.g. TOMS shoes[9]), socially conscious marketing and advertising campaigns (e.g. Jigsaw's Love Immigration[10] or Nike's Dream Crazy[11]), as well as media campaigns (e.g. Make Friday Green Again[12]).

The context of climate crisis, racial and social injustice, as well as the COVID-19 pandemic further influenced how market actors shape their promotional communication. Francesca Sobande comments that brand responses to COVID-19 commodify notions of care and mask 'stark inequalities between how people are affected by the COVID-19 crisis – from their experiences of work, healthcare, relationships, violence, state surveillance and family life, to the likelihood of them surviving this challenging time' (2020: 1035). Similarly, Chatzidakis et al. argue that discourses of care have exploded during the pandemic and require a move away from 'carewashing' (using care for promotional communication) and towards 'a radical caring politics' in which 'we are all collectively responsible for hands-on care work as well as the work necessary for the maintenance of communities and the planet' (2020: 893).

Within the context of backlash politics and the COVID-19 pandemic, brands have actively pursued inclusion of care and social consciousness in their promotional communication. Within the US, the Black Lives Matter (BLM) movement against systemic police brutality and the general precarity of black lives, as well as the legacy of Donald Trump's administration and January 2021 US Capitol attack following his incitement to insurrection, demonstrates a contentious, racialized and polarized political context. In that context, the communication of brand values tends to produce hopeful arguments as to the possibility of their fostering better futures (Einstein, forthcoming; Kozinets and Jenkins, 2021). Yet brands tend to pick out from a universal playbook for social change (as Ogilvy's 2019 report would suggest). In the context of Greece, for instance, following the #metooGR movement and the pandemic, global and national brands have also promoted diversity and care for the first time in the history of the country's advertising, to produce problematic normative stories and solutions for gender justice (Lekakis, forthcoming). Again, context matters.

Promotional communication (advertising, marketing, branding) to inaccurately, vaguely, or irrelevantly communicate environmental responsibility and justice ('greenwashing'), gender equality and justice ('pinkwashing'), and racial justice ('wokewashing') is routinely undertaken by market actors. Greenwashing varies in relation to the balance between 'advertising techniques of companies with well-established positive and negative records of social and environmental responsibility' (Jones, 2019: 734). Richard Maxwell and Toby Miller write that the problem with an institutional embrace of environmentalism is that '[i]t is contradictory, valorizing "a green commodity discourse" that promotes the magical fusion of environmentalism with growth, profits, and pleasure' (2012: 25). 'Pinkwashing' is evident, for instance, in Primark's launch of Pride-themed clothes and accessories in association with Stonewall, the UK's biggest LBGTQ charity (for which they held 80 per cent of profits on full prince items and donated the remaining 20 per cent to Stonewall), and their harassment of a trans employee (a case the employee unanimously won in an employment tribunal) (Tyler and Vachhani, 2021). Pinkwashing is explored in context in Chapter 4. 'Wokewashing' is expressed in socially conscious marketing commercials that aired during mega-sporting events in the US that 'conspicuously demonstrate the leagues' moral values without altering the conditions that produce the crises' (Montez de Oca, Mason, and Ahn, 2020: 3). Yet the extent of market actors' engagement in 'greenwashing', 'pinkwashing' or 'wokewashing' deserves further analysis, particularly in terms of the implications of inclusion, exclusion, and hierarchy of voices and issues. Ultimately, market activism can promote consumer solutionism and negate all nuance from causes, to produce an accessible (though often ambiguous) path to social change.

Celebrities: From Promoting Change to Promoting Consumption and Vice Versa

Celebrities are the fuel of consumer culture, provoking or producing lifestyle trends. Yet celebrities have also embraced ethical or green consumerism. Michael Goodman (2010) identifies a shift in fair trade representation from farmers to celebrities. As Abidin and colleagues posit, 'the strategies celebrities use (such as promoting awareness and raising funds through consumerism, YouTube campaigns, letters to newspapers, and appearances at protests or before policy makers) can be applied to almost any cause' (Abidin et al, 2020: 390). Celebrity campaigning for change is often connected to opportunities for ethical or sustainable consumption. For instance, actress and UN Women Goodwill Ambassador Emma Watson founded a site dedicated to sustainable fashion and natural beauty in 2010, has worked with an ethical British brand to create new lines of clothing, while she has been documenting the sustainable clothing she is publicly fashioning in a separate Instagram account. Another example is that of the K-pop girl group BLACKPINK, goodwill ambassadors for the 26th Climate Change Conference (COP26) and honorary ambassadors for the United Nations' Sustainable Development Goals. In their speech during the Google event 'Dear Earth' they called for our increased attention to the urgency of climate change.[13] The relationship between celebrities and consumer activism is extensively discussed in Chapter 6. Here I will only mention a couple of examples of celebrities advocating consumer boycotts, to highlight how celebrities perform ordinariness through engagement with long-standing consumer tactics.

The first is the case of actor Rupert Everett who joined a boycott of Starbucks when the opening of a store was announced near his home in Bloomsbury, London in 2006: 'Starbucks is spreading like a cancer. Nobody in the neighbourhood wants it, including me. There are plenty of diners and coffee shops there already.'[14] In 2019, George Clooney, Elton John and Ellen DeGeneres, among others, called for a boycott of Brunei-owned hotels over the country's new criminal law (which included death by stoning for sex between men or for adultery, and punishment of 40 lashes for sex between women).[15] George Clooney, wrote in *Deadline*:

> let's be clear, every single time we stay at or take meetings at or dine at any of these nine hotels we are putting money directly into the pockets of men who choose to stone and whip to death their own citizens for being gay or accused of adultery. Brunei is a Monarchy and certainly any boycott would have little effect on changing these laws. But are we really going to help pay for these human rights violations? Are we really going to help fund the murder of innocent citizens?[16]

As a result, Brunei retracted the law and ratified the United Nations Convention against Torture.[17] This was not the first time celebrities called for a boycott of the Bel-Air in Beverly Hills and other hotels owned by the Ministry of Finance of Brunei,[18] but it remains a paradigmatic contemporary case of (celebrity) consumer activism against the violation of human rights. What the case illuminates is a key tension between celebrities and consumer activism: on the one hand, they use the same tactics as citizens, while on the other hand their boycott is of luxury goods and services, demonstrating an inherent issue with their involvement in social change. This is that they are hyper-promoters of individual action for social change, and importantly they embody wealth and media power, which sets them aside from ordinary citizens. Yet the issue at hand is that because of their increased visibility within promotional culture, their causes can spread faster and to a broader audience, and often advocate consumerist solutions to global challenges (see Chapter 6).

Subvertisers: From Lone Jammers to Collective Movements

Much of the literature on consumer activism reviewed earlier in this chapter also discusses culture jamming. Yet the extent to which advertising has been targeted by activists to claim voice and contest commercialization has altered significantly since the emergence of famous examples such as Adbusters (a media education foundation, founded in Canada in 1989, which started the Adbusters magazine as well as Buy Nothing Day and Buy Nothing Christmas campaigns) and Reverend Billy and the Church of Stop Shopping (a radical performance community that stages guerrilla theatre actions against consumerism and its consequences). Since Naomi Klein's (2005) *No Logo*, which spoke of lone activists toiling away at defacing advertising in public spaces, the field of anti-consumerism has evolved, evident in the formation of Subvertisers International, a transnational alliance between subvertising activists (Lekakis, 2021). But while its agencies and tactics have proliferated, the topic remains largely unexplored. Chapter 7 unpacks subvertising (the act of subverting advertising to correct, distort or completely replace its meaning) as anti-consumerism, and grounds it in debates around incorporation, play, participation, and law. This section focuses on how subvertising activism manifests as collective organizing against climate change and for commercially free lives, as well as new forms of digitally native activism against programmatic advertising.

There remain many individuals and collectives scattered in cities in the global North, fighting against the commercialization of everyday life, the sexualization and objectification of women, the pollution of the environment, and the corporate and corrupt politics of neoliberalism. One such example is Brigade Anti-Sexiste (Anti-Sexist Brigade) in France which has been tampering with advertising that objectifies women since 2016 (e.g. by posting stickers with 'sexist' on them).[19] Yet groups have sought to create networks of groups concerned with advertising. In the UK, AdFree Cities is a national network of groups mobilizing against 'the impacts of corporate advertising on our health, wellbeing, environment, climate, communities and the local economy'[20] since 2017. Through local campaigning work to prevent digital advertising screens in localities, lobbying to ban advertising in public spaces, and inviting people to imagine spaces differently, AdFree cities prioritizes community, builds grassroots networks, and uses creativity to 'fight against billboards as part of a wider struggle for social, ecological and economic justice'.[21] While the network does not focus on creative direct action such as subvertising, they consider themselves as part of 'the wider subvertising and anti-advertising movement'.[22] In Argentina, Proyecto Squatters is a network concerned with advertising as corporate propaganda, engaging in subvertising activism (ad takeovers) in the streets, developing communication networks, and running educational projects in schools since 2008.[23] In their Manifiesto de la Contrapublicidad (Anti-Advertising Manifesto), they offer a review of their concerns with advertising:

> Advertising is a political weapon that the centers of power use for the ideological and cultural conquest of audiences. This form of corporate propaganda is omnipresent, insidious, and has colonized our own subjectivities, selling us a false and stereotyped version of reality, constantly telling us how to think, how to see ourselves, what to eat, how to dress, what music to listen to … [as well as] what, how much and how to consume. (Proyecto Squatters, 2019)

They also state the objectives of their movement as assisting in the formation of critical thinking, operating as an instrument for a creative and constructive response against corporate propaganda, as well as offering a communication strategy for different social struggles and demands. Those examples further suggest that various forms that consumer activism takes are not always geared towards individual action.

Finally, the rise of programmatic advertising has brought to light many additional contentious issues that can be diagnosed in advertising beyond the concerns of the groups above. The automated buying and selling of online advertising can privilege regressive and far-right voices, and thus presents grave dangers for democracy (by way of disrespecting and even attacking minorities, or women) through the rise of hate speech. In some cases, browser extensions have been created to warn citizens online about problematic advertising and/or sites. One such example is La ultraextensión, created after the Spanish elections of 2019 in opposition to the far-right party Vox that won 24 seats in the parliament, in a first win for a far-right party since the fascist era of Francisco Franco. The browser extension changes the name of the party to 'the far right' across various news sites. Furthermore, there are examples such as Stop Funding Hate in the UK, a pressure group that asks companies to divest from advertising in (thus, to defund) certain British newspapers that 'spread hate and division'.[24] Stop Funding Hate involves citizens to act in protest of advertising in outlets that allow hate speech by using social media to lobby companies. Then, there is the case of Sleeping Giants in the US which also invites citizens to protest hate speech (particularly to lobby advertisers to withdraw their advertising from target sites). Citizens take screenshots of a brand's ad that appear on *Breitbart News* or other sites, and then post them to Twitter in a tweet that tags both the brand's Twitter account and the Sleeping Giants account. Francesca Colli (2020) calls this 'indirect consumer activism'. Hence, there are multiple ways in which resistance to advertising produces collective anti-consumerist activism, and, importantly, targets advertising, rather than brands, as part of the struggle for social and environmental justice. At this point, it is useful to turn our attention to the technologies that have enabled (as well as disabled) consumer activism historically and presently.

Media and Consumer Activism: Methods and Approaches

Contemporary consumer activism appears within larger processes of economic, cultural, and technological change and demonstrates both continuities and changes. We can trace continuities from 'white lists'[25] or boycott bulletins of the past to the consumer activist magazines of the present. For instance, the UK-based *Ethical Consumer* magazine and website publishes boycott lists to everyone, as well as 'lists' of ethical alternatives (mostly) to its subscribers.[26] Do you want to avoid shopping through Amazon? Here are some alternatives, which they propose.[27] Furthermore, anti-consumerist magazines such as Adbusters (reader-supported and advertising-free magazine) remain in operation and offer both print and digital versions, while past examples such as Consume Hasta Morir's anti-consumerist *Malababa* had three issues printed but remains digitally available free. We also trace changes. We now see more complex and interactive organizational web pages, petition sites, ethical consumption apps, and digital communities espousing new forms of consumption or utilizing consumption as a tool of political intervention. Those give rise to claims about the broadening of politics and consumption and the readdressing of power between different agencies; 'new communication technologies have altered the balance of power between citizens and corporations in that everyday people can now press political claims through social media' (Heldman, 2017: 23). Such claims are true, to a certain extent, but not new. Margaret Scammell wrote that 'we, as consumers, are increasingly aware of our political power and increasingly willing to use it' (2000: 352) and that 'some of the most celebrated, and arguably successful, consumer actions were led on the Net' (ibid.: 355). Indeed they were, as this was the time of the Nike e-mail exchange, when Jonah Peretti (then-MIT postgraduate student, now-Buzzfeed CEO) decided to request a pair of personalized shoes that featured the word 'sweatshop' or a picture of the underage worker that made his shoes in a discursive stand-off with Nike. Peretti's email exchange is considered one of the first viral campaigns as it reached over 11 million people globally and he personally received 3,655 emails about it (Peretti with Micheletti, 2004). Yet it is not indicative of all campaigns that have used consumer activist tactics to augment their cause through media technologies.

Consumer activism is shaped through and by media and various agents, as outlined in the previous section. The way in which academics have approached the relationship between media technologies and consumer (activist) practices has largely varied in relation to the methods chosen. Locating the presence of political consumerism through survey data, for instance, leads scholars to argue that people who use social media are more likely to engage in political consumerism than those who do not (Gil de Zúñiga et al., 2014). Through a similar approach, Kelm and Dohle (2018) question the extent to which online information (measured by how often citizens had used the internet for information on reasons to boycott and buycott) and communication (measured by whether citizens had used the internet for political expression or to communicate about consumer politics with others) activities influence the intensity of political consumerism. Again, scholars find a positive correlation between media and consumer activism. What does that mean? Such data are useful to the extent that they offer a window into the presence or absence of a phenomenon but remain limited in explaining how meaning is made and negotiated. Analysing the communication of fair-trade brands through discourse analysis, on the other hand, can produce arguments about the way in which solidarity (though buycotts) is constructed (Polynczuk-Alenius and Pantii, 2017). Rather than merely asking whether solidarity exists, it is also important to ask how it manifests and what it means.

Within popular commentary (and, often, academic research), the notion of 'digital solutionism' (Morozov, 2014) persists. This is the idea that technology can be used to create solutions for all sorts of issues, from poverty to climate change. To offer a constructive and holistic analysis, research on (media) practice has made key contributions to the study of what people do with media and how, avoiding the trap of media determinism and offering perspectives on hybridity and complexity (Barassi, 2015; Couldry, 2004, 2012; Enghel and Noske-Turner, 2018; Treré, 2019). In *Digital Economy*, Tim Jordan (2020) highlights how an economy requires the identification of practices and culture and treats 'digital economic practices as repeated and patterned habits of creating, exchanging and consuming a huge range of goods and commodities that make up the wealth of society'. In *Activism on the Web*, Veronica Barassi argues that a media practice approach 'challenges techno-deterministic assumptions on the pervasiveness and agency of internet technologies in the everyday life of social movements by considering the tension between "old" and "new" media and by highlighting the complex relationship between media structures, practices, and beliefs' (2015: 9). In *Hybrid Media Activism*, Emiliano Treré (2019) conceptualizes a paradigm for thinking about social movements in relation to communicative complexity and argues for the importance of approaching activism through theories of media practice. Treré's approach invites us to explore ecologies, imaginaries, and algorithms. As already discussed in relation to programmatic advertising, these can spread propaganda, manipulation, and disinformation.

Whether algorithms can be manipulated to promote social and environmental change is questionable, though there are efforts to do so. 'Profsarahgrace' posted a video on Tik Tok of herself dancing to the superimposed text 'When you spent 4 years getting a PhD in marketing to realize that doggos and tiktok dance challenges are the best way to promote your account that deconstructs consumer culture [shopping bag emoticon, knife emoticon] and promotes conscious consumerism [comet emoticon]'. Can 'doggos' and dances really be used to further conscious consumerism? Is conscious consumerism the only way to practise politics within promotional culture? Media practices such as this can only be read within context, to grasp their complexity and evaluate their impact.

To address the complexity of contemporary consumer activism, here and continuing from previous work where I have drawn on ethnographic methods such as interviews, participant observation, and document analysis, I also embrace the practice turn. Consumer activism is a terrain of consumer practices; questions of who engages in this and how, how they use media objects and intermediaries, as well as how those practices are mediated deserve our attention. In this section, I review the literature and explore examples of consumer activism as digitally enabled (e.g. Facebook groups of fair-trade supporters) or digitally native (e.g. communities emerging and existing entirely online, such as Sleeping Giants in the US), and suggest that we can illuminate three key areas of consumer activism vis-à-vis the media: ecologies, publicities, and responsibilities.

Ecologies

How can we approach the relationship between media technologies and consumer activism? Media ecology is a holistic approach that combines media, agencies, and meaning to the study of communication and social change; it constructively surpasses what Treré (2019) calls the 'five fallacies of communication reductionism' (virtual/physical binary, one-medium perspectives, fascination with the present, technological visibility, and celebration of digital alternativeness). We can start by problematizing media technologies. Rather than, for instance, celebrating TikTok activists as entities separate from physical contexts, enabled by the specific platform, enchanted with its present success, enthralled in what appears rather than what is hidden, and revelling in the alternative traits of TikTok, an ecological approach asks for deeper questioning. Are activists not people connected to places, present, and past times, or as Merlyna Lim (2018) argues, grounded in spatial, temporal, and historical roots? Media ecology 'explores multiplicity and hybridity, overcomes dichotomies, assumes a diachronic perspective, and invite us to recognize the political and critical nature' of mediated phenomena (Treré, 2019: 18). In other words, media ecologies refer to the continuities and changes in the media and communications environment and include all technologies at the disposal of consumer activists who are embodied presences making decisions largely informed by their local contexts. A media ecology approach is a constructive response to 'digital solutionism' (Morozov, 2014).

Research on consumer activism and digital media has emerged in the last few years, identifying a gap in the field. Some have studied the shaping of consumption in and by social media (Sörum and Fuentes, 2019), the process of online consumer activism within the petition site Change.org (Minocher, 2019), or the process of construction of the Yellow Economic Circle in Hong Kong (Lee and Fong, 2021). Others have questioned the role of apps through digital ethnography (usually, a combination of interviews with app developers and consumers, as well as observation of apps) (Eli et al., 2016; Fuentes and Sörum, 2019; Hansson, 2017; Sörum, 2020), or an analytical survey of ethical consumption apps (Humphery and Jordan, 2018). These scholars do not agree on the digital affordances of consumer activism. For some, the way in which apps are scripted as 'ethical' choice prescribers promotes consumer choice and ignores forms of consumer activism such as consuming differently (through community-supported forms) or consuming less (reducing consumption) (Hansson, 2017). For others, 'there is scope for such apps to ably demonstrate how a "consumer agency" can sit alongside more collective or associational forms of political action' (Humphery and Jordan, 2018: 536). The digital marketplace includes a number of established apps, as well as some emerging apps (e.g. Sojo[28]) which raise questions about digital technocultures and their agency within a politics of consumption; do they 'promise a consumer agency, but then technologically displace it'? (ibid.: 535). However, there can be no quick conclusions when it comes to apps, as this would fall into the fallacy of one-mediumness. Whether digital affordances enclose or further emancipate consumer activist agency is best explored through the question of what people do with media – they could be using apps to start their own campaign (e.g. Buycott[29]) or to connect to local exchange communities (BuyNothing[30]). In addition, they might be involved in other forms of local or transnational politics in and through other media platforms. An ecological approach to consumer activism requires a careful exploration of how technologies, agencies, and moralities circulate in order to identify examples of technology that assists in processes of change.

Publicities

How does consumer activism become public and how do causes compete in a hierarchy of publicities? Publicity is the keystone of public information and communication, the basis of a public sphere and, in a Habermasian reading (the way in which the industrialization of societies and mass media have resulted in the decline of a sphere of political discussion and debate), advertising has replaced 'critical publicity' with 'manipulative publicity'. Borrowing these terms from Habermas (1989), we can call 'critical publicity' the campaigns of citizens and community groups that advocate for change through consumer activism, aim to provide information about causes, and engage stakeholders in communication. Then we can call 'manipulative publicity' the dominance of advertising industries and the routine normalization of consumer surveillance (Turow, 2017). Within media ecologies, these two competing publicities exist in a dialectical relation. A number of studies further enforce this point regarding dialectics. Veronica Barassi argues that 'the relationship between social media and political activism is defined by activists' negotiation with the "self-centered" logic of these web 2.0 technologies' (2015: 79). Julie Uldam similarly illustrates how the affordances of social media visibility to activists are counterbalanced due to 'visibility asymmetries that privilege corporate actors' (2018: 55). Zizheng Yu (2021) shows how, in China, engaging in online consumer activism is not encouraged by government officials, who mention the resulting loss of personal privacy. Indeed, as Yu writes, this was what happened to the woman who protested the faulty vehicle she had bought from a Mercedes dealership in Xi'an, who unwillingly found her personal information publicly disseminated. To summarize, the intersection of 'critical publicity' with 'manipulative publicity' is not simply a win-win scenario. The dialectics of publicity is about the constant counterbalancing of benefits that can be gained and losses that can occur by public exposure.

Even within 'critical publicity', there is an 'asymmetry of publicities'. An asymmetry of publicities refers to the agents, as well as the meanings of consumer activism. Regarding the first, Emiliano Treré and Zizheng Yu (2021) also note different consumer activist tactics employed by ordinary consumers and highly influential internet celebrities or We-media operators. Chapter 6 also sheds light into the publicity affordances of celebrities in relation to consumer activism. Regarding the second, Minna Santaoja and Piia Jallinoja's (2021) netographic (social media content, digital media coverage, and interviews with group moderators) study of a Facebook group of vegans in Finland demonstrates how meanings connected to veganism resist ethical or health-related discussions and instead celebrate the light-hearted and joyful discussions on indulgent veganism. In short, as far as publicities go, consumer activism is conditioned by asymmetry, whereby already visible agents receive advantageous publicity, while topics that are less contentious or complex are curated and promoted accordingly. Yet this is not conclusive. To understand consumer activism from a media practice perspective we need to account for the complexity of technologies, agents, and meanings. Here, meanings are explored through publicities, but extend beyond them, from the presentism of what we see online to the imaginaries of activists and the lived experience of citizens.

Responsibilities

How is responsibility related to consumer activism framed within media ecologies? Here we encounter a number of responses from the responsibility of the consuming individual to the emergence of collective campaigning responsibility, and, finally, networked campaigner–individual–corporation responsibility. For some, media technologies foster individualized responses to ethical or environmental issues. In their study of how the Buycott app frames political engagement, Eli et al. find that with its 'brand of prepackaged activism, subscribers become consumers – not only of products, but also of the app itself' (2016: 71) and thus the activist habitus which is constructed through the app is 'a consumer habitus' (ibid.). Similarly, Allison Page analyses the responsibilization of consumers through slaveryfootprint.org (a platform and app launched by a non-profit and the US State Department), and finds a blurring of slavery within capitalism and a reconfiguration of the notion of freedom:

> Through the use of algorithms and digital platforms, one can abolish slavery while also making a profit and strengthening the market overall. With companies as the 'new' leaders of the 'free world,' the site's complicity with neoliberal racial capitalism is clear, as is the line they draw between slavery and capitalism. Freedom here means a trickle-down logic of corporate freedom: corporations set the terms and Made in a Free World hopes that corporate freedom means freedom for everyone. (2017: 52)

While the use of algorithms and digital content delivery is hailed as revolutionary by the partners behind slaveryfootprint.org, there is a tendency to reproduce 'digital solutionism' (Morozov, 2014), which conceals structural inequalities and puts the consumer at the heart of a 'consumer solutionism' narrative.

There are also arguments, however, for the significance of media technologies in fostering collective responses and responsibilities to social and environmental change. Communities such as freecycle.com[31] exist to reduce consumption by operating as international grassroots groups based on the free exchange of goods. In this sense, 'virtual spaces help create feelings of belonging and solidarity and support for alternate ways of living' (Nelson et al., 2007: 146). Their study drew from survey data, and they admit that such a statement is speculative, as it is important to question what people do with media. A study by Rufas and Hine (2018) which draws on interviews with Freecycle users in south-east England suggests that they imagined users while projecting their own values onto them and making assumptions about socioeconomic types. Yet despite the limited possibilities for overcoming existing social divisions, 'most interviewees were very positive overall about their experiences of these local online platforms and the platforms' impact on their view of people in general' (Rufas and Hine, 2018: 3891). Also examining Freecycle from a practice theory perspective, Sally Eden (2017) identifies the blurring of binaries such as consumption/production, digital/material, and mainstream/alternative. A practice approach enables the location and illumination of affordances by platforms such as Freecycle that can subvert the individual responsibilization of 'consumer solutionism'.

Finally, others conceptualize responsibilities as collective through activist–consumers–corporations engagements. In part, this can be explained by digitally native forms of consumer activism such as Sleeping Giants who ask citizens to force corporations to be responsible by divesting from hate speech and intolerance culture (Braun et al., 2019). Relevant examples that engage activists, consumers, and corporations are also Carrotmob[32] and GoodGuide.[33] Constance Kampf (2018) argues that social media shift activism from targeting businesses to restructuring their field of operations to connect consumer social responsibility (CnSR) with corporate social responsibility (CSR). For Kampf, we need to understand '*how social media-based activists use practices and knowledge* to engage consumers in social movements who are positive toward both business and their activist concerns' (2018: 2, italics in original). Connected responsibilities can also be explained by the increasing engagement of market actors with consumer activism, which is what Jenkins calls 'treacherous territory' (quoted in Kozinets and Jenkins, 2021: 5). Jenkins continues:

> Companies should not be co-opting these social movements, but they should recognize that they live in a world where these social movements are occurring and they are dealing with consumers who feel strongly, one way or another, about these issues. As we think about the current moment, I am seeing lead footed and facepalm responses from companies on all sides. How to describe some of the inane ways that brands initially attached themselves to Black Lives Matter? There was one bathroom product which

said, 'We got your backside' to the Black Lives Matter movement so that they celebrated their commitment to fight for anti-racism. You know, we just don't need a toilet paper brand to affirm a social change movement. (ibid.: 8)

To summarize, a media practice approach is essential in disentangling the entanglements of consumer activism within promotional culture and media technologies. Understanding what consumer activism is, what its goals are, what the role of consumers (or, better, citizens) are and what are the media technologies at our disposal requires an understanding of media platforms and practices that extends beyond fast celebration or criticism.

Conclusion

This chapter has defined and debated consumer activism within interdisciplinary approaches. Consumer activism manifests through questioning mass and unsafe consumerism and its social and environmental consequences, campaigning for institutional change, practising consumption differently, and imagining life beyond consumerism. It is about how advertising and promotional culture, as well as brands and celebrities become platforms or indeed players in social or environmental change. Consumer activism can appear at the local, national, and transnational level, promoting or protesting communities, corporations, nations, and the planet. Conceptualizing consumer activism within a broad yet directly relevant interdisciplinary research sheds lights onto the centrality of consumer activism in the post-COVID-19 era, and necessitates its grounding within context, its exploration within both progressive and regressive causes, and its uncomfortable relationship with individual choice. Celebrating consumer activism without approaching it analytically can lead to 'consumer solutionism', the popular narrative pushed forward by promotional intermediaries such as corporations and celebrities.

Locating the agents of consumer activism, we can both confirm and contest the centrality of 'the politics of choice' (Fenton, 2017: 74). On the one hand, popular narratives of change habitually highlight citizens as change agents through narratives of 'reduce, reuse, recycle'. On the other hand, collectivities connected around anti-consumerism (especially advertising critique and regulation) have been forming both physically (e.g. AdFree Cities) or virtually (Sleeping Giants). Furthermore, promotional intermediaries such as market actors and celebrities come to take centre stage in the performance and practice of consumer activism. Conceptually, therefore, the complexity of agents in the articulation and action concerned with consumer activism necessitates a contextualized, practice-based approach. Consumer activism, as historian Lawrence Glickman (2009) reminds us, waxes and wanes, and by understanding its history and practice, we can avoid disconnected and deterministic readings of contemporary manifestations of the phenomenon.

Consumer activism is central to contemporary causes and politics, but the extent to which it is empowering to citizens or effective for social change requires interrogation. Overall, different methodological approaches produce different perspectives on consumer activism: to name a few, survey data find it and correlate it with other forms of political participation, discourse data deconstruct it and identify its tendencies and tensions, interview data contextualize it and ground it within lived experiences. All these approaches are useful in different ways, but a combination tends to provide more holistic approaches. Particularly within the study of consumer activism and the media, we need to move beyond 'communication reductionism' (Treré, 2019). This means we need to understand that while the advent of digital/social/mobile media has both routinely and rebelliously reconfigured consumer activism, it is not a panacea. We can interrogate how consumer activist agency is constituted, mobilized, and connected to technologies, agencies, and meanings. By exploring the ecologies, publicities, and responsibilities of media and consumer activism, we can appraise consumer activism from a practice approach.

Notes

1. Some of the ways in which the campaign urges individuals to act in support of sustainability are to save energy at home; drive and fly less; eat more plant-based foods; cut food waste; reduce, reuse, repair, recycle; get wind or solar energy; switch to an electric vehicle; choose eco-friendly products; and speak up. (www.un.org/en/actnow) (14 September 2021).
2. https://vimeo.com/470768963 (13 September 2021).
3. At the time of writing, Sarah Grace's (PhD in Marketing) account 'Profsarahgrace' had over 11,000 followers (25 October 2021).
4. https://vimeo.com/466740743 (14 September 2021).
5. The authors define a foodie as 'a person who devotes considerable time and energy to eating and learning about good food, however "good food" is defined' (Johnston and Baumann, 2015: x).
6. http://trashartmuseum.weebly.com (26 November 2021).
7. www.ogilvy.com/ideas/making-brands-matter-generations-come
8. GREEN B was launched on Earth Day 2021 to connect the Benetton Group's brand initiatives for sustainability (www.benettongroup.com/media-press/press-releases-and-statements/green-b-sustainability-according-to-benetton/) (25 November 2021).
9. TOMS is a company that runs on the 'one for one concept', gifting one pair of shoes to a child in need for every pair of shoes purchased.
10. As part of their autumn/winter 2017 marketing strategy and in retaliation to the uncertainty of Brexit, British fashion brand Jigsaw launched a pro-immigration campaign on print, social media, and digital ads, as well as an advertising

takeover of Oxford Circus tube station in London and the website of *The Times* newspaper. (https://uk.fashionnetwork.com/news/jigsaw-launches-high-profile-pro-immigration-campaign,879818.html) (25 November 2021).

11. In 2018, for the 30th anniversary of the *Just Do It* marketing campaign, Nike's *Dream Crazy* advertisement featured former NFL quarterback Colin Kaepernick, who in 2016 refused to stand and took the knee during the national anthem to protest police brutality and racial injustice. The advertisement received polarized responses from Trump's call for a Nike boycott (www.reuters.com/article/us-nike-kaepernick-idUSKCN1LL1WS) (25 November 2021) and Trump supporters burning their Nike shoes (www.bbc.co.uk/newsround/45433923) (25 November 2021) to celebrities and supporters praising Nike and buying more Nike gear.
12. Over 300 (mostly French) brands formed the *Make Friday Green Again* collective (www.makefridaygreenagain.com/), and asked consumers to boycott Black Friday and instead spend the day looking in their wardrobes at what they can repair, sell or recycle (Foster, 2019).
13. www.koreatimes.co.kr/www/art/2021/10/732_317539.html (1 November 2021).
14. www.thetimes.co.uk/article/your-cappuccino-moment-xkknwr7gnhm (2 October 2021).
15. www.nytimes.com/2019/04/03/world/asia/brunei-hotel-boycotts.html (20 September 2021).
16. https://deadline.com/2019/03/george-clooney-sultain-of-brunei-hotels-boycott-beverly-hills-hotel-anti-gay-laws-brunei-1202584579/ (2 October 2021).
17. www.forbes.com/sites/rachelsandler/2019/05/06/brunei-rolls-back-gay-death-penalty-after-a-month-of-global-protest-and-boycotts/?sh=40dc8af36c0b (20 September 2021).
18. www.bbc.com/news/world-us-canada-27303085 (20 September 2021).
19. www.ibtimes.co.uk/brigade-antisexiste-masked-feminist-group-vandalising-sexist-posters-1651152; www.vice.com/en/article/bjdn5q/the-masked-feminist-brigade-vandalizing-misogynistic-ads (20 September 2021).
20. https://adfreecities.org.uk/ (22 October 2021).
21. https://adfreecities.org.uk/our-vision-and-values/ (22 October 2021).
22. ibid.
23. http://proyectosquatters.blogspot.com/2008/12/los-objetivos-de-squatters.html (22 October 2021)
24. https://stopfundinghate.info/ (22 October 2021).
25. In the early 1900s, the US National Consumers' League published 'white lists' of firms approved by unions (Hilton, 2009).
26. www.ethicalconsumer.org/about-us/celebrating-30-years-ethical-consumer (14 October 2021).
27. www.ethicalconsumer.org/ethical-campaigns/boycott-amazon/shopping-without-amazon (26 October 2021).
28. Sojo was launched in 2021 as the UK's first clothing alterations and repairs app which supports the 'reuse' model through repairs. Through the app, consumers can find a local seamster service, have a 'rider' pick up their order and deliver it to them when it is ready (www.home.sojo.uk/).
29. Buycott is an app launched in the US in 2013, featuring a number of crowd-sourced campaigns and product barcode scanning that provides information about the product history.

30. BuyNothing is an app launched in the US in 2021, as part of the international network Buy Nothing Project that focuses on reduced consumption. Buy Nothing groups are different to Freecycle groups in that they are smaller and based on the idea of hyper-local gifting economies which foster a sense of community (www.ethicalconsumer.org/technology/beyond-consumerism-buy-nothing-app) (1 November 2021).
31. Freecycle was launched in the US in 2003, and can currently be found in over 100 countries (www.freecycle.org/pages/about) (2 November 2021).
32. Carrotmob is a non-profit organisation in the US, which employs the tactic of buycotts where consumers collectively purchase from one particular business to reward it for its social or environmental responsibility. This campaign tactic is used by community organizers around the world, and businesses compete for the title of the most socially responsible, which guarantees support by a network of consumers.
33. GoodGuide.com is a B-corporation standing as an intermediary between businesses and consumers, and provides the latter with third party scientific information at the point of purchase.

THREE
NATIONALISM, RACE, ETHNICITY, AND CONSUMER ACTIVISM

Introduction: Can a Consumer Save the National Economy?

> Here are some reasons why he could not find work in Greece: Yannis began his day by setting his alarm clock (made in Japan) at 6 o'clock in the morning ... He made his coffee in a coffee pot (made in Turkey), shaved with his electric shaver (made in Germany), put on his shirt (made in Sri Lanka), his branded jeans (made in Singapore), his shoes (made in Italy). He ate some Gouda cheese from the Netherlands, Milner cheese from Germany, two Frankfurt sausages, tomatoes from Israel, two apples from Chile, and an orange from Spain. Then he checked his email on his laptop (made in Mexico), while checking his watch (made in Taiwan). Next, he locked the door (made in the USA), got in his car (made in France), and filled up the tank with petrol (from Saudi Arabia). At the end of yet another fruitless and frustrating effort to find work and after he printed some more copies of reference letters from a printer (made in Malaysia), Yannis decided to rest a bit. He put his slippers (made in Brazil) on, poured a glass of wine (made in France) and turned on the TV (made in Indonesia). Then he was thinking why he could not find work in GREECE.[1]

The above story appeared in the Greek blogosphere at the aftermath of the financial crisis of 2008, propagating the idea that citizens should recall their responsibilities towards their nation and its economy. The moral of the story goes like this: if you do not support your country, it will not support you. This storyline appears at different points in time and sustains the belief that if you support your nation's economy your nation will make you a part of its economy; or in even simpler terms, if you consume the 'right' way, you will be rewarded. Following on, if you consume the 'wrong' way, you will be reprimanded, like Yannis, who couldn't find work in his country, despite being able to surround himself with commodities from around the world. The story of Yannis is not unique to the Greek context. Appearing under different names and projecting different characters who deviate from the 'right' kind of consumption, the same moral story appears in many countries at different points in their history. To think about consumption and the nation involves questioning how consumption has been used as a powerful mobilizer of citizens to behave in the 'right' way, from the inception of the nation to moments of national crisis. Elected governments, right-wing nationalists, patriotic citizens, and everyone else can and do promote consumer activism, whether through implicit or explicit connections to the nation. Importantly, thinking about consumption and the nation also involves questioning what nationalism means in relation to race and ethnicity to those who promote it.

Consumer activism can appear as a reminder of the contested and contentious nature of contemporary nations. The COVID-19 pandemic disrupted the flow of everyday life and brought the ideology of nationalism to centre stage, and the mundane but also malevolent aspects of nationalism have been exacerbated: governments competed with each other for equipment, there were concerns about people being stranded 'abroad', and stereotypes and schisms between nations grew. What are nations, how are they imagined and experienced, and how do consumption and consumer activism intersect with contemporary nationalism? To respond to these questions, we will first go through key concepts regarding nationalism and then go through key theories that will provide a fundamental theoretical framework to examine the relationship between nationalism and consumer activism. We will map out critical issues and key arguments from the relevant literature, reflect on their methods and analyse the case of the Yellow Economic Circle in Hong Kong that started in 2019, before presenting key questions for future analyses of consumer activism. This chapter addresses the politics of nationalism, race, and ethnicity in relation to consumer activism and argues for the importance of recognizing, analysing and critically appraising cases based on specific considerations: 1) history, 2) ideology, 3) agency, 4) justice.

Key Concepts

The discursive and practical constructions of the nation are often routinely produced and reproduced in everyday consumption. In popular discourse, the terms nation, race, and ethnicity are often conflated. They tend to be regarded in simpler, blurry terms, understood and misunderstood, and in those misunderstandings intolerance can rise. We see this conflation in representations of criminals, refugees, and sufferers as originating from 'dangerous', 'dark' and (excuse the language) 'shit' countries.² From a narrative of developed and developing world, we have degraded to a narrative of 'great' world versus 'shit' world. To think about the nation is to remember that representation is a powerful mechanism in creating ideas, myths, and narratives of ourselves and of others, often based on race and ethnicity. Then we can think about consumer activism and map out its dynamics, its possibilities and its limitations, as well as its signification.

Race and Ethnicity

Ethnicity refers to cultural processes that we are all conditioned by. As Lisa Peñaloza and Christopher Chávez posit, 'ethnicity remains a major source of dynamism and conflict in many nations, cities, neighborhoods, work spaces, and marketplaces' (2016: 1). It is a kin term to nationhood, often conflated in the presupposition that all nationals come from the same ethnos and share a language, history, and culture. For Stuart Hall, there are two discourses of ethnicity: a closed one and an open one whereby the first is essentialist and exclusive and the second creates and converges ethnicities and considers 'the boundaries of belonging as permeable' (Mercer, 2017: 5). Such competing conceptualizations of ethnicity make nationhood an arena for cultural, political, and economic contestation. Ethnocentrism is the belief that one's ethnicity is central and superior to others. In *Consuming Race*, Ben Pitcher speaks of ethnicity as a generally preferred concept to race, 'precisely because it references culture, not biology' (2014: 30). Yet Pitcher also identifies two issues with replacing the concept of race with that of ethnicity: first, it tends to seek application and authenticity in particular communities and, second, it is essentialist in that it is determined by place or community of origin from birth and through language, culture, or skin colour. Pitcher's focus on race rather than ethnicity allows for a broader set of dynamic identifications that give people a local and transnational sense of belonging. Opposition to ethnicities different to the dominant ones thus signifies a closed discourse of ethnicity and a clear discourse of racism.

Like ethnicity, race is socially constructed. In those social constructions, hierarchies, stratifications, and boundaries are discursively, legally, and culturally perceived, and performed. Du Bois (1903) wrote of racial stratification and segregation in relation to 'the colour line' where whiteness is privileged and blackness is ousted. The privilege afforded to whiteness in the post-colonial Western world has persisted through its insistence on studying, classifying and stereotyping 'Otherness', as Edward Said (1978) posited in his canonical book. Orientalism is a key contribution to post-colonial theory. As Said notably argued, 'the Orient is not Oriental in the commonplace sense, but it was made to be Oriental' (1978: 41). Furthermore, Hazel Carby offers an incisive definition of race:

> Race is not a material object, a thing; it has not to do with what people are but with how they are classified. It is a practice or series of practices, a technology that calculates and assigns differences to peoples and communities and then institutionalizes these differences. It is a verb not a noun. The only way to understand the complex configurations and connotations of 'race' is in the context of particular times and places. I use the word racialisation to capture the practices and processes involved in the calculations and impositions of difference, all of which have their own logic but are not eternally fixed. (2019: 65)

We are all affected by our ethnic and racial appearance and subsequent categorization. We also produce and reproduce racial meanings in our daily lives (Pitcher, 2014). Yet processes of racialization tend to produce difference based on appearance rather sameness based on than belonging.

Nations and Nationalism

Nations are geographical territories governed by a state structure. They are organizational units for the promotion of political and economic (and often a dominant religious) ideology and they legally inscribe rights and responsibilities to their nationals in the form of citizenship. There are long-standing debates on what constitutes citizenship, starting with Marshall's (1950) approach and extending to more cultural conceptualizations (Couldry et al., 2010; Miller, 2007; Stevenson, 2003; Vrikki, 2020). They also culturally inscribe norms and rituals to their citizens, in the form of national identity. As will be discussed later, connecting consumption with citizenship has been a tactic of the construction of modern nations (Figure 3.1).

What is nationalism then? Nationalism is an ideology that is hardwired in our everyday practices and perceptions. Nationalism is also not fixed, but rather a social construction. As Benedict Anderson wrote, nations, ethnicity, and race are all 'cultural artefacts of a particular kind' (1991: 4). Their meaning and salience change over time. For Anderson, nations are 'imagined communities', imagining the values, rituals, and loyalties they share with people they have never met before, that inhabit the same national borders. In *Media Nations*, Sabina Mihelj (2011) argues that nationalism is best understood through the prisms of discourse, legitimacy, and power and how these are entangled in specific social spaces; social context, social position, and social power all matter. Nationalism is an ideology that can and does create attachments to particular nations, speaking to a basic human need (the need for a sense of belonging) and connecting that to a particular territory and its cultural associations. Some become part of a territory by birth, while some are required to pass 'citizenship' examinations in countries where the majority of citizens might not be able to answer. Yet these fixtures of nationhood persist.

Figure 3.1

Copyright: Adbusters, permission granted.

We can understand nationalism as the discursive construction of the multiple possible relationships between race, ethnicity, and the nation, the 'fateful triangle' according to a collection bringing to light Stuart Hall's lectures in Harvard in 1994 (Mercer, 2017). Consumption comes to play an instrumental part in the daily construction of nationalism, both in the form of support or opposition towards a nation as a whole or an ethnic group.

Nationalism is further exacerbated in the digital age. Sabina Mihelj and César Jiménez-Martínez (2021) argue for the importance of acknowledging the subtle, less visible ways in which digital technologies reproduce nationalism. Drawing on some of the key theoretical approaches outlined below and connecting with studies of digital media, they demonstrate how digital nationalism and nations differ qualitatively to analogue articulations of these through diversification, polarization, and commodification. Diversification refers to the way in which citizens can enjoy accessible participation to digital technologies that (despite structural or societal constraints, such as lack of access or knowledge of access and use) have the potential to produce different national narratives. Polarization refers to fragmented participation that can lead to the disjunction between inclusive and excusive approaches to national belonging. Finally, commodification concerns the mediation of participation through the marketplace where a complex ecology of actors reproduce nationalism: commercial actors connect to national narratives alongside nations connecting to commercial narratives (Kania-Lundholm, 2014). On the other hand, 'the web offers a perfect environment for selling far-right goods, such as the merchandise sold online by Thor Steinar, White Trash Rebel, Dirty Tees and Doberman's Aggressive' (Mihelj and Jiménez-Martínez, 2021: 341). At the same time, citizens engage with a #BoycottGermany hashtag campaign to oppose austerity measures in Greece (Lekakis, 2017b). As Mihelj and Jiménez-Martínez (2021) also argue, the appearance of digital nationalism is not new, but is rooted in analogue theories and histories. This is what the following section examines.

Nationalism and Consumption: Key Theories

Nationalism is an ideology connected to the economic growth of nations; it has also always been connected to struggles for and against nations or ethnicities, which are marked as 'different'. The study of nationalism is and must be interdisciplinary and theories of nationalism have historically tended to focus on the frameworks of primordialism, modernism, and ethnosymbolism (Özkırımlı, 2000). Primordialism is an ethnocentric conceptualization of nationalism where the nation stems from the persistence of ethnic identities and struggles and where it is legitimated by ethnicity and culture. This strict conceptualization of nationalism through the prism of engraved and enduring ethnic identities does not recognize the fluidity and dynamism of ethnic articulations through migration. Modernism is an approach according to which nationalism belongs to a broader discourse of Westernization, growth, and progress. Ethnosymbolism is another school of thought focusing on the significance of national symbols, myths, values, and rituals, focusing more on the cultural construction of the nation rather than its economic construction as modernism does.

To understand how the nation intersects with consumption campaigns and practices, and more specifically how nationalism intersects with consumer activism, we can look at how nations are constructed and reconstructed through representations, discourses, practices, and performances. As Samuel Sadian (2018) argues, it is possible to think of consumer studies as critical social theory in unpacking how economic action undertaken by social actors can explain social change. What we can find out by looking at situated approaches to consumer activism can open up ways of understanding history and questioning its reproduction. 'Buy national' campaigns, for instance, appear historically and are appropriated in times of crisis with various motivations. The US has been constructed as a consumer republic (Cohen, 2003), and China's nation-building project was founded on its products (Gerth, 2003), while the British Empire used the Empire Marketing Board to legitimate the Empire and problematically broaden Britishness through colonial trade (Kothari, 2014). Communicating the nation and national belonging has tended to envelop consumption practices and condition the possibilities for consumer activism where governments, market actors, and citizens of all ideological persuasions all fight for their right to represent (and sometimes impose) a national narrative.

Religion further complicates consumer culture. Guillaume D. Johnson, Kevin D. Thomas, and Sonya A. Grier (2017) demonstrate how French secularism exhibits certain problematics when it comes to marketplace inclusion of halal meat. Consumers rebelled against a popular burger chain in France deciding to serve exclusively halal meat at about 2 per cent of their stores, claiming disempowerment and reclaiming equality and secular 'freedom' in the marketplace, thus further reinforcing the privilege of white French consumers. Similarly, in the UK, halal consumption in mainstream supermarkets has been contentious; the country's struggle for multiculturalism reveals long-routed assumptions of Britishness as white and of non-white people and consumption practices as to be avoided, while 'Britishness' is produced both as secular and at the same time as Islamophobic (Lekakis, 2019). Religion persists as an area of consumer contention. Whether mobilized by intolerance or rejection of intolerance, it can connect contentious consumers at a local level (a neighbourhood group resisting the sale of halal products in their supermarket) or at a transnational level, as the transnational boycott of Chinese products by Muslim (and non-Muslim) consumers over the violation of Uighur human rights suggests.[3] Furthermore, a study of everyday nationalism in unsettled times suggested that the pandemic transformed 'routines of everyday life, suddenly conferring new significance on doing normal things as a way of performing one's nationhood and calibrating national solidarities' (Goode et al., 2020: 1). Yet everyday nationalist practices such as 'performing the nation' and 'consuming the nation' demonstrated both solidarities and exclusions. Take the example of Victory in Europe Day in the UK when British councils called for stay-at-home street parties (taking afternoon tea, listening to the Queen, decorating the house, and having a garden party):

> the assumption that everyone involved in the celebration has access to a backyard where they could have tea and scones excluded lower class citizens and residents … from participating in this invented national ritual. It similarly neglects the fact that the Muslim British population was celebrating Ramadan, which automatically excluded them from the daytime, food-based merriment. (ibid.: 16)

The example serves to highlight how nationalism as an ideology tends to produce a narrative for collective behaviour that aims to unify, but often fails to grasp different social positions particularly pertaining to class and religion.

The next section breaks down different articulations of the power of nationalism through the concepts of banal nationalism and everyday nationhood, as well as the relationship between them (for an extensive review of the literature on consumption and nationalism, see Lekakis, 2018). Then, key theorizations of nationalism in economic terms (economic nationalism and consumer nationalism) are explored and forwarded into the present through an exploration of resistant consumption practices in relation to 'backlash politics'. Significantly, there is a highlighting and problematization of race and ethnicity within consumer activism.

Banal Nationalism and Everyday Nationhood

Michael Billig's (1995) *Banal Nationalism* remains a highly influential framework for making sense of the way in which the rational (in terms of systems of governance) and irrational (in terms of emotional attachment) belief in the nation is reproduced on a daily basis in subtle and symbolic ways. The main contribution of this thesis is that we are all always already hardwired to experience life through the prism of the nation. Working against mainstream theories of the time that equated nationalism with its extreme manifestations ('hot nationalism'), Billig noted how within the Western context (UK and US) we experience latent manifestations of nationalism, 'banal nationalism', evident for instance in the image of the unwaved flag. Yet Billig does not make a distinction between 'banal' (typically associated with 'good') and 'hot' (typically associated with 'bad') nationalism, as Özkırımlı (2000) does not make a distinction between patriotism (good) and nationalism (bad), as both terms are united in the harnessing of nationalist ideology. The point is that banal nationalism is an ideology shared by nations and one that is repeatedly 'flagged' to us, lest we forget where or who we are, or are supposed to be. This ideology also conditions our activism through various forms of sympathy or antipathy.

The salience and success of *Banal Nationalism* is also evidenced by the plethora of scholarly responses – from 'banal cosmopolitanism' to 'everyday nationhood'. Ulrich Beck approaches banal cosmopolitanism as 'closely bound up with all kinds of consumption ... the huge variety of meals, food, restaurants and menus routinely present in nearly every city anywhere in the world [and] also penetrates other spheres of everyday culture' (2004: 151). Banal cosmopolitanism does not engage critically with the 'banality' of cosmopolitan ideology, in the same way that banal nationalism does: it is not evident in discourse, but in consumption and it is not covert, but conspicuous. Banal nationalism manifests in the way in which ethical consumption such as fair-trade coffee aims to connect producers in the coffee-growing regions in the world (typically in the global South) with consumers in the global

North. As I argue, in this case, '[b]anal is synonymous with kitsch' (Lekakis, 2013: 155). Yet banal nationalism is not so much about the consumption of commodities or ideology, but the embracing and becoming of the latter.

Approaches connected to 'everyday nationhood' have interrogated how citizens negotiate the nation in everyday life. Scholars engage constructively but critically with the idea of a top-down approach of banal nationalism (Fox and Miller-Idriss, 2008; Skey, 2009, 2011; Skey and Antonsich, 2017). A key differentiation has been an approach to the nation that 'is not simply the product of macro-structural forces; it is simultaneously the practical accomplishment of ordinary people engaging in routine activities' (Fox and Miller-Idriss, 2008: 537). Jon Fox and Cynthia Miller-Idriss (2008) focus on four ways of analysing the reproduction of nationhood in everyday life: 1) discourse (how the nation is constructed and legitimated as discursive construct), 2) choice (how nationhood frames the choices people make), 3) performance (how the everyday meanings of national symbols are negotiated), and 4) consumption (how 'ordinary people' engage with the nation through consumption). What is interesting for consumer activism in relation to everyday nationalism is what Tetiana Bulakh suggests: 'Unlike implicit everyday consumer behavior, boycotts and patriotic consumption present a mixture of all these four modalities' (2017: 81). There have been long debates between scholars regarding the extent to which the nation is shaped through media and political discourses and then consumed by the masses, or whether nationhood is a more dynamic process, experienced differently by everyone, approved, appropriated, but also contested. This simplification of the debate does not do justice to situated studies exploring people's relationships with national symbols that might uncover tensions between closed and open understandings of ethnicity as Stuart Hall perceived them. An edited collection called *Everyday Nationhood* acknowledges the dialectical relationship between banal nationalism and everyday nationhood (Skey and Antonsich, 2017). There are both top-down and bottom-up forces in the crafting and recrafting of an understanding of the nation and national identity, and we cannot make sense of the ideology of nationalism without considering the dynamics of their interaction.

Twenty years after the publication of *Banal Nationalism*, Billig reiterates his thesis that 'the established nations of the West are deeply nationalist although their citizenry and sociological theorists often overlook this nationalism' (2017: 310). Contrary to several subsequent theorizations of the role of nations and nationalism in everyday life, Billig does not offer an uplifting approach to our attachment with nationalism, but rather warns that banal nationalism can morph into 'hot' nationalism at a moment's notice. As Sophie Duchesne argues:

> nationalism is therefore not the result of an impulse for identity and a process of categorisation. It is not an internal sentiment. It is an ideology that not only has not been eradicated after the horrors of war, but one

which seems more powerful than ever today, because of the dichotomy established between 'hot' bellicose nationalism (which drives the masses to wave their flags) and the nationalism of established nations (which goes unnoticed but which, by its omnipresence, restricts our thought). (2018: 852)

Consumer activism is conditioned by the ideology of nationalism. All of us have been routinely exposed to unwaved (or even waved) flags, and are continuously reminded of the ideas, values, and beliefs of the nations that we inhabit throughout public and privately owned spaces, across analogue and digital media. When invited to buy nationally, we are reminded where we belong, and we are invited to act on our belonging through our consumption.

Economic Nationalism

Economic nationalism concerns the ways in which the establishment of modern nations is oriented towards the creation of a citizenry that expresses their affiliation for the nation through consumer culture; in other words, nations, in the moment of their inception, appeal to their citizens through 'buy national' campaigns. The British case is one of the first. Liah Greenfeld argues that the origins of economic nationalism are found in England in the 19th century with 'a refraction of national consciousness in the consciousness of particular – economically active – strata' (2001: 33). Dana Frank lays out a rich history of economic nationalism in North America, noting that 'a Buy American campaign gave birth to the United States of America' (Frank, 1999: 4). In fact, the Continental Association was founded two years before the signing of the Declaration of Independence to ban trade between America and Great Britain (1774). Another significant contribution is Karl Gerth's (2003) *China Made*, which charts the co-evolution of the Chinese nation with 'Chinese products'. Like 'Yannis' in the opening anecdote to this chapter, 'Ms. American Consumer' appeared in the United States[4] as 'The Lin Family Shop' had appeared in China[5] to tell a variation of the same story of economic nationalism; if you buy imported goods, you punish yourself. Their stories are the same in that they reinforce the ideology of the nation and recreate the belief that citizens have a duty as consumers.

Economic nationalism then is a form of 'consumer regime' (Glickman, 2004), where the state uses the marketplace for strategic purposes, namely, the creation of a consumer society that taps into the ideology of nationalism. It is also important to note that 'buy national' campaigns can and do resurface in times of political or economic crises. The vignette that opened this chapter was part of a campaign to revive the nationalist sentiment of Greeks following the financial crisis in the early 2010s. One campaign even used exactly the same video showcasing one 'Yannis' walking around a social security building and in a queue to receive his benefits while exhibiting his imported clothing (Lekakis, 2017a). Another example is the politicization of consumption in Ukraine during the Orange Revolution of 2004–5 and the EuroMaidan revolution of 2014, when consumption 'became an area for civil activism and proactive interactions with [the] state' (Bulakh, 2017: 77). A study by Tetiana Bulakh illustrates how consumer practices (boycott of Russian goods and buycott of Ukrainian goods) are 'a site where ideas about the state, nation and citizenship are actively shaped and reproduced from below' (2017: 74) and argues that 'consumer activism represents how citizens manifest loyalty for the state, or, rather, a fantasy for the state' (ibid.: 87). Economic nationalism furthers the crafting of the ideology of nationalism in and through the marketplace.

Economic nationalism has historically been and presently remains a version of nationalism which is driven by the state and business elites (Greenfeld, 2001). Colonial rule augmented and distorted the conception of the nation. For instance, for the British Empire, economic nationalism did not just manifest as supporting British workers in Britain, but also the interests of the Empire in British occupied territories. For instance, industrialist entrepreneur Sir Williams Morris started the 1931 Buy British campaign to persuade 'British consumers to buy, the British traders to sell, products made in Britain or in the British Empire overseas at the expense of foreign suppliers' (Constantine, 1987, p. 44). The campaign appeared in the context of a financial crisis and the Empire Marketing Board gave it the motto 'Buy British – From the Empire at Home and Overseas'.[6] The campaign attempted to positively stereotype empire goods and produce consumer culture that operated to legitimate the very existence of Empire (Kothari, 2014).

It is particularly illuminating to explore continuities and changes in the rhetoric of nation building (Lekakis, 2018). For example, the 1932 Buy American campaign was inspired by the Buy British Campaign. Media mogul William Randolph Hearst (whose life is portrayed in the film *Citizen Kane*) complemented the campaign with an anti-immigrant campaign through the newspapers he owned. In response, the civil rights movement appropriated the phrase in a 1933 editorial in the *Pittsburgh Courier* (a prominent African American paper with a national circulation) challenging Hearst's one-dimensional 'Buy American' campaign with the phrase 'Buy American, hire American', demanding equal rights to labour opportunities for African Americans (Frank, 1999). In 2017, in a regressive re-appropriation of the phrase, Donald Trump signed the 'Buy American and Hire American Executive Order', as part of his broader anti-immigration strategy. Buy national campaigns are ambiguous and tend to appear as grassroots campaigns during times of crises, though they are closely linked to political parties and persons (Lekakis, 2017a).

Nascent studies of consumption during COVID-19 have highlighted consumer preference for a country's own brands and products (Verma and Naveen, 2021). Yet economic nationalism is not always the best framework for making sense of buy national campaigns and their popularity. The same dialectical relationship that exists between banal nationalism and everyday nationhood also exists between economic nationalism and consumer nationalism.

Consumer Nationalism

Consumer nationalism concerns citizens' support for their nation or rejection of a nation other than theirs through acts of consumption or non-consumption. Consumer nationalism also envelops 'buy national' campaigns and the extent to which they are adopted, embodied, and actualized by citizens. For the most part, the main difference is that economic nationalism has been studied by economists and historians, whereas consumer nationalism has been studied by sociologists, communication, and cultural studies scholars, adopting different questions and methodological approaches. Furthermore, the latter also foreground the interplay between the 'political' and the 'symbolic'. As Jian Wang maintains, 'nationalism is symbolic and cultural as well as territorial and political' (2006: 190). Wang's study of the Toshiba incident (the upheaval of Chinese consumers once the Toshiba Corporation effectively admitted selling faulty floppy disk drives in the US in 1999, as the same products were sold in China)[7] illustrates how historical resonance, advocacy groups, and media practices become entangled in the production of consumer nationalism. The dynamics of consumer nationalism vis-à-vis state narratives and citizen responses are of course dependent on histories, agents, national ideology, and struggles for justice.

Enric Castelló and Sabina Mihelj (2018) break down consumer nationalism into two categories, 'political consumer nationalism' and 'symbolic consumer nationalism'. By political consumer nationalism, the authors refer to the research on political consumerism, which aims at specific targets through the selection or abstinence of specific products related to a nation. A relevant example is the Greek boycott of German cars following the financial crisis of 2008 (Fouka and Voth, 2016). By symbolic consumer nationalism, Castelló and Mihelj refer to discourses and actions aiming at cultural ends, such as in the example of a pro-independence retailer in Catalonia (vam.cat) that sells clothing and accessories adorned with national symbols.

Consumer nationalism is a complex formation between the push towards economic nationalism as propelled by the state and the pull of consumers as citizens, who of course can experience this in variation, depending on their socioeconomic background. For example, Laura Nelson's (2000) ethnography of women from different class backgrounds during the 1990s, a period of ongoing development for South Korea, illuminates tensions between the strategies of industrial development of the South Korean state and their embodiment, negotiation, and resistance by citizens. Entitled *Measured Excess*, the book explores the way in which the development of consumer culture in South Korea affected the sense of national community that was central to the country's economic development. Buy Korean campaigns in the early 1900s were concerned with supporting limited consumption, savings, and the purchase of South Korean products. By the 1990s, Korean society was witnessing a rich market of consumer imports, as well as a domestic consumer market and the negotiation of excess was more complicated.

Consumer nationalism thus manifests as the appeal of national identities in the process of consumption, where individuals respond to or initiate consumer activist practices to engage in the reproduction of national ideology and struggles that are defensive, offensive, or neutral. Complex interplays between grassroots struggles and contemporary politics also manifest in the ambivalent dynamics of consumer activism.

Nationalism, 'Backlash Politics', and Consumer Activism

In the contemporary context, environmentalist, feminist, anti-racist, and justice movements have further intensified their use of the tools of consumer activism, drawing on historical lessons and combining these with tools of the digital age. In the US, for instance, Black Lives Matter supporters organized a 'Boycott for Black Lives' to boycott companies which have not aligned with the movement during Juneteenth. Since 19 June 2021, Juneteenth National Independence Day is celebrated as a US federal holiday that commemorates the emancipation of African–American slaves that started in 1866. However, at the same time, there is a rise of 'backlash politics', which, according to Alter and Zürn (2020), has the regressive objective of returning to a previous social condition, utilizing unexpected and extreme tactics, and having the ability to enter mainstream public discourse.

A case in point is consumer activism towards Starbucks. In the early 2000s, Starbucks boycotts were called for to question justice in their supply chain. In 2012, UK Uncut called for a boycott of Starbucks over the corporation's tax avoidance. So far, consumer activism has mostly been exemplary of social movement attempts to lobby corporations to be more responsible and more transparent. Then, Starbucks boycotts in the US turned into an extraordinary version of what Bryant Simon (2011) calls the 'out-sourcing of politics in the branded world'. In 2015, Donald Trump threatened to boycott Starbucks over its decision to remove 'symbols of the season' from their Christmas-themed cups. In 2017, Starbucks received both threats for boycotts and pledges for 'buycotts' following its decision to hire 10,000 refugees. In 2018, two black men were arrested in a Philadelphia Starbucks as they were sitting without having purchased a drink and calls for a Starbucks boycott proliferated on the basis of racial justice. In 2020, Starbucks banned employees from wearing Black Lives Matter (BLM) clothing or accessories because they advocate 'a political, religious, or personal issue'. Following calls to boycott Starbucks over hypocrisy, the corporation reverted its decision, and even said it would print

250,000 BLM shirts for baristas who wanted them. What this historical snapshot of Starbucks boycotts shows is twofold. First, market actors are finding themselves in the midst of backlash politics where consumer activism sways like a pendulum from progressive to regressive goals. Second, market actors are increasingly becoming powerful agents in the mediation of consumer activism. Brands do not escape backlash politics, as indeed we see more and more contention when it comes to brands taking a stance in terms of social or environmental justice (for a further illustration of this, see Chapter 4).

Nationalism is an international ideology shared by all nations, that nations agree is the best possible format for organizing and governing communities. Yet how the nation is discursively constructed and routinely reproduced, as Billig (1995) posits, has the potential of turning banality into heat in the wake of populism. In popular, but also academic, discourse what qualifies as populism remains highly contested, with disagreements about its definition, its agencies, its consequences and even its usefulness (Brubaker, 2020). This chapter does not engage theoretically with the concept of populism, as this has often been discussed in an ahistorical perspective, thus erasing long histories of colonial, ethnocentric or xenophobic nationalism. Instead, here, I take issue with the way that nation, race, and ethnicity have been at the centre of consumer activism, as part of the constant negotiations of nationalism. The politics of consumption have historically addressed ethnic and racial injustice, sometimes in the form of state apartheid or segregation. In order to construct a framework for understanding these, we need to consider the historical and cultural contexts of consumer activism, as well as the openness and closeness of perspectives of race and ethnicity in the action being advocated.

There Is Nothing Post-Racial about Consumer Activism

To think about consumption as post-racial is to assume that people make choices in their daily consumption practices without drawing the colour line. Consumption and consumer activism are racialized. Any arguments suggesting that we are living in post-racial times can be countered through historical examples. Numerous studies highlight the long history of consumer activism, ranging from anti-slavery campaigns in 19th century England (Glickman, 2004; Midgley, 1996; Soper and Trentmann, 2008) to the iconic case of the Montgomery bus boycott of 1955 in the US (Cohen, 2003; Friedman, 1999; Glickman, 2009) and beyond. In the United States, going back to the nonconsumption or nonimportation movement of British products, consumer activism has shaped consumer culture in the nation. Specifically thinking about the disenfranchised black, Hispanic, Asian, and Native American communities of the US, life had been one of forced sacrifices and long struggles, where one of the tactics used was boycotting. What Mukherjee (2011) refers to as 'black consumerism' is consumption practices that are connected to political standing and signify a space for struggles over black political subjectivity.

Several historical studies have developed an understanding of how, in the US, the civil rights movement drew on boycotts (and buycotts) to demand or reinforce desegregation. Nicole Marie Brown specifically discusses 'racialized political consumerism' as a political project of black Americans; case studies include business initiatives (especially the Black Star Lines) from the Universal Negro Improvement Association. Brown defines the term as consisting of cases where:

> (1) race is invoked to help encourage, describe, or explain consumption patterns and experiences, and (2) marketplace sites of consumerism are used or targeted for some political purpose that is designed to influence how resources are allocated toward a specific racial group. (Brown, 2015: 239)

For Brown (2015), the use of racialized political consumerism has been effectively used to mobilize groups in nationalist struggles. Mia Bay and Ann Fabian have noted that 'race and ethnicity have long shaped the economic wellbeing, purchasing power, and daily consumption experiences of all Americans' (2015: 5), highlighting that 'there is nothing postracial about American shopping' (ibid.: 6). The volume *Race and Retail* (2015) features at least two chapters that explore campaigns supporting black consumption or struggles for economic freedom during the years of the civil rights movement. Mia Bay's (2015) chapter 'Travelling Black/Buying Black' highlights the difficulties faced by African Americans during (but also after) the Jim Crow laws and practices, as well as alternatives such as the short-lived 'Jitney' services (black-owned intercity bus lines) or travel guides such as Grayson's Guide, *The Negro Motorists' Green Book*, and the *Negro Travelers' Green Book* (identifying accommodation and dining facilities in their route that would welcome African Americans). Another chapter, by Traci Parker, documents African American consumer protests which 'focused on winning equal access to and respectful treatment in public accommodations and markets' (2015: 77), highlighting particularly the importance of consumer–worker alliances. Regina Austin (1994) documents ongoing service discrimination against black people, as well as the construction of black consumption as a form of deviance. Austin also connects the critique of forms of racialized consumption to the importance of linking production and consumption. Consumer activism practices had been significant for disenfranchised (especially African American) communities in the US, but, when they were successful, they were never separated from collective struggles between workers and consumers, and the production of alternatives.

It is not only US shopping that remains tainted by difference. Farida Fozdar discusses economic nationalism in the Australian context where, despite it being a settler nation:

due to the White Australia Policy, a set of policies and practices that from 1901 to 1973 sought to keep Australia White, the population is often conceptually divided along the lines of White-European background/mainstream and migrant or 'ethnic', often 'visibly different'. (2021: 542)

Here, ethnicity appears more prominently than race. Similarly, in a comparison of the United States to France, Bo Yun Park (2019) points out that the context is different, in that France does not emphasize race as much in its constution as the US does. Without arguing that France is a post-racial society, Park shows how 'race' and 'ethnicity' play different roles, depending on the context: how citizenship is discursively constructed in the constitution and how each state is involved in different historical, colonial, and civil conflicts which permeate the present and taint consumer culture and its activism. Post-racial consumerism suggests that the nation is a homogeneous composite of people who share the same national identity in a simplified way, where racial and ethnic tensions are erased. Yet a historical approach to consumption that pays attention to race illustrates the underwritten violence of national ideology and the persisting legacies of racialized consumption.

Critical Issues

How does the relationship between the state and citizens manifest in consumption? To what extent are citizens encouraged or empowered as citizens through nationalist consumption? How accessible and impactful is consumer activism for citizenship struggles? Is consumer activism a universal phenomenon? How just can consumption be? In providing answers to these questions, there are several key considerations to reflect on. History, ideology, agency, and justice are integrated in a matrix of core considerations that should underscore any study of consumer activism.

The importance of history, especially social history, in relation to race and ethnicity

History is taught and told in many different narratives, often consistently obscuring minority struggles and rendering cases of oppression as exceptional. Historical approaches to consumer activism and nationalism indicate both convergence and divergence between the state's approach to democracy and justice and communities' struggle towards the same goals. Enjoying citizenship rights is enshrined in the constitution of many modern nations, and yet many of these were late in extending these to women, people of colour, and other minority groups.

The importance of nationalism as banal ideology

Following Billig, ambivalence is at the heart of modern nationalism. Nationalism is a cohesive narrative for the pursuit of economic goals. Yet it can blur existing ethnic and racial differences, potentially leading to the exclusion of minorities. Scholars warn of the ambivalence characterizing racially and ethnically motivated consumer activism. For Brown (2015), for example, the use of racialized political consumerism has been used effectively to mobilize groups in nationalist struggles. Cheryl Greenberg's (2004) study of consumer protests involving black communities in the US (1930s–50s) explores campaigns of or against racism through consumption (Boycott Jewish and Buy Black); she suggests that sometimes the struggle for black economic emancipation targeted the businesses of Jewish people in Boycott Jewish campaigns. Drawing on the example of Black Lives Matter and Blue Lives Matter, Bo Yun Park's (2019: 22) study underscores the idea that one of the democratic challenges of racialized political consumerism is the way in which it 'actually will reinforce the divisive lines that are already present in society'. Castelló and Mihelj also emphasize the pendulum that is consumer nationalism:

> On the one hand, it can have the effect of limiting the scope of democratic engagement, enclosing citizenship empowerment in the realm of everyday consumption, and reproducing parochial thinking and exclusion. On the other hand, however, it can also be used strategically to revitalize local economies and communities, limit the environmental costs of long-distance trade, and engender a sense of empowerment among individuals and communities that may otherwise feel alienated from traditional instruments of political engagement. (2018: 572)

At the same time, consumer activism against forms of everyday racism has been significant in highlighting the colonial histories and controversies that are often found in consumer practices.

The importance of agency

There is a key distinction between consumer regimes (initiated by the state or economic elite) and consumer activism (initiated by citizens or social movements). As Dana Frank (1999) notes, it was an entrepreneur and media mogul (William Randolph Hearst) who started the Buy American campaign in 1932 and promoted it through the newspapers that he owned, complementing it with an anti-immigrant campaign. In more recent years, the 'Buy American, Hire American' executive order of Donald Trump is a very different kind of consumer politics to the 'Buy American, Hire American' demands of black Americans. Ideological oppositions such as this are often hidden in plain sight and evident through in-depth exploration.

From the civil rights movement's progressive use of the marketplace for democratic ends to the Trump administration's regressive policies towards women and minorities and from anti-austerity sentiments to anti-lockdown protests, who calls for action matters.

The importance of justice

Questioning commodity production through a critical political economy approach is essential, and is sometimes overlooked in the emotional entanglement with the nation and national belonging. What use is it celebrating a 'buy Greek' discourse without questioning justice at the level of production when scandals about inhumane labour conditions have been publicized?[8] Nationalist discourses without just national production mean nothing, as scandals exposing the outsourcing of merchandise in the 'Backing Britain' campaign had noted,[9] and as was the case with the British post-Brexit blue passport where the company that designed it was the Franco-Dutch company Gemalto and the passports themselves are to be made in Poland. Yet it is also important not to remain at the surface level of this critique, as this has often been used in a rush to uncover the obvious dissonance between performances and practices of economic nationalism or manipulated to further enforce economic nationalism. An example is the rumour that Make America Great Again (MAGA) hats were made in China, as an image circulating on Facebook pointed out. This gives further credibility to the MAGA narrative, which can appear more 'authentic' in its claims to economic nationalism.[10] What is more important is to ask who makes the products and under what conditions they labour away. Consumer activism can be effective, but it also needs to be connected to production and workers' struggles.

Researching Consumer Activism and Nationalism: Methodologies

To summarize, there is nothing fixed about consumer activism in relation to nationalism. The line between 'hot' and 'banal' manifestations of nationalism (as that between 'nationalists' and 'patriots') is blurred and there is no 'real' race or ethnicity to capture. The relationship between nationalism and consumption can be both democratic and democratically dubious (Lekakis, 2019; Micheletti and Oral, 2019; Park, 2019). Economic nationalism is mostly studied in historical and organizational terms, exploring modes of governance and government campaigns. Manifestations of economic nationalism are historical and often include contestations over race and ethnicity through consumption practices; in doing so, they can operate as market-bolstering, nationalist smokescreens. Consumer nationalism is about people's engagement with ideas of the nation through their consumption (or anti-consumption) practices. Similar to this, racialized political consumerism brings race to the forefront of the struggle in its analysis and expects no normativity. It can also extend shared struggles beyond the nation, based on a transnational collective racial identity.

Let us now reflect on the way in which such theories have been produced, in order to explore the methodological options available for further explorations on consumer activism and nationalism. Given that nationalism is a dialectical process, a variety of methods is available to researchers, ranging from quantitative (especially regarding economic nationalism approaches) to qualitative (typically analysing consumer nationalism). Regarding top-down approaches to nationalism and consumption, scholars have drawn mostly on mixed qualitative and quantitative methodologies. For instance, Vasiliki Fouka and Hans-Joachim Voth (2016) analyse a leading Greek newspaper's reportage of clashes between the German and Greek governments during the years of the financial crisis in combination with statistical data on new passenger vehicles registered in each prefecture during that period. Similarly, Xavier Cuadras-Morató and Josep Maria Raya (2015) conduct an econometric analysis of sales of different types of Catalan cava in the Spanish market in combination with reporting on the Catalan cava boycott in the main Spanish daily newspapers to explore its effect at the national level. From a bottom-up perspective of citizens and their engagement with nationalism in the marketplace, scholars have opted for methods such as archival research of historical documents (Greenberg, 2004; Brown, 2015): a combination of ethnographic methods, including participant observation, interviews, and surveys (Fox, 2006), interviews with small entrepreneurs, consumer and social activists, as well as marketing professionals (Bulakh, 2017), focus groups (Fozdar, 2018), critical discourse analysis or thematic analysis of news stories (Johnson et al., 2017; Wang, 2006), immersive, interpretative netography (Page, 2017; Minocher, 2019), and analysis of social media content (Kang, 2012; Lekakis, 2017a, 2017b).

In-depth qualitative approaches allow us to problematize normative neoliberal narratives about marketplace effectiveness or post-racial nationalism. They allow us to look deep into the cracks of consumer culture, where hierarchy and privilege persist. Mixed methods are also favoured as they explore both the discourses and practices of consumer activism. Limitations aside, it would be fruitful to design a project which examines a combination of these factors; the (newspaper and social) media discourses, citizens' negotiations of nationalism and consumer activism and, if possible, statistical data of the effectiveness of the action. Merely examining the 'success' or 'failure' of the action does not yield a compelling analysis as to why the action happened in the first place, and whether (given ripe conditions) it might reappear. As Greenberg points out, 'we must always keep in mind that whether it [the consumer action] succeeds (is the goal achieved?) and whether we want it to succeed (is the goal desirable?) are two distinct questions that must be kept separate' (2004: 64).

There are several relevant contemporary examples, which reveal the multiple ways in which consumer activism and nationalism intersect. The struggles involving the nation are plenty, and they mobilize based on identity politics (race, ethnicity, religion), as well as political orientation. In the first case, we can observe struggles around halal produce in England and France (Johnson et al., 2017; Lekakis, 2019), while in the second case there are struggles around sovereignty such as the cases of Ukraine vs Russia or Greece vs Germany (Bulakh, 2017; Lekakis, 2019). It is worth turning our attention to a specific example of contentious consumer activism that implicates the nation.

Case Study: Consumer Activism in Hong Kong's Yellow Economic Circle

Some Context about the Dispute between Hong Kong and China

The historical economic and cultural make-up of Hong Kong is a succinctly unique case of a Special Administrative Region (SAR) with its own government, two administrative bodies and strong government–business collaboration. The handover from the British government to China in 1997 coincided with the Asian Financial Crisis, and a new set of political negotiations characterized by various forms of tension. As a SAR, Hong Kong would maintain separate governing and economic systems from those of mainland China under the principle of 'one country, two systems'. However, tensions arising from mainland China's attempts to blend the 'two systems' into one caused waves of protest across the city from 2014, with Occupy Central (Umbrella Revolution) and again in 2019 (Anti-Extradition Law Amendment Bill Movement or pro-democracy movement) (Lee, 2015; Lim, 2018; Wong and Liu, 2018). The 2019 movement was characterized by the youthful profile of protesters (almost half of them millennials), self/leaderless mobilization, technologically enabled action, solidarity, and a coherent set of motivations regarding abuse of power by the police and lack of representation in the political system (Lee et al, 2019). The movement's five demands were:

1. Withdrawal of the extradition bill
2. Retraction of 'riot' label for protesters
3. Amnesty for those arrested during protests

4. Independent commission of inquiry to investigate political crisis and police operations
5. Universal suffrage (direct elections) for chief executive and all legislative members.

The struggle for these demands started with political strikes attended by hundreds of thousands of people. They witnessed a first indication of businesses' approach to the movement: some were sympathetic, and thus (as we will see) penalized, while some were adamantly against the protests (Chan and Pun, 2020). Yet following four months of escalating protests, Carrie Lam, the Chief Executive of the SAR government, withdrew the Anti-Extradition Law Amendment Bill in September 2019. This did not stop the protesters, who continued to push for recognition and approval of their other four demands. It is around this time that the yellow economic circle became part of the toolkit of tactics of the pro-democracy movement.

Yellow Economic Circle

'Yellow economic circle' is the term given to the waves of economic resistance in the double form of boycotts and buycotts by the protesters. This colour coding originated in the use of yellow umbrellas during Occupy Central and was granted to businesses that were in support of the movement, while blue was designated to businesses supporting the police or mainland China. Yellow shops included a number of businesses from restaurants to fitness studios. There was a 'Bye Buy Day' in August 2019, targeting pro-regime businesses in a boycott, and the 'Buy Yellow, Eat Yellow' movement took off soon after. In the yellow economic circle, citizens expressed their political identity in their consumer patronage: buy yellow and boycott blue if you support the movement, and, as this can swing both ways, buy blue and boycott yellow if you do not.

This is a digitally enabled form of consumer activism, relying on crowdsourcing and applications such as Google Maps, WhatsGap, Wolipay and Wolieat, many of which are shut down by Google, as 'a violation of our Terms of Service and/or policies', but pop back up through dedicated sites. There are also relevant Facebook pages such as HK Shoplist, Yellow Alliance, and Heung Shing Online Yellow Economic Circle. At the same time, hashtags such as #yelloweconomiccircle, #yelloweconomy, #yellowshop, #yellowcafe, #yellowfood, #yellow_foodhk appear on social media such as Instagram, Facebook, and Twitter, promoting businesses that support the pro-democracy movement. There are also Facebook pages specifically signposting Blue Shop lists, requesting that people avoid these and report them to administrators.

Analysing the Yellow Economic Circle through Consumer Activism and Nationalism

We can gain a closer understanding of this phenomenon by questioning it in relation to consumer nationalism, ethnicity, and the response of different actors. The yellow economic circle can be read as consumer nationalism, by way of consumer activism by citizens in Hong Kong aiming to contribute to the pursuit of political independence from the mainland China government. Drawing on Castelló and Mihelj (2018), two types of consumer activism manifest here: political consumer activism appears as a tactic of the movement and symbolic consumer activism as a tactic of local businesses. For example, a gelato store served flavours such as 'teargas' and specials such as 'Five Big Snow Balls' (which in Cantonese sounds almost like 'Five Big Demands'[11]), while local businesses in support of the movement created mooncakes with messages such as 'Hong Kong People', 'We're in it Together', 'No Withdrawal, No Dispersal', 'Add Oil' (an expression of encouragement, in this case towards the protesters) and 'Be Water' (a reference to Bruce Lee's philosophy and style of unpredictability, which has been taken up by protesters during their clashes with the police).[12] Beyond promoting protest symbols, businesses also actively aided protesters by offering water and food, use of their toilets and refuge in times of clashes.

In relation to ethnicity, while the majority of Hongkongers are ethnically Chinese, there is a difference between those who are 'localists' and those who support a pan-Chinese identity. In the post-handover era, the 'imagined community' (a pan-Chinese cultural identification) to which Hongkongers ascribed to changed through the concept of 'localism' (Veg, 2017; Lee et al., 2019). Localism has repeatedly transformed in the post-1997 era, changing the mode of identification of Hongkongers from ethnic to civic. In other words, instead of experiencing cultural identification through their shared ethnicity, for Hong Kong people ethnicity remains a ground of contestation where they position themselves and their civic engagement. The Beijing government and the SAR government promote ethnicity as a glue to the nation, while the pro-democracy movement promotes Hong Kong independence (Lee et al., 2019; Yuen and Chung, 2018).

In relation to state narratives and responses, officials from the SAR administration have spoken against consumer activism of the yellow economic circle, whether by stressing the importance of a 'free and open economy'[13] or by arguing that it will harm small businesses.[14] Yet sociologists suggest that this type of consumer activism supports businesses in favour of the pro-democracy movement and reprimands big businesses (e.g. Maxim's, Best Mart 360), which are typically pro-China because of their economic dependence on the mainland (Chan and Pun, 2020). The patronage of these small businesses is typically local residents, rather than tourists.[15] The practical response from the Beijing front has been more direct.

The case of Taipan Bread and Cakes is exemplary. The business suffered great losses as huge amounts of pastries were returned after mainstream media targeted the owner's stance in support of Hong Kong protests.[16] This illustrates that when businesses have voiced a political claim for the pro-democracy movement or against the official lines of the Hong Kong and Beijing governments, Chinese commercial organizations have responded by shutting that business out of their operations. This is a strong reminder that the economic power of market actors is significantly larger than that of citizens.

The Hong Kong Economy and the Impact of the Yellow Economic Circle

The particular case of the yellow economic circle manifested as consumer nationalism rather than economic nationalism, as it was not initiated by economic elites or organizations. It did not manifest as an ethnic struggle, but as a struggle of political identity. Focusing on how the nationalist struggle between China and Hong Kong manifests in terms of the ideology of nationalism, there is again ambivalence. As Debby Sze Wan Chan and Ngai Pun suggest, 'it is too early to judge the impact of economic resistance by Hong Kong protesters, or to judge whether this economic resistance embodies localist sentiments that produce an exclusive approach' (2020: 2). What is more certain is the direct political and financial impact of the phenomenon.

During 2019, continued challenges in political trust resulted in an economy in decline. Following on, the COVID-19 pandemic rendered the 'business as usual' model of the economy difficult, if not impossible, let alone attempts to protest through the economy. Furthermore, as the legal grip of China over Hong Kong has tightened since 2020, despite strong resistance in the form of protest mobilizations and consumer activism, the outcome of the yellow economic circle appears limited. Businesses that sympathized with the movement are now facing closure. For example, Chickeeduck, a Hong Kong retail chain that took a strong anti-government stance during protests closed local stores in late 2021, having been subjected to smear campaigns.[17] Yet the extent to which digital media facilitated the emergence of the yellow economic circle and the mobilization of symbolic resources by protesters illustrates a positive correlation between consumer activism and democratic struggle.

Questions for Future Case Studies

When exploring consumer activism and the mobilization of consumer choice for purposes related to the nation (whether it is its defence or its attack) there are key issues to consider. First, the way in which we conceptualize nationalism and the processes through which its power is replenished and, second, the extent to which the practice of consumer activism with national identity in mind recreates or challenges existing hierarchies and stratifications in global societies. More specifically, we question:

- What is the relationship between nationalism and consumption in countries experiencing conflict or crisis?
- How can we theorize nationalist consumption?
- What types of agents and campaigns can be identified in terms of the promotion and organization of nationalist consumption?
- What are the narratives they are using to communicate these?
- What are the ways in which they produce and promote these narratives?
- Does the action belong to the phenomenon of economic nationalism or consumer nationalism?
- At what scale does this phenomenon occur (local, regional, national, or transnational)?
- Is the struggle based on race or ethnicity and what is its historical context in terms of oppression and resistance?
- (How) does the ideology of nationalism manifest as ambivalence?
- What does a political economy of production suggest about the coherence of consumer action?

Conclusion

Nationalism is a powerful mobilizer. It can raise citizens to fight for independence or against authority. In either case, they are fighting for their 'imagined community'. From their inception and throughout their histories, particularly in times of crisis, nations appear to demand good citizenship through dutiful politicized consumption. Evoking notions of 'oneness' and 'belonging', buy national campaigns are often coupled with boycott campaigns against those that they consider adversaries. The ideology of nationalism is shared both within and beyond the borders of nation states; the belief in the 'good' people of the 'great' nation draws on old stories and recreates them through discourse. Classic stories starring 'Yannis', 'Ms. American Consumer' and 'The Lin Family Shop' belong in the repertoire of 'consumer regimes' (Glickman, 2004) where consumer activism is orchestrated by governments. As a more dynamic form of consumer activism that appears as a political or symbolic form of action, consumer nationalism can be added to the toolkit of a broader campaign of social justice, and can possibly support individuals, communities, and businesses.

However, consumer nationalism can also be easily integrated into the blurry nationalist narrative of extremist or exclusionary groups, and hence, like economic nationalism, its racial and ethnic politics must always be checked. Particularly in unsettled times, racialized/ethnicized discourses around consumption can either be heightened or hidden (think of the example of anti-Asian racism in the west during the outbreak of COVID-19). The politics of consumption cannot merely concern the choice of a classless, genderless, and raceless consumer, but individuals and groups who are situated within specific social positonings and who might or might not negotiate their national identities within consumer regimes.

This chapter argues that nationalism is an international ideology of organizational and mobilizational character, as it can evoke sentiments and direct action, and include [individuals and groups] or exclude [them] from its bureaucracy and quotidian practices. The nation is discursively constructed and susceptible to both banal nationalism and banal cosmopolitanism. Yet it is also formed by different races/ethnicities, who produce complex negotiations in the formulation of national identity. Nationalism, race, and ethnicity are also inseparable in relation to consumer activism. This is evident in the emergence of 'backlash politics' where victories by progressive movements are antagonized by regressive movements enabled by mainstream political (and media) discourse. Whichever way you look at it, there is nothing post-racial about consumption and consumer activism. The politics of consumption can range significantly when you place the nation at the centre of your investigation. Whether the nation is constructed and communicated as a brand or contested due to the violation of human rights, its exploration necessitates a clear appraisal of the histories, agents, ideologies of nationalism, and notions of justice.

These are some of the key insights drawn here. When it comes to consumer nationalism, there are many nuances along the margins, as symbolic and political are not easily distinguishable, particularly when it comes to static and dynamic understandings of nationalism or open and closed dynamics of ethnicity. First, we cannot afford to ignore the historical context of consumer activism, in relation to race and ethnicity. Second, we cannot afford to overlook the importance of ideological ambivalence and the contradicting claims to civic rights and responsibilities. Third, we cannot afford to neglect the importance of agency and questioning who, when, and under what conditions the call to action is raised. Fourth, we cannot afford to forget the importance of justice broadly and the importance of labour justice more specifically. While nations are imagined constructs and nationalism is a banal ideology, which can morph into a heated conflict, our analysis can focus on unpacking such tensions, as a dedication to the illumination of unjust systems of global production.

Notes

1. Lekakis, Eleftheria J. 2017a. 'Economic Nationalism and the Cultural Politics of Consumption under Austerity: The Rise of Ethnocentric Consumption in Greece'. *Journal of Consumer Culture* 17 (2): 286–302.
2. This is a reference to former US President Donald Trump's racist comment towards certain countries in January 2018 (www.theguardian.com/us-news/2018/jan/12/trump-shithole-countries-lost-in-translation) (1 December 2021).
3. www.aljazeera.com/news/2019/12/muslim-boycott-chinese-products-urged-uighur-treatment-191220122039763.html (30 March 2020).
4. Dana Frank (1999: ix) charts an 'import panic attack' in US newspapers during the 1980s and 1990s where the same story is repeatedly told; an average American consumer finds herself contemplating the loss of 'good American jobs' and then strolling into the mall to discover that there are no products made in the USA.
5. 'The Lin Family Shop' (1932) is a short story by Mao Dun where the young daughter, demanding a dress made with Japanese material, becomes the initiator of a series of social tensions between herself, her family, their neighbours and the nation. As Karl Gerth (2003) writes, this story reveals the tensions that characterize the relationship between consumerism and nationalism in the country.
6. The Empire Marketing Board was set up in 1926 by the Secretary of State for the Dominions to financially support the British Empire by growing resources across colonies and encourage intra-imperial trade.
7. The Toshiba incident refers to the upheaval in China after Toshiba Corporation settled for $1.05 worth of compensations in a class-action lawsuit in the US in 1999. The corporation had been accused of selling faulty floppy disk drives in its notebooks, and the US settlement angered consumers in China, as the same notebooks had been sold there. As a result, media and public discourse in China played the tune of national pride and dignity.
8. https://g2red.org/el/category/manolada-watch/ (11 November 2021).
9. For example, car stickers, mugs, badges and T-shirts featuring the Union flag circulated broadly during the late 1960s Buy British campaign, although it became apparent that they were made in Portugal (www.ft.com/content/3573bd46-99e7-11df-a0a5-00144feab49a) (24 November 2021).
10. https://apnews.com/afs:Content:6391630154 (13 November 2021).
11. www.nytimes.com/2020/01/09/opinion/sunday/hong-kong-protests-food.html#click=https://t.co/vYadJXqC5K (26 November 2021).
12. www.hongkongfp.com/2019/09/13/hong-kongs-mid-autumn-festival-mooncakes-get-protest-makeover/ (26 November 2021).
13. https://news.rthk.hk/rthk/en/component/k2/1498197-20191217.htm (27 March 2020).
14. www.scmp.com/comment/opinion/article/3048090/hong-kong-protests-yellow-vs-blue-economy-might-push-small (25 November 2021).
15. https://thediplomat.com/2019/12/buy-yellow-eat-yellow-the-economic-arm-of-hong-kongs-pro-democracy-protests/ (27 November 2021).

16. www.scmp.com/news/china/society/article/3025883/chinese-importer-says-entire-stock-taipan-mooncakes-will-be (25 November 2021).
17. www.scmp.com/news/hong-kong/politics/article/3156578/hong-kong-retail-chain-chickeeduck-famed-anti-government (2 December 2021).

FOUR
GENDER, FEMINISM, AND CONSUMER ACTIVISM

Introduction: Can Gender Justice Be Progressed through Consumer Activism?

Feminist t-shirts. Homophobic boycotts. Boycotts over sexism and gender-based violence. Chocolate or cereal brands fighting sexual discrimination. Lingerie brands using celebrities as feminist ambassadors. These are only some of the many complex ways in which gender becomes contentious in consumer culture. In 2016, the #GrabYourWallet boycott campaign of Trump-related brands and businesses rose in resistance to the former US president's rampant sexism. In 2018, two years before the Arcadia group went into administration, the #PinkNotGreen boycott of Sir Philip Green's UK brands and businesses was the response to accusations of sexual harassment and racism. To what extent is it possible to use the marketplace to augment feminism or resist sexism? From influencers to politicians, feminist slogans on T-shirts articulate the voices and struggles of innumerable feminists before them. Yet the slogan and t-shirt raise questions over the meaning of feminism itself: what does it mean? What are feminists fighting for? Which feminist voices matter? Does it matter who wears it? Does it lose its meaning? What is feminism beyond a slogan on a T-shirt? Who is a feminist and who is not a feminist?

This chapter addresses such questions from the perspective of consumer activism. It explores the relationship between feminism and consumer activism, drawing on research on the politics of consumption, (feminist) commodity activism and advertising campaigns aiming to promote female empowerment and equal rights to all regardless of age, race, ethnicity, body image, or sexual orientation. On the one hand, the entanglement of feminist politics in brand culture has tended to improve the visibility of women and queer persons in popular communication, while, on the other, it has tended to silence or erase the difficulties of achieving gender justice. Furthermore, boycotts sometimes rise in response of femvertising or advertising campaigns promoting social diversity. I argue that the dialectics between feminism and consumption are best explored through the recognition of four critical issues:

1) gendering consumer activism, 2) highlighting collective struggles, 3) remembering and recognizing histories (or 'herstories'), 4) the critical conceptualization of a feminist politics. In this chapter, we will explore the case of an advertising campaign promoting social diversity undertaken by Greek chocolate brand Lacta, which demonstrates the complex dynamics between commodity activism and social justice. The chapter concludes with a series of questions to pose to consumer activism in relation to feminism.

Key Concepts
Gender

Gender is a social construct, a bureaucratic category to belong to, but also a main determinant of everyday life. The recognition that gender is a social construct is the result of fights won by feminist movements, to the extent that the World Health Organization (WHO) currently uses the same definition.[1] Yet arguably, from birth, we are conditioned to see, perform, and then buy (into) gender. Deviations from the blue–pink binary can result in confusion if someone insists that the baby you are caring for is of or 'looks like' the opposite gender despite what you might tell them. Such clichéd and rigid colour coding generally remains prevalent around the world, despite the range of consumer commodities geared towards the very young. Gender, when equated with biological sex, is a binary that separates 'boys' and 'girls', 'men' and 'women', and typifies these categories into the many assumptions associated with them in popular culture: boys don't cry, girls just want to have fun; 'real' or 'strong' men; 'sensitive' or 'sexy' women. Consumer markets not only thrive on selling these categories, but also thrive in subverting them – just think of 'femvertising' (advertising coveting and covered in seemingly feminist meanings and messages) such as Dove's 2004 'Real Beauty' or 2013 'Real Beauty Sketches' ads or 'woke' advertising (advertising that challenges discrimination and stereotyping) such as Gillette's 2019 'The Best Men Can Be' ad.

Gender is an area of contestation. The 2019 Gillette ad was met by highly polarized responses, the most contentious of which threatened to boycott the brand for its 'betrayal' of 'real' men.[2] Why is gender an area of contestation? Feminist theorists argue that the way in which gender has historically organized societies in terms of politics, (domestic) labour and everyday life, as well as the way in which history itself has been written produces a hegemonic order. By this, I mean that hegemony (the dominance of certain ideas over others in society that lead to the ruling of that society through their embracing and reproduction) is closely related to gender. Concept such as 'gender hegemony' (Schippers, 2007), 'hegemonic masculinity' (Connell and Messerschmidt, 2005), 'androcentrism' (Fraser, 2013) have precisely brought to light the way in which (heterosexual and able-bodied) male-centred societies have produced and reproduce the undermining of women. The subjugation of women, in itself, might appear as a contested phrase, especially as anti-gender contemporary ultra-conservative movements resist the usefulness of 'gender' as a critical category and oppose so-called 'gender ideology'. The conservative backlash against the contestation of patriarchy is telling of contemporary feminist politics. Gender equality at the organizational level has been mediated by the United Nations (e.g. 1995 Beijing Platform for Action), NGOs, civil rights organizations and innumerable feminists around the world. Yet reports such as the 2020 Global Gender Gap Report[3] or the Gender Equality Index of the same year[4] suggest that we are several decades away from gender equality, when care work at home and in the relevant sectors is still mostly undertaken by women.

Broadly speaking, sexism is an ideology that perpetuates a hierarchical and deterministic relationship between genders. Heterosexism is 'the systemic nature of oppression against queers through cultural, political and economic structures favouring heterosexuality and heterosexuals' (Jeppesen, 2010: 464). Similarly, heteronormativity is the ideology that normalizes heterosexuality, and excludes or discriminates against queer bodies. At the same time, promotional culture has increasingly incorporated lesbian, gay, bisexual, transgender, and queer (LGBTQ) consumers and attempted to produce homonormativity in the marketplace, which is hardly ever uncontested. In addition, the promotional normalization of homosexuality can nullify the diversity of queer bodies and standpoints and privilege a uniform middle-class consumer who engages in 'pink' or (dare we say) 'rainbow' consumption, while co-opting feminist and LGBTQ movements through 'pinkwashing' or 'rainbowwashing'. Look at the 2009 Absolute Vodka's Rainbow limited edition bottle commemorating the 40th anniversary of the Stonewall riots. In 1969, a police raid led to the riots in Stonewall Inn in New York where patrons and neighbours rebelled against police harassment and social discrimination, inspiring the rise of numerous gay rights organizations and the growth of the social movements for gay rights in the US.[5] Forty years later, a vodka brand capitalizes on the history of LGBTQ activism. As Sandra Jeppesen puts it, '[q]ueer activism, in earnest attempts to challenge hetero-normativity, has inadvertently reinscribed a homonormative subject complicit with capitalism, racism, environmental destruction, ableism, patriarchy, beauty myths and so on' (2010: 472). Queer activism and theory are about a more fluid understanding of gender, beyond binaries (male/ female, homosexual/ heterosexual) and within the complexities that sexuality can manifest. From the above, the conundrum of gender and consumption is evident. Whether cisgender or queer, whether female or male, whether into pink or not, marketing campaigns testify to the market's inclusion and the consumer's uniformity, aiming to capture queer consumers. What we increasingly observe are market(ing) performances of gender equality, but the capturing of queerness in market terms can also simplify and silence gender justice.

From Feminism to Postfeminism?

Feminism is, as bell hooks (2000) wrote, for everybody. I share her fundamental definition of feminism as a movement 'to end sexism, sexist exploitation, and oppression' (ibid.: 117). Launching from this simple definition, in *Feminism is for Everybody*, hooks offers insights into the many aspects of equality and justice with which the movement is concerned, from critical consciousness of gender to reproductive rights, beauty politics, race and class inequalities, post-colonialism and transnational struggles, employment and life in the labour market, gender-based violence, masculinity and parenting, spirituality, as well as the politics of sex, marriage and partnership. Feminism is for everybody and, as Sara Ahmed writes, '[a] feminist movement is a collective political movement. Many feminisms means many movements. A collective is what does not stand still but creates and is created by movement' (2017: 3). Feminism is also a historical narrative, a way of writing and understanding history, and reclaiming herstory. The role of women as carers, consumers, and labourers is extrinsically connected to the history of modern nations (Hilton, 2002). Feminism is a movement for gender equality and gender justice. It is a material and symbolic fight, always taking place at many levels: law and policy-making, institutions and organizations, as well as public debate and everyday life. It takes place at work, at home, and in the spaces in between.

Feminism is an ongoing consideration of how to achieve gender equality and justice. As a movement towards deeper egalitarianism, feminism has (at different points in time in different geographic and cultural settings) won fights towards the rights of women for self-determination, political participation, employment, and broader recognition. Feminists have mobilized through consumer culture in different historical times to achieve different goals. In the global North, the intersection of feminism and consumer culture has varied significantly. In the early 20th century, before women's full citizenship rights were fully established, feminists used the market to intervene in political struggles (Finnegan, 1999; Frank, 1997). In the mid-20th century, feminists rejected capitalist consumption as a hegemonic practice which seeks to further the domestication of women (Martens, 2009), while in later years feminists have been involved in a debate on the way in which neoliberalism produces postfeminist subjectivities through consumer choices and the ways in which these subjectivities are reified (Dosekun, 2015; Gill and Scharff, 2011).

Postfeminism is a critical concept that allows us to describe and debate contemporary feminism. As a popular media approach (which celebrates young women and girls but does not scratch the surface of social inequalities) it focuses on the successes of individual women and sets up unrealistic expectations for those who cannot fit such a success story. As Simidele Dosekun posits, '[i]t is effectively a co-optation and commodification of the language and principles of liberal feminism, telling women, *selling* to them that they have equality and freedom, or enough, at last, to go forth on their own terms. All this is cheery fiction' (2020: 2, italics in original). Postfeminism is thus the universalizing pull of neoliberal capitalism through its consumer markets and the pull of neoliberal subjectivities that are interpellated through it. But feminism (and postfeminism) are also bound in specific times and spaces. As Sara Liao writes, 'postfeminism is considered a contemporary sensibility rather than a culturally specific historical moment, in which women are proclaimed to be "empowered," to be freely choosing, knowing, and self-pleasing but also paradoxically self-disciplined and -regulated' (2021: 666). In the Chinese context to which she is referring, Liao regards it as a post-socialist femininity that is patriotic in its complicity in the market-state nexus that propagates nationalistic sentiments in the pursuit of social and economic advantage.

'Mainstream', 'popular', 'neoliberal' are some of the epithets used to characterize the feminist context of today. As discussed in the previous chapter, post-racism is an illusion that we are living in a world where we do not need to fight for racial equality and justice. Similarly, postfeminism is an illusion that we are living in a world where we (or some of us, at least) do not need to fight for gender equality and justice. This is what Sara Ahmed calls 'the postfeminist fantasy' (2017: 5). Sometimes social change is so evident within one generation (entry of women into political spaces, ascent of women in labour markets, life choices beyond conventional societal expectations) that it becomes easy for some (media commentators) to argue that we are living in the era of postfeminism, and even that (young) women are more able, successful, and privileged than men. This shift of focus from 'older' feminists to 'younger' feminists (and correspondingly from 'old' feminism to 'new' feminism) creates another problematic illusion. As Angela McRobbie puts it:

> feminism is celebrated in such a way as to suggest that the politics of feminist struggles are no longer needed. Seemingly supplanting feminism per se, and appearing to adopt the interests of girls and young women, commercial culture finds a licence to speak on their behalf. (2008: 533)

For Rosalind Gill, such attempts set postfeminism up as a sensibility. As Gill reminds us, we need to differentiate between 'corporate/neoliberal feminism ... [that] may have little in common with—and indeed may be antithetical to—the activist feminism of those protesting budget cuts to women's services or deportation of migrants' (2016: 612). Neoliberal feminism, for Catherine Rottenberg (2014, 2018), refers to the capture and projection of feminism as a manageable condition in which women are thriving both at work and at home. Sarah Banet-Weiser (2018) further theorizes a particular style of feminism as a popular phenomenon which relies on affective power and media visibility and which is entangled with popular misogyny. We need to defend postfeminism as a critical concept and analytical tool and consider this in relation to contemporary consumer activism.

In defining and debating feminism, we cannot afford to overemphasize the power of consumption to challenge systematic inequalities, which have underwritten our shared histories. As hooks writes, '[t]he significance of feminist movement (when it is not co-opted by opportunistic, reactionary forces) is that it offers a new ideological meeting ground for the sexes, a space for criticism, struggle, and transformation' (2005: 233). Feminism is a movement against oppression (against gender-based discrimination and violence) and for rights: for the democratic rights of participation and representation (the right to elect and to be elected), for reproductive rights (the right to one's body) and for rights to communication and fair representation (in media and advertising). Feminism is an intersectional movement for gender equality and justice. In the next section, we explore theories and arguments connecting gender and feminism to consumer culture and activism.

Feminism and Consumption: Key Theories

The many advocates and adversaries of feminism do not often converge on the same ideas, means and goals; and the extent to which individuals, communities, institutions, and states aim for gender equality and justice remains contentious. Understanding how gender intersects with consumption is part of a broader line of inquiry in the social sciences. Victoria de Grazia (1996) argues that there has been a historical feminization of consumer practices due to the development of capitalism and industrialization. Research has interrogated various aspects of gender and consumption, from how domestic labour (literally, work to maintain the home, shop for food and cater and care for children) has been distributed to women and men in different societies in different times to how women have organized to support or reprimand businesses or brands that fail to provide safe or suitable commodities, as well as how femininities and masculinities have been communicated through advertising. Understanding gender in relation to the politics of consumption requires an exploration of key theoretical approaches to feminism, consumer politics, and commodities. This section offers such a discussion in relation to gender and political consumerism, feminist consumerism, commodity feminism and feminist commodity activism and concludes with a summary of critical issues arising from such research. These concepts outline different practices of communicating gender through advertising and promotional culture and offer key theoretical perspectives for studying gender and consumer activism.

Gender and Political Consumerism

Political scientists approach the parameter of gender (as well as age, class, and education) as a potential participatory bias in the individualized responsibility-taking in the marketplace known as political consumerism (Chapter 2). Survey data allows for a noticeable reverse gender gap when it comes to political consumerism; this means that women are more likely to act politically in the marketplace than men are. Thus, as Dietlind Stolle and Michele Micheletti highlight, 'women stand out as more engaged political consumers' (2015: 76). Yet the fact that women engage more than men in political consumerism is explained by their historical barring from traditional political participation (within representative political institutions) (Forno and Ceccarini, 2006; Micheletti, 2004; Micheletti and Stolle, 2008). And gender inequalities, when it comes to the level of political participation, persist. Jasmine Lorenzini and Matteo Bassoli (2015) question the extent to which gender ideology (broadly defined as beliefs around gendered labour) contributes to their political participation and argue that when women embrace beliefs of equality and justice, they are more likely to act politically in the marketplace. Yet they also add that the employment status of women (in full employment, in precarious employment or unemployed) shapes and reshapes their gender ideology, so unemployment tends to make women less likely to embrace beliefs of equality. The coherence between women's beliefs and their actual situation can trigger political participation. Yet precarious labour can demonstrate either more active engagement in political consumerism when coupled with egalitarian gender ideology (dual-earner stance) or withdrawn engagement in political participation more broadly when coupled with a less egalitarian (male as breadwinner stance) gender ideology.

From such studies, we can draw two significant conclusions. First, understanding the extent to which gender is a determinant of political consumerism is significant as it launches from an understanding that socioeconomic and gender inequalities affect political participation more broadly. Yet they tend to equate biological sex with socially constructed gender and have not focused, for instance, on the way in which the feminist movement has affected political participation in the marketplace and the political repercussions of consumer activism. Andreas Chatzidakis and Pauline Maclaran (2020) push forward an argument for 'gendering' the field of consumer ethics research, which we can apply to consumer politics. In doing that, they invite us to understand gender in consumption through socioeconomic, embodied–affective and representational terms. The socioeconomic strand includes contributions made by feminist scholars aiming to connect the material and cultural conditions marking women's participation in the marketplace (McRobbie, 1997), which reflects broader political-economic injustices and cultural silences. The embodied–affective strand draws from Judith Butler's (1999) theories of performativity and can be found, for instance, in theorizations of the way in which the body, the self and power are constructed and resisted in consumer culture (Zanette and Brito, 2019). The representation and gender strand refers to a long array of feminist critiques of advertising and gender stereotyping (Chapter 7). We need to 'gender' the theory and practice of consumer activism.

Second, importantly, gender ideology and increasing precarity in employment makes women and minorities less able to engage fully in political participation more broadly and political consumerism or consumer activism more specifically. Consumer activism is 'gendered' and, as discussed in Chapter 3, consumption is also 'racialized'. In addition, Nicole Marie Brown (2017) unravels the silenced role of African–American women in the 'Don't Buy Where You Can't Work' campaigns of the 1920s to 1940s, as well as the incongruity between their activist leadership and social class. In other words, we need to think of gender alongside race and class within specific contexts, as well as in light of and despite pressing inequalities. As Brown argues, '[t]he power of the boycott may yet again be useful in empowering this often marginalized and invisible group to achieve goals for the larger community' (2017: 257). To develop a conceptual understanding of the power of the boycott, and the politics of consumption more broadly, I invite you to a review of further key theories related to feminism and consumer politics below.

Feminism and the Politics of Consumption

There is a convoluted relationship between feminism and consumption where feminine and feminist identities appear to clash or collapse, and where media and market industries (especially advertising) reproduce a certain brand of (neoliberal or popular) feminism. Feminist studies have regarded the politics of consumption with cautious optimism. Primarily, it has attempted to move beyond the classic Marxist critique of manipulation through commodity consumption, a tradition continued by the Frankfurt School and North American concerns of hyper-consumerism. In the early 1990s, Mica Nava proposed that 'consumer politics is able to mobilize and enfranchise a very broad spectrum of constituents, and moreover that it is productive of a kind of utopian collectivism lacking from other contemporary politics' (1991: 158). Following on from the reclaiming of popular culture from a purely political economic lens and looking at contemporary examples of the time (green consumerism and the South African boycott), Nava sought to reclaim 'the power of consumerism' (ibid.) and consumer activism which appeals 'to groups who historically have been marginalized from both the production process and the politics of the workplace and government, namely women and the young' (ibid.: 169). The contention that designates consumer culture as 'bad' is also challenged by Joanne Hollows (2013) who attributes this to the absence of feminist research. Her analysis addresses this gap by exploring how the feminist magazine *Spare Rib* (1972–93) communicated feminist consumption in the UK. Hollows illustrates that while *Spare Rib* promoted responsible consumption practices that also criticized capitalism consumer culture, it also projected an ideal 'feminist' consumer who undertakes these practices and articulates such critique, against the subjugated standard housewife consumer who reproduces her gender role and oppression (and capitalist accumulation). For Hollows, '[i]n both *Spare Rib* and second-wave feminism more generally, it became increasingly difficult to think about how women could use consumption practices as part of a feminist politics' (ibid.: 281). Thus, feminist scholars who have directly interrogated the politics of consumption do not appear to find radical opportunities in consumer activism.

What we can find is a blurring of what constitutes the political in neoliberal promotional culture. In *Promotional Culture*, Andrew Wernick (1991) presents an analysis of the ideological work of advertising through the example of cigarette ads directed towards women, illustrating a trend of the industry in response to second wave feminism. Wernick argues that advertising 'typifies what is diverse, filters out what is antagonistic or depressing, and naturalizes the role and standpoint of consumption as such' (1991: 42). Similarly, Goldman et al. (1991) introduced the idea of 'commodity feminism' to refer to an advertising strategy which arose in the 1970s to capture the informed, fatigued, and cynical female consumer through the commercial appropriation of feminism. In *Reading Ads Socially*, Goldman elaborates on this idea, arguing that advertising and media culture represent 'a feminism tailored to the demands of the commodity form' (1992: 132). This definition of commodity feminism manifests as advertising and attempts to co-brand with ideas and symbols of feminism. Rosalind Gill further defines commodity feminism as an example of postfeminism, which 'represents an aesthetically depoliticized version of a potentially oppositional feminism' (2008: 583). A popular synonym of commodity feminism is 'femvertising', which signifies contemporary advertising and marketing attempts to channel female empowerment. Commodity feminism is, thus, promoted as a stylish, feminine and enjoyable way of being one's 'true' (read 'authentic') self (Gill, 2008; Goldman, 1992; Goldman et al., 1991; McRobbie, 2008). Tsai et al. (2021) bring to focus the ways in which gender-themed empowerment advertising demonstrates fundamental differences in the representation of female vs male empowerment, thus perpetuating gender hegemony.

Promotional culture's address of authenticity is key. In *Authentic*™, Sarah Banet-Weiser (2012a) outlines the transformations of marketing from Fordism to post-Fordism and neoliberal branding targeting the individual and performed by the individual. This has created ambivalence (between feminist and feminine, between struggle and style) in popular communication of feminism; 'commodity feminism… reshapes and reimagines forms and practices of social (and political) activism into marketable commodities and takes specific form within brand culture' (ibid.: 16). Similarly, 'commodity activism' (Mukherjee and Banet-Weiser, 2012) concerns the way in which consumer behaviour merges with activism in neoliberal culture.

Commodity activism exists precisely as the ambivalent political position of consumers and the territorial corporate culture that produces commodities for every style and belief imaginable. In other words, brand culture sets the pace of contemporary politics in the marketplace.

A classic example of commodity activism is the Dove Real Beauty campaign. Banet-Weiser (2012b) elsewhere demonstrates how commodity activism (in this case, commodity feminism) and corporate appropriation go hand in hand. A similar study which compared the same example of brand communication with the fat-activist organization Pretty, Porky, and Pissed Off (PPPO) in Canada was conducted by Josée Johnston and Judith Taylor (2008). They argue that this 'feminist consumerism', 'a phenomenon with the potential to partially disrupt gender norms' (2008: 943), exists at the push of hegemonic brand communication and the pull of grassroots campaign communication. For Johnston and Taylor, the core difference between the two examples are to be found at the emotion cultures and emotion work of each of the discourses that attempt to challenge beauty standards; neoliberal brand communication in the case of Dove presents an easy path to self-consciousness and self-confidence, while PPPO organized performances and articulated discourse where self-worth comes from a long process of collective storytelling, emotional transformation and, finally, assertion. Breaking down gender norms is not as easy as brands would have it. Johnston and Taylor conclude that while Dove's approach to feminist consumerism 'provides a critique that partially disrupts the narrowness of western contemporary beauty codes, at the same time it systematically reproduces and legitimizes the hegemony of beauty ideology in women's personal lives in the service of expanding sales and corporate growth' (ibid.: 961). Another key difference, and one to underscore here, is the way in which feminism is communicated as an individual or collective project. Commodity feminism and feminist consumerism signify the ideological dominance of neoliberal consumer culture. Feminism is constantly rebranded as a choice, a style, a way of being one's true self, a way of liberating one's self from patriarchy, through smiling against adversity, in the Saturday shopping spree or late night online shopping marathon.

Commodity activism is the (un)comfortable blending of consumption with attempts to bring about social change within neoliberal brand culture. Though their focus is in the US, Mukherjee and Banet-Weiser's commodity activism approach has been adopted to analyse the intersection of political and commercial campaigning in different geographies too. Cara Wallis and Yongrong Shen (2018) analyse the #changedestiny campaign by a beauty brand in China which attempted to combat the stigma of single women over 25; Wallis and Shen find that the market-based intervention to fight gender discrimination is less successful in doing so, and more successful in spearheading a neoliberal culture of individualization, personal fulfilment and self-care. Through the sale of feelings, values, and relations, the campaign presents an invitation to consumers to engage in the buycotting of a brand whose values they share and stands as a channel for social change. While the similarities between commodity activism in the US and in China are striking, the differences need also be noted. When we are talking about commodity activism, we are still talking about a culture of activism, and, as such, it needs to be grounded in context. In the US, the challenges of activism have long been noted, especially in terms of commodification and so-called 'slacktivism'.[6] Yet in China, demonstrations are increasingly controlled by the state and consumer activism often reproduces Chinese nationalism. Hence, as Wallis and Shen note, 'unlike the Dove "Real Beauty" campaign, which utilized videos but also workshops, toolkits, user-generated content, and voting …, the #changedestiny campaign allows agency through one activity that also presents itself as a solution—purchasing an expensive beauty product' (ibid.: 384). How commodity activism manifests is thus reliant on the political context, global capitalism, and the history of consumer struggles in each case.

Queerness further complicates the notion of (commodity) feminism through the 'pink economy'. The race for the 'pink dollar', the 'pink pound', and the 'pink yuan', and their various advertising and marketing campaigns, present LGBTQ movements with both opportunities and constraints. There are many different layers to this. First, sexuality can be as controversial as gender and race or ethnicity in that it is socially constructed. As Lisa Peñaloza (1996) points out, the targeting of gays and lesbians as consumers constitutes them as a particular type of reified consumer who can be identified (and contested by those who challenge their full incorporation into society). Yet Peñaloza also points out that the market has historically presented a significant arena for social contestation, while Sender (2004a) notes how the deployment of consumer boycotts is also relevant to the present. Second, advertisers and marketers have tended to imagine the queer consumer as a uniform subject, typically, a white man based in the west (Ginder and Byun, 2015; Sender, 2004a, 2004b). In *Business, Not Politics*, Katherine Sender (2004a) argues that marketers are concerned with producing and reproducing difference, while at the same time typifying all queer consumers as 'a recognizably gay citizen: usually white, male, affluent, discreetly sexual, apolitical, gay subject' (2004a: 23). This identity is globalized through pink tourist guides, such as *Pink Map: The Gay Guide to Cape Town*, as Bradley Rink (2019) argues, and diffused from the West to the non-West, annihilating diversity and lack of purchasing power across queer individuals. Third, the way in which lesbian women have been excluded in both feminist concerns over consumerism (Clark, 1991) or marketers' attempts to approach them as consumers (Sender, 2004b) signifies undercurrent tensions between certain exclusionary, so-called feminists (who tend to be both misogynistic and transphobic) as well as hidden biases in the so-called inclusive marketers. Finally, queerness within promotional culture has had the same predicament as commodity feminism;

'commodity lesbianism' treated as a 'style', 'it is easily appropriated, reconstructed and divested of its original political or subcultural signification' (Clark 1991: 193).

The co-optation of queer identity and activism is possibly inescapable in the marketplace (Chasin, 2000; Whitney, 2006; Corey, 2019). It is also important to consider 'how consumers suffering from prolonged discrimination negotiate the political tension as they forge market relations beyond their subcultural context' (Tsai, 2012: 42). Wan-Hsiu Sunny Tsai (2012) demonstrates how queer consumers make sense of gay window advertising (an ambiguous advertising strategy covertly targeting lesbian and gay consumers), demonstrating a tension between pleasure, identification and empowerment and uneasiness, ambivalence, and commodification. The pink economy can, on the one hand, offer an affirmation through LGBTQ-friendly promotional culture, but also further stereotyping. The tension that is most prominent in these studies is not necessarily that between acceptance and rejection of queer-friendly marketing, but the negotiation of what is 'normal', the negotiation of different individual experiences of socialization with collective struggles for recognition, and the negotiation between business and politics (as in what will sell and what will impact positively on the queer community).

What is at stake when feminism is mediated through promotional and consumer culture? What possibilities exist for challenging gender hegemony and gender and sexuality-based injustices? What challenges do movements for equality and justice face when promotional communication takes hold of the symbols and messages of feminism? When feminism meets (ethical) capitalism much is at stake. Examining the political economy of the feminist T-shirt, Jemima Repo argues that the western rendering of feminism into a marketable commodity presents challenges for feminist politics in terms of 'accountability, collective action, depoliticisation, and the disposability of feminist ideas' (2020: 3). Calling this 'feminist commodity activism', Repo identifies three key shifts in terms of the 'commodification of the aesthetic experience of feminist protest, the entrepreneurialization of grassroots activism, and the production of the feminist as a subject of value' (ibid.: 13). We can further problematize feminist commodity activism by queering the concept; who is included in feminist protests, how LGBTQ subjects are represented, to what extent queerness as enterprise contributes to the visibility of the movement and its quest for justice and how the value of queer subjects is produced. What does it mean, for instance, when 'period-proof' underwear 'ethical' brand THINX advertises a gender-neutral period-proof boy short to raise awareness of transgender rights or when Caitlyn Jenner features in H&M's 'Every Victory' 2016 advertisement? Is there such a thing as 'transgender commodity activism' and to what extent does it run the same risks as feminist commodity activism? Is transgender justice up for sale?

The feminist revolution will not be marketized. When it is marketized, it reproduces a problematic binary between 'developed' and 'developing' world, as well as 'saviour' and 'sufferer' (Iqani, 2016). We need to think within and beyond the global North in terms of how capitalism speaks to gender movements across countries and continents. Critical studies have also noted the deep impact of neoliberal capitalism on the way in which western ideologies of consumerism and feminism have become interdependent with neo-colonialism. Ofra Koffman et al. (2015) scrutinize the so-called 'girl powering' of humanitarianism, which reproduces postfeminism as post-humanitarianism (where the concept of 'girl power' is mobilized by corporate branding, celebrity endorsements, and consumer culture). Similarly, Lisa Daily further identifies 'the paternalistic logics of colonialism' (2019: 145) in the way in which 'commodity feminism canonizes the ideal feminine subject—whether as a savior or a "damsel"—while ensuring her social reproducibility as a figure of capitalist productivity and the corporeal reproduction of future generations' (ibid.: 152). Commodity feminism epitomizes gender as a dualism, if not necessarily between genders in the west then between women in the global North and global South.

Furthermore, the ways in which race becomes entangled in feminist commodity activism and specifically brand communication disguises another dangerous simplification of social change. Francesca Sobande's work on how brands draw on Black social justice activism to highlight 'who and what is framed as brave in marketing tied to interdependent issues pertaining to race and gender' (2019: 2724) further illustrates this. Sobande scrutinizes the marketing of 'wokeness' by identifying key subject positions within marketing examples: White Saviour, Black excellence, Strong black woman (and mother), and the ambiguous 'Woke' change agent (which can include the White Saviour). The latter is particularly suitable for ethical capitalism as it 'enables brands to depict historically under-represented and oppressed individuals, as a means of virtue signalling, rather than explicitly calling out specific and overlapping social injustices' (ibid.: 2738). Feminism is for everybody. But when 'feminist' is used as a trope, an aesthetic, a style, a marketing campaign or a set of commodities in the marketplace, it nullifies the persisting need to recognize, react to, and redress gender injustices.

Critical Issues

Postfeminism is the embracing of feminism by promotional culture. It is the situatedness of feminist ideas, symbols, and discourses within specific times and spaces, and within the contexts and remits of promotional industries, communication, and culture. Many questions have arisen in response to the presence of feminist symbols in the marketplace and the proliferation of feminism commodities: What are the dialectics between feminism and consumption? To what extent can the marketplace be used as a space for expressing and practising a feminist politics? What are the histories (or herstories) of feminism and how has a politics of consumption been communicated in relation to a gendered subject? What are the different subject positions within 'woke' marketing campaigns in so-called ethical capitalism? Can the politics of consumption be mobilized to further the work of social change agents? To respond to these questions, we should highlight four key issues.

1. *The importance of gendering consumer activism.* Gender is a social construct which is expressed in consumer ethics and politics through various approaches. Chatzidakis and Maclaran's (2020) gendering of the field identifies three such tendencies: socioeconomic, embodied–affective and representational. In other words, you cannot point at someone in the supermarket and say, for instance, 'a woman is shopping' without asking what her purchasing power might be, how shopping might be labour, how she performs her gender and draws on emotional regimes or draws pleasure from her choices and how she responds to gendered advertising. Gender is not a single indicator that fully explains consumer behaviour.
2. *The importance of collectivity.* Of course 'Individual struggle does matter; a collective movement depends upon it' (Ahmed, 2017: 6), but the feminist movement is much more than a collection of individual white cisgender women who shop for change and their sisters wherever they might be. The feminist movement is the identification of key injustices over women at home, on the street, in the workplace, and everywhere in between. The feminist movement is the recognition of the work of women in the struggles against gender-based violence. It is listening, sharing, and advocating.
3. *The importance of history.* We also need to think of gender beyond the West and in relation to post-colonialism. The false narrative of feminism travelling from west to east produces 'a history of how feminism acquired utility as an imperial gift' (Ahmed, 2017: 4). For instance, continuities from colonial times persist in visual representations of women in ethical commodity advertisements, as Kalpana Wilson reminds us, where sexualized images of beautiful African women stand in for fair-trade chocolate, their representation itself constituting a 'guilty pleasure' (2011: 328).
4. *The importance of identifying a feminist politics.* A feminist politics should be intersectional, meaning that gender is only one parameter, which explains a subject's position (Crenshaw, 2017). We need to think of gender in relation to race, class, sexuality, migration, disability, and other conditions. When we think of a feminist politics we think of a hopeful politics, but not a politics of instant self-actualization, as femvertising would have it. The feminist movement is not a consumer alone in the marketplace looking for the best possible way to exercise 'girl power'. As Sara Ahmed writes, '[w]e learn about the feminist cause by the bother feminism causes; by how feminism comes up in public culture as a site of disturbance' (2017: 21). Feminism is as significant as ever. Through its entanglement with promotional culture, commodity

activism has tended to provide an easy, happy, soluble narrative of female empowerment. Yet as Repo argues, '[t]he feminist critique of capitalism is thus lost in the mass production of the feminist T-shirt' (2020: 15).

Researching Consumer Activism and Feminism: Methodologies

We cannot simply celebrate or condemn the power of consumer politics. Research on feminism and consumption has brought into sharp focus a critique of neoliberal capitalism in relation to gender. Scholars have highlighted how promotional culture draws on gender and feminism and how this process dilutes the difficulties that women and marginalized groups face in voicing and claiming their rights. Call it 'pinkwashing' or 'rainbowwashing', and nothing changes. What can bring change is remembering that feminism is not irrelevant or irrational (as anti-gender movements claim). And it is not for sale. Primarily then, we come to understand consumer activism in relation to feminism as a dangerous liaison, characterized by a set of dynamics which reimagine a feminist politics in relation to promotional culture. On the other hand, it is also important to consider the way in which consumer activism has come to the aid of many feminist movements, as a tool in their repertoire of actions. Additionally, we need to assess how ethical commerce has provided opportunities for economic empowerment to women. Such questions remain pertinent in relation to globalization and consumer culture.

Let's reflect on the way in which knowledge around gender and consumer activism has been produced. For the most part, this has been constructed through qualitative methods with the exception of political scientists studying political consumerism who have tended to draw on available survey data (Forno and Ceccarini, 2006; Stolle and Micheletti, 2015). Jemima Repo has engaged with a political economy of feminist protest with a focus on T-shirts, reconciling the research on commodity feminism, neoliberal feminism, and commodity activism. Working within historical sociology, Nicole Marie Brown (2017) develops an extensive literature review of secondary sources to bring to light the hidden role of African–American women in relation to economic boycotts from the 1920s to the 1940s. Within critical marketing studies, scholars have also undertaken a literature review to highlight the centres and margins of academic knowledge on queer consumer markets between 1993 and 2013 (Ginder and Byun, 2015).

Many studies have analysed media texts in different ways to probe questioning which had been largely missing in instrumental studies, which have tended to explore the 'hows' and not the 'so whats'. Critical advertising studies have examined advertising texts to bring to light 'types of social power depicted in advertising' (Tsai et al. 2021: 19). Drawing on content analysis, Tsai and colleagues explore advertising that communicates empowerment towards women and men and find significant differences. The initial conceptualization of 'commodity feminism' also relied on a close reading of advertisements (Goldman et al., 1991) and the way in which advertising has emulated feminism and black social justice has been explored through an interpretive and critical discursive analysis (Sobande, 2019). Hollows (2013) analyses the construction of the politics of consumption in a British feminist magazine during the first two years of its operation. Finally, Molander and colleagues (2019) analyse a photography project of Swedish fathers through a critical visual analysis to bring to the fore issues about the context, gender politics and the constitution of consumer subjects. Textual analysis and the discursive construction of gender and consumer politics remain valuable in highlighting previously under-researched topics.

A case study approach is also useful in synthesizing textual data with contextual data. Sara Banet-Weiser analyses the 2004 Dove 'Real Beauty' campaign as '[p]art advertising, part pedagogy, part social activism' (2012b: 47) to demonstrate how brand culture comes to mediate female empowerment, thus illuminating the inner workings of postfeminism and commodity feminism. Similarly, Wallis and Shen (2018) explore the 2016 '#changedestiny' campaign by Chinese high-end beauty brand SK-II to challenge the patriarchal stereotype of young unmarried women. They thoroughly contextualize China's biopolitical projects, consumerist gender norms, and familial ethics and obligations and closely analyse a video called *Marriage Market Takeover*, where women hijack their parents' attempts to match them. Their analysis demonstrates the similarities between the Dove 'Real Beauty' campaign and the '#changedestiny' campaign, suggesting that the latter is 'emblematic of the logics of China's post-socialist gender politics, as well as western post-feminist media culture' (ibid.: 385), but also highlight the importance of context, suggesting that in China 'consumer subjects take precedence over consumer citizens' (ibid.: 384). Poignantly, they conclude: 'in contrast to a western neoliberal brand culture that emphasizes the individual consumer citizen who "freely" chooses and/or remakes her identity through consumption, in China a neo/non-liberal state sets definite parameters for its self-optimizing consumer subjects' (ibid.: 386). Lisa Daily (2019) analyses two brands which engage in commodity feminism and link consuming 'saviour' subjects in the west with women 'in-need' in the global South, thus demonstrating how neoliberal logic perpetuates neo-colonial capitalism. Koffman and colleagues (2015) have also similarly drawn on the 'Girl Up' campaign by the United Nations Foundation which has included a series of partnerships with entrepreneurs such as Ivanka Trump to demonstrate how this postfeminist and post-humanitarian 'girl-powering of development' masks inequalities and injustices. A case study approach, and particularly one which draws comparisons with other cases, is thus useful in highlighting the politics of commodity activism.

Scholars who have engaged in critical consumption studies tend to draw from an assortment of ethnographic methods. Katherine Sender (2004a, 2004b) interviews professionals who produce gay advertising, marketing strategies, market research, and analyses media texts such as advertisements and articles in newspapers and magazines to showcase how sexually ambivalent marketing has attempted to capture the LGBTQ consumer market in the US. Zanette and Brito (2019) utilize interviews with overweight Brazilian women, as well as a netography of fashion blogs, the website content of an online retailer, and a fashion magazine to explore processes of subjectification and resistance in the plus-size fashion field. Interviews are the method of choice of a number of scholars who employ these to reflect on the everyday lives, embodied experiences and agentic practices of women who encounter fashion, brands, marketing attempts, consumer choices, and the world of fashion (Dosekun, 2020; Johnston and Taylor 2008; Lorenzini and Bassoli, 2015; McRobbie, 1997; Tsai, 2012). There are innumerable questions related to gender, politics, and consumption that can be answered through ethnographic methods.

Case Study: When a Chocolate Brand Sells Love and Diversity

Some Context about Feminism and LGBTQ Justice in Greece

Greece is considered a western democracy, where women have been able to vote since 1934 and have achieved full political citizenship (the right to vote and to be elected) since 1952. Homosexuality was decriminalized in 1951, although it took half a century more for law-making to protect queer persons against discrimination in the job market,[7] though not in other realms of social life. Homosexual couples cannot adopt a child, while there is abundant heterosexist commentary in public speech and in the media. Austerity policies implemented after the financial crisis of 2008 have further dampened campaigns for social justice, and press freedom has significantly worsened. In 2021, Greece ranked 70th in the World Press Freedom Index, a position that has slightly improved over the last few years (it ranked 89th in 2016), but which had dropped severely from the 35th position in 2009. In addition, the fascist organization and political party Golden Dawn gained parliamentary representation between 2012 and 2019, during which time they administered the persecution of LGBTQ people, migrants, and leftists. In 2012, a prominent Golden Dawn MP slapped a Communist Party MP on live TV.[8] The murder of hip-hop artist Pavlos Fyssas (aka Killah P), the attempted murder of Egyptian fisherman Abuzid Embarak, and the attempted murder of members of the Communist Party and trade unionists brought Golden Dawn members to trial where they were found guilty of all charges and are presently serving time in jail.[9]

The hegemonic neo-conservative approach of mainstream media has tended to promote a narrative of austerity acceptance against alternative voices (Doudaki et al., 2016). For instance, in 2013, Syriza MP Zoe Constantopoulou (who later served as President of the Hellenic Parliament) was protesting the sudden (and undemocratic) closure of the public service broadcaster when she was surrounded by riot police and later mocked for her actions by opposition politicians and mainstream newspapers.[10] The gender hegemony of mainstream media is also evidenced by the violation of human rights of 27 HIV-positive women who were arrested in central Athens in 2012. These women (some were homeless, drug users, or sex workers) had their personal details, mugshots and full body shots aired on mainstream (commercial) TV channels, opening them up to outrageous and violent victimization.[11] Then, in 2018, the killing of LGBTQ activist Zak Kostopoulos (aka Zackie Oh) sparked the campaign Justice for Zak/Zackie.[12] Zak's death was announced shortly after he was arrested after being violently kicked on the floor of a jewellery shop and divided public debate, exposing deep-seated homophobia and stigmatization. What's more, at the beginning of 2021, Olympic medallist Sofia Bekatorou detailed her sexual assault two decades previously, sparking the Greek #metoo movement and a contentious public debate on the existence, nature, and extent of gender-based violence. A few weeks later, sexual abuse statements by minors finally led to the arrest of Dimitris Lignadis (then Artistic Director of the National Theatre of Greece). Throughout 2021, femicides were continuously reported, one man after another killing his lover, girlfriend, wife, demonstrating an urgent need to address sexism, stigma, and gender-based violence.

Background on the Lacta Brand and Its Advertising History

What does chocolate have to do with all this? Lacta is a chocolate brand owned by the Greek company Pavlidis until 1991 when it was sold to Kraft Foods Inc., which was renamed Mondelēz International in 2012. Mondelēz Hellas has been employing Ogilvy Greece for the production of Lacta advertising, which has a long history of capitalizing on the idea of love. From the 1990s up until the 2000s, the recipe used to advertise the chocolate had been simple: take a man who is determined to do his own thing, go to work, ignore affection, or have the last word, present him with a chocolate and make him remember, recognize, or reconcile with his loved one. An iconic 1995 advertisement featured a man eating a Lacta chocolate and reminiscing about a lover who appears when he goes to open the door to his apartment (not expecting anyone to be there), and who hands him another chocolate bar. Cue happy end. Sad man eats chocolate, gets woman whom he thought he had lost, eats another chocolate, is happy. A 2010 ad called 'I'm Sorry', for instance, showed the scene of a lovers' quarrel, ultimately mediated by the chocolate brand. In black and white, we see a young man quarrelling with (presumably) his girlfriend, storming off in anger, pushing street vendors and passer-bys aside before he reaches a kiosk where we see (in its red emblematic colour) a Lacta chocolate bar in focus. As expected, Lacta, as a uniting influence on their love, makes him forget his fury and transforms his erratic behaviour into the very opposite; within seconds, he returns to the young woman, balloons and flowers in hand, as her passive, grateful look meets him.

Ogilvy had been experimenting with digital innovations in advertising since the late 2000s. In 2008, they curated 'Love at first site', an interactive love story and the first branded entertainment campaign in the country.[13] In 2009, they produced 'Love in Action',[14] an integrated promotional campaign which put consumers to work by asking them to crowdsource love stories, one of which was chosen and written into a script by a well-known writer and director. In 2018, 'The Taste of Love' branded entertainment campaign featured a lonely middle-aged affluent man who lives in the future with an AI robot who can satisfy his every need, but does not know what love is. Audiences were again invited to 'help ELLi learn, by submitting a photo that captured love for them'.[15] Their photos were then analysed and positioned on a 3D map and they were able to look into ELLi's mind and see what she was learning in real time. In short, over the last two decades, Lacta advertising had been based on a heterosexist narrative where male protagonists are centred, their emotions privileged, while women have appeared as mostly passive subjects, someone to return home to, their emotions unquestioned, and their youth eternal.

The #ActForLove Campaign

The campaign was, as before, produced by Ogilvy and launched in February 2019 to coincide with Valentine's Day. This campaign was significantly different to Ogilvy's previous strategies both in narrative and in structure: it did not focus on a single (and typically white) male protagonist and it did not rely on digital innovations, like interactive media or artificial intelligence. The campaign's innovation (possibly identifying the rise of a feminist movement and an LGBTQ consumer market) was that it did not attempt just to sell love, but socially diverse (multicultural, homosexual, dis/abled) couples in love. Mondelēz Hellas stated:

> Part of our work is listening in on society. For the last ten years we have been narrating love stories through the specific product. We thought that now, in parallel with international developments, with movements such as #MeToo on gender equality, difference and inclusion, public opinion in Greece has progressed.[16]

Ogilvy Greece employed a freelance photographer whose portfolio includes refugee and anti-fascist protests, as well as women photographed in protest of human trafficking. The campaign included a video of 28 real couples, a photography exhibition in a high-end shopping mall in downtown Athens and further video content of each couple in Lacta's YouTube channel. The blurb of the campaign read:

> Love has no colour, age, ethnicity or gender. It has no rules and conditions. Love does not discriminate. Every couple in love feels it differently. That's why love does not have one taste, but innumerate tastes, all of which deserve embracing.[17]

#ActForLove was a very different ad in relation to previous Lacta advertising, asking audiences to break down stereotypes when it comes to love. Yet while the corporation stated that they thought that public opinion in Greece had progressed, much contention surrounded the ad campaign, reminiscent of other 'wokewashing' advertising campaigns around the world.

Analysing #ActForLove as Commodity Activism

Ogilvy drew from the playbook of advertising and social justice. The choice of a female photographer, the choice of real couples, the careful performance of diversity, and the moment upon which the advertising campaign was launched attempted to establish another 'first' in Greek advertising (first branded entertainment example, now first social justice campaign). As an example of commodity activism, #ActForLove is also '[p]art advertising, part pedagogy, part social activism' (Banet-Weiser, 2012b: 47). The brand asks consumers to participate in social change (to accept love in all its 'tastes') by consuming the chocolate, downloading posters of diverse couples in love, as well as viewing and sharing branded content on social media. The profiles of real couples in love are short and often aim to erase the idea of difference; 'they believe that all couples have one thing in common, and that is love', 'we are no different to other couples, we just have some bigger difficulties', 'I don't feel different. I feel one with everyone else', 'where there is love there is no obstacle'. Lacta plays on 'the potential to partially disrupt gender norms' (Johnston and Taylor, 2008: 943), but continues to capitalize on love and presents a version of social change which can be consumed through visuals and commodities. Different to the US and Chinese examples analysed by Banet-Weiser (2012b) and Wallis and Shen (2018), #ActForLove is closer to the western example, but with limited options for consumer citizens. The participatory aspects of the campaign were limited to viewing the photographs and profiles of each love story, and downloading black and white posters of each couple featuring a bright red Lacta bar.

The liberal campaign promoting gender and racial diversity in advertising is a welcome interruption of Lacta's previously heterosexist advertising but raises questions as to who the ideal target of such a campaign might be and how to continue the public debate after the positive impact of the campaign.[18] The campaign became a trending topic on social media as it sparked a public debate about diversity and inclusion, and received threats of a boycott from conservative constituencies. Similarly, an anti-LGBTQ group in the US, the American Family Association, called for a consumer boycott of the US multinational Kellogg Company because of its limited edition 'Together with Pride' cereal. Both the Lacta and the Kellogg cereal campaigns prompted boycotts focused on the brand's so-called attempt to promoting 'homosexual propaganda' and lack of respect towards 'family life'. When consumer activism launches from such regressive ideology, it is clear that the promotional culture can usurp both progressive and regressive attitudes and actions.

Ultimately, the critical question behind the emancipatory potential of branded consumer activism is the extent to which innovative attempts to engage publics in processes of social change can be a step towards gender justice. On the one hand, #ActForLove challenged heteronormativity in Greek popular culture (and thus received the backlash of conservative agents) and promoted an inclusive approach to romance. Yet this 'romance diversity' (Lekakis, forthcoming) serves the brand more than it serves the cause. The specific framing of diversity is associated with the power of romantic love, but also framed within homonormative terms. There is little space for queerness to be expressed or included in 'romance diversity'. Media and public discourse around femicides or the killing of Zak Kostopoulos, a queer activist, and drag performer under the name Zackie Oh, illustrates persisting heterosexism. While promotional campaigns that challenge this and can expand the public debate beyond stereotypes are important, they also attempt to capture consumers by providing a new twist to an old recipe.

Questions for Future Case Studies

Appraising consumer activism in relation to gender requires careful consideration of the agents spearheading social change (as we have seen there is a difference between brand culture and grassroots organizations in terms of the stories told about social justice). It also requires deep contextualization of where, when, and how consumer activism emerges. The following questions are helpful in beginning to question gender justice in relation to the politics of consumption:

- What are different articulations of feminist consumerism and what are the opportunities and challenges of each case?

- How has consumer citizenship been constructed through feminist media historically and presently?
- How have social movements mobilized consumption to further their political outcomes? To what extent are boycotts still successful following #metoo revelations?
- What are the aims of utilizing the marketplace and consumer culture in relation to gender justice and to what extent are these achieved?
- To what extent do women in a particular place and time participate in consumer activism and what other parameters condition their participation? What is the context of gender ideology within which they are acting?
- How can we draw on a comparative case study to appraise the opportunities and challenges of feminist commodity activism?
- How can we dismantle the post-colonial logics of commodity activism and to what extent is it possible to do so through the marketplace?
- To what extent does empowerment advertising represent male and female empowerment on equal terms?
- To what extent can feminist entrepreneurship empower women?
- To what extent does queerness as enterprise contribute to the visibility of the movement and its quest for justice and how is the value of queer subjects produced?
- Is there such a thing as 'transgender commodity activism' and to what extent does it run the same risks as feminist commodity activism?

Conclusion

This chapter has interrogated how gender becomes embroiled in consumer activism. Feminism is not a commodity for sale. Of course, wearing a t-shirt that features a feminist slogan does not make you a bad feminist or a non-feminist. The very point of the feminist movement (that I want to belong to) is not to perform feminism or to create divisions between feminists and others, but to act in everyday life, in public and in private, gender equality and justice. It is to unite and fight when it is time to fight. Feminist commodity activism, as highlighted by Repo (2020), is part of the broader neoliberal tendency to fashion, enterprise, and brand the self in a way that dismantles the political power of the feminist movement. The value derived from social justice goals is gained by brands embracing feminist values and performing social justice to the extent that they generate profit and publicity, all in one ad campaign. But feminism is not irrelevant, and it is not passé.

The idea that feminism is no longer useful, relevant, or necessary is a position divorced from an understanding of what gender equality and justice is. In the European Union, during the Covid-19 pandemic, women have been the overwhelming majority in the care sector, as well as in essential services (cashiers, domestic cleaning, etc.) (European Parliament News, 2021). The historical and presently exacerbated feminization of labour, coupled with the historical feminization of consumption testify to the extent that, despite the typical fulfilment of political citizenship, women remain underpriviledged in most advanced capitalist societies. Queer citizenship rights are further away from fulfilment. The 'power of the boycott' (to go back to the beginning of the section), is evident in the chant 'We're here, we're queer, and we're not going shopping', sung by movements such as Queer Nation. Will the marketplace be a valuable arena to gain some of those rights?

What conclusions have we drawn so far? We need to 'gender' consumer activism and 'queer' consumer activism, as we need to 'race' consumer activism. Gender is socially constructed, and gender identity and gender expression are different ways of internalizing and externalizing gender choices and characteristics. Gender equality is inescapably connected to gender justice, and attempts to promote equality without discussing justice are vacuous. We need to think globally and we need to think locally, in context. This chapter has attempted to ask the broader question of the extent to which it is possible to use the marketplace to augment feminism or resist sexism. Many examples have been presented to showcase the debate on the power of the politics of consumption, as well as the limitations of commodity activism.

We ask, what happens when empowerment becomes a discourse in neoliberal brand culture. The answer we get depends on the context. The Dove Real Beauty campaign in the US, the #changedestiny campaign in China and the #ActforLove campaign in Greece are all examples of (feminist) commodity activism, yet the consumer agencies they mobilize depend on the culture of contention in each geographical setting and the state of gender in relation to state ideology. The feminist revolution will not be marketized. When it is marketized, it reproduces a problematic binary between male and female empowerment, as well as 'saviour' and 'sufferer'. We need to think within and beyond the western context in terms of how capitalism speaks to gender movements across countries and continents.

Notes

1. www.who.int/health-topics/gender#tab=tab_1 (May 28 2021).
2. www.bbc.com/news/newsbeat-46874617 (11 November 2021).
3. www.weforum.org/reports/gender-gap-2020-report-100-years-pay-equality (10 November 2021).
4. eige.europa.eu/publications/gender-equality-index-2020-report (10 November 2021).
5. www.absolut.com/au/products/absolut-rainbow/ (27 June 2021).
6. *Slacktivism* typically refers to political activities that have little political impact, but which presents individuals with the sense of political fulfilment.

For instance, changing your social media profile to a symbol of resistance, sharing a petition online or looking up your 'slavery footprint' (Heynen and van der Meulen, 2021) are examples of slacktivism.

7. In 2005, a law for the application of equal rights despite racial, ethnic, religious or other belief system, disability, age or sexual orientation. In 2010, a law against for the equal treatment of men and women in relation to employment barred any discrimination between the two genders. In 2021, a law against violence and abuse at the workplace also includes the elimination of any form of behaviour against sexual orientation, gender expression, and identity or gender characteristics of a person. This is particularly important, as it now includes the protection of queer persons more broadly, beyond the strict categorisation of biological sex.
8. www.theguardian.com/world/2012/jun/07/greek-golden-dawn-mp-assaults-females-tv (27 July 2021).
9. https://goldendawnwatch.org/?lang=en (27 July 2021).
10. www.opendemocracy.net/en/5050/misogyny-in-greek-parliament-and-media-problem-no-one-wants-to-deal-with/ (28 July 2021).
11. The case is well documented in the 2013 documentary *Ruins: Chronicles of an HIV Witch-Hunt*. Available: www.youtube.com/watch?v=LlbL4sQ3_Fo (28 July 2021).
12. www.zackieohjustice.watch/en/ (6 June 2022).
13. https://ogilvy.gr/feed/lacta-love-first-site (29 July 2021).
14. The campaign put the consumers to work, asking them to vote who will lead the film, where the film will be shot, what the protagonists will be called, and some of the audience would also participate in the shooting as extras. All stages of production of the campaign was continuously promoted on social media.
15. https://ogilvy.gr/work/lacta-the-taste-of-love (29 July 2021).
16. www.kathimerini.gr/culture/arts/1009563/diafimisi-enantion-tampoy/ (29 July 2021).
17. www.actforlove.gr/ (29 July 2021).
18. The campaign received a number of awards and increased sales by 13.5 per cent (https://ogilvy.gr/work/lacta-actforlove) (29 July 2021).

FIVE
CONSUMER ACTIVISM IN THE ENVIRONMENT

Introduction: Can We Consume Ourselves out of the Climate Crisis?

We will probably not consume ourselves out of the climate crisis. The planet is in deep ecological crisis, characterized by the decline of biodiversity and the rise of climate change. The very phrase 'climate change' can be either a conversation stopper or opener for citizens, a field of decade-long action for civil society, a pre-emptive or contentious political statement by politicians, or a pledge or performance by corporations. If we look inside a household in the global North, some worrying facts about consumer commodities and their impact on the environment appear. Making a pair of jeans requires 10,000 litres of water[1] – and, yes, by the way, according to Levi's you should really avoid washing your jeans.[2] The fashion and footwear industry produces over 8 per cent of total greenhouse gas (GHG) emissions (Quantis, 2018). Livestock supply chains account for over 14 per cent of all anthropogenic GHG (FAO, 2016), while it takes 75 per cent less land to feed someone on a plant-based (vegan) diet.[3] Approximately 30 per cent of the food produced worldwide is lost or wasted every year.[4] Plastic defines our lives, with 368 million tonnes produced globally in 2019, a rise from 359 million tonnes the year before. In 2019, e-waste amounted to 53.6 million metric tons (Mt), more than the equivalent of the weight of all adults in Europe. Environmental movements have long lobbied for state regulation, industry change, and consumer responsibility in using the planet's resources. The Paris Agreement (COP21) recognized 'that sustainable lifestyles and sustainable patterns of consumption and production … play an important role in addressing climate change' (UNFCCC 2015: 21). Negotiations at COP26 highlighted again the necessity to change consumption patterns to meet the shared goal of keeping climate warming to less than 1.5 degrees Celsius, but in largely equalizing terms, making no mention of the vast volume of consumption and subsequent pollution by rich and middle-class consumers (mostly based in the global North). Universalist approaches to consumption and environmentalism require urgent questioning.

When we think of consumption and the environment, we can think about consuming less or consuming differently, and pose questions to our systems of provision: How and where are things produced and how do they reach us? How does sustainable consumption and green consumerism intersect with (individual) projects of the self, lifestyle politics, and everyday life? What are green identities and how do they connect to broader campaigns for environmentalism? How can we, as consumers, demonstrate environmental awareness and responsibility in our daily life? To what extent does our background, socioeconomic status, and location determine our ability to be 'green'? To what extent can individual consumer behaviour transform industrial systems of provision? What happens to post-consumer waste? The points raised here are not intended to moralize environmental consumption, though moral economies are very much part of consumer activism. This chapter highlights key debates in relation to growth and development that relate to consumption and consumer activism. Following an interrogation of concepts such as climate change, sustainable development, sustainable consumption, and green consumerism, this chapter presents arguments and analysis on environmentally conscious consumption and highlights critical issues related to 1) justice and inequality, 2) challenges of individualization, 3) the environmental paradox of information and communication technologies, and 4) the importance of consuming less. Finally, we will explore a case study of the nearly omnipresent smartphone.

Key Concepts
Climate Change, Sustainable Development and Alternatives

National Geographic defines climate change as 'a long-term shift in global or regional climate patterns' and it is acknowledged by the United Nations and the Intergovernmental Panel on Climate Change (IPCC) that human activity, by way of post-industrial economic progress, has had an alarming effect on this.[5] Mass and fast consumerism – especially in the global North – is harmful to the environment. During COVID-19 lockdowns in 2020, the air became temporarily cleaner (Cohan, 2020) and animals took to the streets (*The Guardian*, 2020), producing interesting insights into the question of what happens when economic growth (the growth of consumption and production as measured by gross domestic product) slows down. If human activity based on the universalizing model of economic growth is the major source of our climate crisis, a consideration of alternatives is more than necessary. The United Nations has been advocating for both 'green economy'[6] and 'sustainable development'[7] through sustainable development goals (SDGs).[8] Yet this agenda for sustainable development is often criticized as disconnected from significant systemic change.

One reason is the disconnect between the environmentalism and environmental justice movements; the parallel existence of the movements has, for some, not adequately aligned in terms of the aims of the environmental justice movement, which seeks to account for and address environmental racism (recognizing that communities of colour are disproportionately exposed to environmental harm) (Sandler and Pezzullo, 2007). Furthermore, indigenous environmental justice (highlighting indigenous knowledge around justice and recognizing the agency of non-human beings including the Earth itself) applies a settler colonial and environmental injustice analysis to highlight the historical conditions that characterize the contemporary climate crisis, as well as alternative routes to it. The alternative People's Summit Rio+20 during the United Nations Rio+20 Summit produced the document *Another Future Is Possible*, outlining concerns about the capitalist nature of the green economy[9] and proposed transition initiatives towards a fair, sustainable, and solidarity economy.[10] A foundational concept behind the document was *buen vivir*, a South American model emerging from indigenous traditions and imagining transition from development as economic growth (and its re-imagination as sustainable development) to development as a synthesis of wellbeing within communities and Nature (Gudynas, 2011). Similar to *buen vivir* are approaches such as ecological swaraj[11] and degrowth which pose decolonial critiques of development and thus treat 'sustainable development' as an oxymoron (d'Alisa et al., 2015; Kallis, 2018; Kothari et al., 2014). Development is a contested term, in many ways the root of systemic inequalities within and across societies, and consumption is very much connected to visions of sustainable development, alternatives towards decolonial ecological futures and the state of planet Earth.

Sustainable Consumption, Green Consumerism and Alternatives

Sustainable development aims to change the gears of consumer economy from a productivist model of planned obsolescence and wasteful consumerism to a model of integrating sustainability in industry planning and everyday life. SDG12 is the United Nations' development goal on sustainable consumption and production (SCP) which 'is about doing more and better with less. It is also about decoupling economic growth from environmental degradation, increasing resource efficiency and promoting sustainable lifestyles'.[12] SCP is presented as a holistic approach to systemic production and consumption, involving different stakeholders such as 'business, consumers, policy makers, researchers, scientists, retailers, media, and development cooperation agencies, among others' (United Nations Environment Programme, 2010: 13). Businesses have increasingly turned towards performances or practices of sustainability, evoking celebration around their ecological citizenship or critique around 'greenwashing'[13] (Chapter 2). For instance, between the mid-1990s and 2011 global sales of natural and organic cosmetics increased from less than $1 billion to $9.1 billion (Sahota, 2014: 7). And in 2019, a collective of over 300 clothing brands called 'Make Friday Green Again' asked shoppers to boycott Black Friday sales because of environmental reasons.

When it comes to consumers and action on climate change, the 1992 United Nations Conference on Environment and Development (Rio Earth Summit) called for 'a better understanding of the role of consumption and how to bring about more sustainable consumption patterns' (UNCED, 1992), signalling a shift of address from producers to consumers. In 2018, the UN launched the 'Act Now' campaign and app, encouraging individuals to save energy at home, drive less, eat plant-based foods, fly less, cut food waste, reduce, reuse, repair, recycle, get wind or solar energy, switch to an electric vehicle, choose eco-friendly products, and 'speak up' for environmentalism. These are all ways of partaking in green consumerism, from the consumer choice of local and seasonal foods, products certified by ecolabels[14] and energy-efficient and ethically sourced appliances to the reduction of food waste, meat, single-use plastic, everyday use of electricity, and transportation. Sustainable (consumer) lifestyles are, thus, regarded as a combination of green consumerism (buying green) and managing individual (and family) carbon footprints.[15] Yet the lack of action on addressing unbridled consumerism stands out among the flaws or weaknesses of the green economy and sustainable development model:

> While there is a welcome focus on sustainable production and consumption, there is no explicit focus on the need to curb and drastically cut down the present consumption levels of the rich in the global North (the so-called 1 percent, including the dominant elites of the South). Without this, the majority of humankind will never have the space needed to become more secure and genuinely prosperous. (Kothari et al., 2014: 365)

Indeed, limiting mass consumerism appears to be one of the biggest challenges, as it would require, as Doyle puts it, altering cultural and social norms 'to meaningfully reveal the ecological unsustainability of many of the behavioural and consumer practices undertaken on a daily basis' (2011: 128). The role of media industries and communication platforms and practices is key here, as will be discussed later. Furthermore, grassroots alternatives to green consumerism exist in the solidarity economy, a socioeconomic framework, based on direct democracy, egalitarianism, and self-management. Arising primarily in Latin America following the economic crisis of the 1990s and in Europe following the economic crisis of 2008, local alternative economic practices have become established such as consumer–producer cooperatives, exchange networks, urban gardening, collective kitchens, parallel currencies, time banks, and cooperative media (Castells et al., 2012; d'Alisa et al., 2015; Lekakis and Forno, 2019).

Theory: Environmentally Conscious Consumption as Consuming Less and Differently

The question of the form and function of consumer behaviour in addressing environmentalism has been posed more broadly following the 1992 Rio+20 Earth Summit, generating terms such as 'sustainable consumption' and 'green consumerism'. Both refer to environmentally conscious alternatives to mass consumerism, although challenges of linking consumption to political considerations persist (Autio et al., 2009; Boström and Klintman, 2019a). Despite their often-interchangeable use, we can discern a key difference between the terms; green consumerism refers to consumption of products that are less harmful to the environment, while sustainable consumption suggests reduced consumption alongside consumption of environmentally friendly products (Boström and Klintman, 2019b; Doyle, 2011; Wilén and Taipale, 2018). For instance, in 2007, British supermarket Sainsbury's sold a designer bag made of unbleached cotton and fashioning the text 'I'm not a plastic bag', prompting claims that 'sustainable is the new black' and became a highly desirable consumer product (Eden, 2016). Often manifesting as commodity activism, green consumerism is a contested site:

> green consumption can be consumed as a middle- or upper-class practice to ramify social divides; it can exist as an isolated act; buying more green goods can ironically mean increased consumption; a corporation can produce a few green lines while also producing deeply environmentally harmful ones (or 'partial greening'); green marketing can be used to update a company's image while the products remain unchanged; or through all-out greenwashing a company can use green branding to try to hide a destructive environmental record. (Littler, 2012: 82)

In many ways, the intersection between environmentalism and consumer activism echoes concerns posed in Chapter 4 regarding the entanglement of brand culture in social change. Within media studies, Mehita Iqani (2020) undertakes an appraisal of representations of waste in popular culture. In addition, a large volume of studies questions the transformative potential of climate-friendly consumption. This is dedicated to a number of issues concerning individual consumers, as well as criticizing the extent to which responsibility for the environment is futilely designated to individuals.

In their review of such studies, Magnus Boström and Mikael Klintman identify five key limitations, or constraining mechanisms, and conclude that 'individually independent and reliant solutions to climate problems are not where society should place its hopes' (2019b: 372). First is the case of the value–action gap where scholars question why people do not act in accordance with their climate consciousness, and finding a number of reasons – from lack of willingness to pay a premium for green products to motivational complexities and social dilemmas (e.g. why pay more when others do not?). Second, critical perspectives highlight that the 'individualisation of responsibility that over time does not produce any tangible result on the aggregate level is likely to lead to a deepening alienation from traditional understandings of active citizenship' (2019b, 366–7). Third, the knowledge gap of citizens regarding the environment is curtailed by the complexity of environmental issues, the risk of misleading climate information or simply limited knowledge. Fourth, ethical fetishism concerns the possibility of fetishizing environmentally friendly commodities which can result in a double fetish rather than defetishization (simply, instead of understanding the processes of production and distribution of a product, one celebrates their self-centred altruism through the purchase of a 'green' product). Again, the banality of branding is partly responsible for the commodification of consumer politics, despite attempts to decommodify ethical products (Lekakis, 2012). Fifth, the rebound effect has to do precisely with the assumption that the sky is the limit when it comes to green consumption, so it is often observed that through eco-labels and other green promotional communication consumers can end up buying more stuff or having a bigger carbon footprint, which is the opposite of what sustainable consumption is. The following review echoes some of these concerns through the inclusion of cultural studies and media and communications disciplines to the sociological and political science approaches reviewed above. First, I engage in the politics of green consumerism and sustainable consumption in relation to individualization and political participation, and then I outline the role of media and communications technologies in the knowledge around consumer activism and the environment, as well as the environmental paradox of media technologies and information and communication technologies (ICTs) used to raise awareness and run campaigns while being contributors to the fastest growing form of domestic waste – e-waste.

The Politics of Green Consumerism and Sustainable Consumption

Who are we buying environmentally friendly stuff for? Many scholars have pointed to the demise of the environment through green consumption. On the one hand, researchers have been critical of green consumerism as an individualized and consumerist response to environmentalism (Giddens, 2009; Hamilton, 2010; Johnston 2008; Katz-Kimchi and Atkinson, 2014; Littler, 2009; Maniates, 2001; Maxwell and Miller, 2020; Meissner, 2019; Szasz, 2007). More than a decade before the COVID-19 pandemic, Andrew Szasz (2007) wrote about the phenomenon of the environmental 'inverted quarantine' in the USA, which he perceived as the 'opposite of a social movement', and where concerned individuals shield themselves and others by consuming filtered water, organic foods and other 'natural' products, and creating 'personal commodity bubbles' for their bodies. Szasz argues that this model of non-toxic consumption has serious consequences in the form of 'imaginary refuge' at the micro-level and 'political anesthesia' at the macro-level. In the first case, consumers fail to fully protect themselves from environmentally harmful consumption, while in the second they experience 'a reduction in urgency' (ibid.: 195), which minimizes their chances to mobilize for general agricultural reform so 'the process of politicization never starts' (ibid.: 211). Littler highlights issues with the 'responsibilization' agenda:

> [T]he new green order is seen to involve burdening the individual with an overwhelming (rather than a partial) responsibility for change. [...] This has significant implications for green consumption, as it implies that, by 'governing the soul' of the individual, by encouraging the idea that tackling climate change is down to the individual rather than corporations or governments, the green consumer might, in effect, be read as a means or conduit to perpetuate and endorse neoliberalism. (2009: 95–6)

The individualized approach of green consumerism is further analysed by Miriam Meissner (2019) through popular narratives in response to overconsumption; Meissner is concerned with the way in which this is framed 'as a vague problem that the individual confronts like an external enemy' (Meissner 2019: 197). This call to the individual to subscribe to a minimalist lifestyle promotes:

> an internal focalization ('Does it spark joy – for me?,' 'Does it annoy – for me?'), which individualizes the perception of 'too much' and – by the same token – systematically blends out systemic perceptions of excess consumption/ labor as a collective economic and eco-political issue. Currently, lifestyle minimalism ties in with an ideology of individual self-responsibility that is instrumental to neoliberalism. (ibid.: 197)

Similarly, Susie Khamis (2019) notes how such decluttering narratives aestheticize restraint and require individuals to be agile, creative, and empowered. Green consumerism is a double-edged sword; buy environmentally friendly products and you are not contributing to climate change, but you are not saving the planet either, so don't get too complacent. As Maxwell and Miller write, the term 'green' has become a misnomer for consumer lifestyles instead of a new understanding of the good life that 'prioritizes the biosphere, ecology, and a balance between human existence and Earth's life-support systems' (2020: 15).

On the other hand, studies that focus on the practices of ethical or green consumers further nuance such claims. Contrary to the false security that Szasz

(2007) argues individuals feel, they often perceive the limits of green consumerism. Norah MacKendrick and Lindsey Stevens (2016) discuss how environmentally conscious consumers perceive personal control as uneven through the concept of the 'contingent boundary'. Accepting that there are settings where they have some control over safe/non-toxic consumption and how they accept that 'inverted quarantine' (Szasz, 2007) cannot exist outside this boundary, is sometimes 'robust and sometimes ... porous and ineffective' (MacKendrick and Stevens, 2016: 324). Furthermore, research with young people in Finland suggests that 'green consumer status is not very attractive or fashionable, unless one gains pleasure from the denial of the fruits of late modern consumer culture' (Autio et al., 2009: 49). Furthermore, a range of alternative consumer practices born out of environmentalism (though exemplary of the usual middle-class and educated suspects of green consumerism) offer opportunities for collectivity and community coalescing: solidarity purchasing groups (Dal Gobbo and Forno, 2020), freecycling (Eden, 2017), clothes swapping (Henninger et al., 2019), second-hand clothing (Lang and Zhang, 2019), and foodsharing (Yang et al., 2019).

Parenting (and especially mothering) is particularly fertile ground for the practices and problematization of green consumerism (AbiGhannam and Atkinson, 2016; Auriffeille, 2020; Cairns et al., 2013). Jo Littler takes the example of the 'econappy' to illustrate how different positions coalesce or clash in green consumerism; from corporations offering their tokenistic environmentally friendly nappy and zealous green consumers fetishizing this environmental object to a discursive backlash against this as classed aspirational consumerism. Kate Cairns et al. navigate the complexities of mothers negotiating the 'organic child' ideal, demonstrating that 'while the maternal pursuit of an organic child undoubtedly reproduces and naturalizes the neoliberal ideals of individualism and consumerism, these practices and ideals rest upon maternal values of love, care, and responsibility' (2013: 113). To move forward, they argue:

> it seems critical to avoid binary positions about women consumers as maternal-heroes or neoliberal dupes, and further investigate how care-work, emotion, and consumption decisions are intertwined in daily shopping habits and food work routines – and how this works differently for women and men in a post-feminist age. (ibid.: 114)

Expecting and new mothers are aggressively targeted by marketing attempts that seek to inscribe a new consumer in them, one that is 'good' and self-sacrificing. The discursive construction of green motherhood through advertising oppresses and restricts the mother, rendering her invisible and indebted to the brand that informs and provides green solutions (Atkinson, 2014). Yet Niveen AbiGhannam and Lucy

Atkinson's research highlights the role of pre-established environmental identity makes expectant mothers 'equipped with the knowledge and determinacy to control their consumption of many of the products that are promoted to new mothers as essential' (2016: 460). 'Good green moms' might know better.

In parallel with the debates on the politics of green consumerism, scholars have also questioned the texture of sustainable consumption, often finding contradictory evidence to the idea that environmentally conscious consumption displaces activism (Dewey and Fisher, 2019; Willis and Schor, 2012). Kristoffer Wilén and Tiina Taipale suggest that green consumerism only tells a partial tale of consumption and environmentalism. They differentiate between 'weak' sustainability that 'can be achieved when individuals, in their role as consumers, change their consumption patterns and purchase goods and services that are environmentally less damaging' and 'strongly sustainable consumption' where 'consumption and production levels and their related ecological impact need to be decreased' (Wilén and Taipale, 2018: 209). They research the discursive construction of environmental awareness to explore the construction of 'green identities' and their implications for strongly sustainable consumption. They find two different ways of constructing environmental awareness, green identity, and relationship to (green) consumption and consumerism, in other words, 'being green' and 'being a responsible consumer'. Both categories oppose consumerism (as 'buy cheap and throw away' culture), but the second avoids environmental activism or moralizing behaviour in relationship to economic growth: 'I'll be a mindful consumer, but don't bring politics into this.' Hence, this distinction between green consumers and ecological selves (or between 'weak' sustainability and 'strong' sustainable consumption). Despite this, 'all of the interviewees seemed to be aware to some extent that individual consumption choices do not offer a solution to sustainable structures' (ibid.: 224). It seems difficult to support an argument that green consumers are ignorant of the limitations of consumption when it comes to saving the environment. Yet as Emily Huddart Kennedy et al. (2018) suggest, despite the sophisticated understandings and commitment of campaigners, causes can be curtailed by their reliance on individual consumption.

There is a specific case of environmental consumer activism that can help drive some of the aforementioned points home: veganism. The v-word, once conjuring a negative image, has now been popularized, after environmental alarm bells went off several times, and publics in the global North became more receptive of the idea of a 'plant-based' diet (Jallinoja et al., 2019; Rodan and Mummery, 2019). According to the Peoples' Climate Vote, UNDP's (Flynn et al., 2021) large-scale survey of 1.2 million respondents in 50 countries, one third of people believe that plant-based diets should be promoted. Varieties of 'plant-based' diets now include various categories of environmentally conscious consumers, such as part-time vegans, reducetarians, and flexitarians (Morris, 2018). Despite ongoing challenges from its commercialization, the transformative potential of veganism is heralded by several scholars (Doyle, 2011; Giraud, 2021; Jallinoja et al., 2019). As Doyle suggests, 'climate change needs to be made culturally meaningful and relevant to people's everyday lives. The linking of food consumption to climate change is an important way of achieving this' (2011: 142). For Giraud (2021), it is 'more than a diet': it is a movement with radical potential. For Jallinoja et al., 'veganism does not simply appear as political consumerism par excellence – concentrating on affecting the markets – but also as a movement of self-realization, identity building, healthism, and the aestheticized food of foodies' (2019: 173). Campaigns to promote veganism have varied significantly from middle-class appeals to encourage bridging the 'value-action' gap by eliminating meat and dairy consumption to campaigns to change government policies which subsidize industrial factory farming (see Doyle, 2011, for a comparison between Meat Free Monday, Meat's Not Green and Friends of the Earth UK's The Food Chain Campaign). Finally, a study of 'carnivalesque online veganism' – veganism with an indulgent and playful approach – explores its transformative potential towards sustainable food culture (Santaoja and Jallinoja, 2021). 'Sipsikaljavegaanit' (Crisps and Beer Vegans) is a Facebook group originating in Finland, which invites vegans of all approaches – regardless of motivation or constancy – to celebrate indulgent vegan food, challenging concerned food discourses pertaining to health, body, and gender. On the one hand, this has helped broaden a positive image of veganism and create 'new vegans'. On the other hand, the group is heavily moderated to exclude discussion on negative food and body talk, or ethics, thus blurring the boundaries of the movement, from activist principles related to animal rights or the environmental aspects of food consumption to ephemeral or indulgent lifestyle choices. This provides the opportunity to cast some light on a key aspect related to the 'knowledge gap' identified by Boström and Klintman (2019b): the role of media industries and communications technologies in relation to environmental consumer activism.

Media Discourses, Technologies, and the Environmental Paradox

When it comes to the environment and consumption, there are at least two fundamental aspects to consider. First, what do we know about the environment, to what extent do we understand it, how did we acquire that knowledge and how can we be sure it is accurate? As Doyle suggests, 'discursive practices shape how we perceive climate change and what kinds of actions are promoted and undertaken' (2011: 6). And second, before we rush to celebrate or condemn the digital technologies that provide knowledge and connection, what is the environmental cost of these technologies and what are environmentally friendly alternatives? It is beyond the scope of this discussion to analyse the 'knowledge gap' of environmental identities and practices. Here, it is important to highlight the discourses that arise in relation to sustainable consumption and media and communications, and the material dimensions of said technologies. As Emiliano Treré argues, social movements (here, environmental activists ranging from individuals to organizations) tend to be 'privileged sites for the reproduction of technological myths' (2019: 19). What I present here is how the technological myth reproduced in relation to environmental consumer activism is that media (especially smartphones) are potential harbingers of change rather than major climate polluters themselves.

The role of media industries remains limited in relation to the discursive construction of sustainable consumption and environmentalism. Justin Lewis (2013) argues that consumer capitalism is not a rewarding system in terms of life quality, and yet 'we remain so deeply committed' to consumer capitalism 'whose benefits are increasingly limited, whose promises are exhausted and whose environmental consequences look increasingly dire' (Lewis, 2013: 48). The reason behind this paradox, Lewis argues, is that media and advertising industries provide no alternatives but continue to promote mass consumerism or sideline climate change. Environmental organization Albert (2021) that works with subtitle data provided by the industry has been producing a report with Deloitte to highlight how environmentalism is being covered by the biggest British broadcasters (BBC, ITV, Channel 4, Channel 5, UKTV, and Sky). Some of their findings are sobering in that in 2020, for instance, the words 'dog' and 'cake' appeared 23 and 11 times more respectively than the phrase 'climate change'. Over the last decade we have seen a proliferation of ethical discourses related to the environment, whether in the popular minimalist lifestyle writings analysed by Meissner (2019) or in ethical consumption reporting explored by Anastasia Denisova (2021). The latter has analysed over 1,000 media artefacts in the UK (magazines to newspapers, gossip weeklies, and Instagram influencers), and identifies the promotion of high consumption in legacy as well as social media, while words such as 'ethical' and 'sustainable' are used in often-misleading ways. A significant approach to environmental communication comes from Michael Goodman et al. who find that 'we are more and more being told about how to "solve" ecological problems through spectacular environmentalisms' (2016: 677; see also Chapter 7 for a discussion on the spectacle). Goodman et al. suggest that popular culture offers flamboyant and various opportunities and hindrances for environmentalism and these are conditioned by mediation (in material as well as symbolic terms), framing (visual and emotional), and relationality (connectivity in the new digital economy). These points are useful guides in any future analysis of environmental communication within popular culture.

Here is a difficult and discrete paradox that lies at the heart of contemporary advanced consumer societies. Consumerism:

offers green consumption choices as the most readily available tool for individuals to act upon environmental concerns, while simultaneously forcing upon them a range of new commodities needed to be able to participate fully in society, such as communication devices. (Wilén and Taipale, 2018: 224)

I can go on my phone to read news on the environment or to see what I can do to be more sustainable in my daily life, while the device itself might be made by toxic chemicals such as phthalates, PVC and brominated flame retardants (just to name one of the many ethical issues raised by smartphones). Beyond the environmental cost of manufacturing a smartphone – which includes over sixty materials (Rohrig, 2015) – there are significant labour justice issues, as materials are often mined by children and heavily exploited workers in areas of armed conflict, while the money has been found to fund armed groups and prolong conflict.[16] The material extensions of the operation of media industries and technologies are brought to light in *Greening the Media* in which the authors discuss the environmental perils that stem from the production and disposal of media technologies (Maxwell and Miller, 2012). Maxwell and Miller do not disregard the power of consumer activism in shaping politics and policy but dispel the valorization of a '"green commodity discourse" that promotes the magical fusion of environmentalism with growth, profits and pleasure' (2012: 25). They also acknowledge that '[i]t is particularly difficult for green consumers to formulate a point of intervention when gadgets are built with components that have seemingly disconnected production histories, such that they are manufactured all over the planet' (ibid.: 30). In their latest book *How Green Is Your Smartphone?* Maxwell and Miller (2020) repeat their warning that not only is your smartphone not green, but you, me and everyone we know should probably never buy another one again. That is not to say that you should never own another smartphone in your life, but that as a device it is one of the most polluting. Of course, there are alternatives; there are 'ethical' smartphones such as the Fairphone (produced by a company founded in the Netherlands in 2013 with the aim to develop an ethical smartphone) that I decided to buy when mine broke down after four years of personal and professional use. Yet, as we will see below, green consumerism is not always the best alternative. Sustainability does not begin in consumption, though the end of consumption can promote sustainability.

Critical Issues

When we think of the environment and commodity consumption, we encounter difficult questions in relation to sustainable development and social change; what are the limits of individual or collective consumption practices in relation to environmental ethics? To what extent can the marketplace be used to express environmental identities and practise a politics of sustainability? What are the histories of environmental communication in relation to consumer culture and politics? What are the ecological ethics of consumer activism? Can the politics of consumption be mobilized to support environmental social movements? To respond to these questions, we cast light on four key issues.

1. Environmentalism is connected to a politics of justice and inequality, and thought and action on the environment needs to recognize movements for labour justice (Hua, 2018; Pun, Tse, and Ng, 2019; Qiu, 2016), environmental justice (Coolsaet, 2020; Seyfang and Paavola, 2008), and eco-feminism (MacGregor, 2021). Green consumerism is a deeply classed privilege that excludes the majority of consumers (Szasz, 2007). Environmentally conscious consumers are typically white and middle-class high cultural capital consumers (Carfagna et al., 2014; Littler, 2012; MacKendrick and Stevens, 2016). As Welch and Southerton remind us, 'sustainable consumption is fundamentally an issue of inequality' and we need 'more equitable distribution of consumption-based emissions within and between societies' (2019: 41).
2. Individuals cannot 'save' the environment through consumption. Environmentalism is more than a moralizing commitment to buying ethically. It is about espousing an environmental politics in everyday life. The 'inverted quarantine' of climate-friendly consumption can appease political will (Szasz, 2007). Individual self-responsibility, a key driver of neoliberal culture, is exacerbated by popular and promotional culture where lifestyle minimalism or advertising of green products restrict the options we have to think and act ecologically. This remains conditioned by persisting inequalities and mass consumerism. The example of veganism, Doyle writes, 'must acknowledge the contextual nature of such a "choice" within a western context, and must be supported by government legislation and incentives which promote sustainable consumption, where an ethics of human, animal and environmental justice are intertwined' (2011: 144).
3. Information and communication technologies allow for spectacular or subversive (see Chapter 7) discourses of environmentalism, although the knowledge gap (Boström and Klintman, 2019b) persists. Digital campaigns can be successful in mobilizing public opinion and action on topics such as veganism, but they also tend to promote a fun, accessible and flexible subject position that does not necessarily engage with the politics of environmental justice. In addition, media technologies themselves have significant carbon footprints, starting from the production moment of sourcing materials to assembling and distributing them as well as in the energy consumption they require.
4. It is important to consume less. Beyond the SDGs, a reduction of overall consumption and production is also essential; wealthy countries and the

global rich are among those that need to take the pledge and practise this first (Alfredsson et al., 2018; Doyle, 2011). As Wilén and Taipale write: '[i]n order to keep alive any hope of steering clear of a track that threatens the planet's life-support systems, consumption and production levels and their related ecological impact need to be decreased, forming the starting point for strongly sustainable consumption' (2018: 209). This can start with our smartphones. As Humphery and Jordan remind us, 'there is a deep complicity with a global digital technologies industry; one based on extensive resource extraction, highly exploitative labour practices and an alarming rate of "e" waste production' (2018: 533).

Researching Consumer Activism and Environmentalism: Methodologies

Sustainable consumption and green consumerism are explored within economics, political science, sociology, media and communications, and cultural studies, with all disciplines asking variations of the same question: what is the role of consumers in relation to environmental politics? The questions vary in relation to the extent of climate-friendly consumption constituting environmental action, the communication, or the practice of sustainable consumption. The methods also vary accordingly. Among the studies reviewed above, there is a literature review on the relationship between consumer action and climate mitigation (Boström and Klintman, 2019b), a few survey-based works, some analysis of texts and discourses, several case studies, and numerous ethnographic approaches.

Scholars who seek to understand the phenomenon from a macroscopic perspective typically use surveys. Willis and Schor (2012) assess the relationship between environmentally conscious consumption and political activism in the USA to find a positive correlation between the two. Similarly, Roser-Renouf et al. (2016) explore the extent to which green consumption goals are connected beliefs about the threat and solvability of climate change in the same country to find that environmentally conscious consumer activism is motivated by personal and social impact goals. Lang and Zhang (2019) study clothes swapping among Chinese consumers to find that social values (frugal consumption) and enjoyment play a key part in participation, while performance risk (product not being what they expected) and social risk (appearing to behave in a way that is not accepted widely) are barriers.

Textual or discourse analysis has been used to explore representations of environmentally conscious consumerism. Atkinson examines green advertising in a US pregnancy magazine (*FitPregnancy*) over the course of the year through critical discourse analysis to 'generate insight into the green mothering discourse these advertisements promote and reinforce to their readers' (2014: 561). Meissner (2019) analyses a selection of five self-help books and one blog that promote lifestyle minimalism through a narrative and thematic analysis in order to interrogate their potential in stimulating de-growth eco-politics through popular culture. Johnston employs discourse analysis to overcome 'a simplistic dichotomy between consumer dupes versus consumer heroes' (2008: 153). To do so, Johnston analyses a wealth of data from a case study of a particular Whole Foods Market (WFM) branch in the US (field notes from two visits per month over a two-year period and participant observation at WFM events, promotional texts on material such as brochures, napkins, shopping bags, website, and product packaging, as well as the business press literature on WFM).

Case studies, specifically, as intensive analyses of specific phenomena, have been used to study public communication campaigns relating to environmental consumer activism (Doyle, 2011; Rodan and Mummery, 2019; Pezzullo, 2011). Szasz provides an in-depth analysis of commodities that enable an 'inverted quarantine' such as bottled water and organic goods (and the current lack of a commodity solution for 'clean air') and compares this to consumption concerns during the fallout shelter panic of 1961. A chapter of Doyle's (2011) book *Mediating Climate Change* compares three UK public communication vegan campaigns from civil society groups and individuals (Meat Free Monday, Meat's Not Green and Friends of the Earth UK's The Food Chain Campaign). Rodan and Mummery (2019) cast light on Animals Australia's Make It Possible vegan campaign. Pezzullo analyses three US-based campaigns that address global ecological crises: the Rainforest Action Network boycott of Mitsubishi, the Farm Labor Organizing Committee boycott of Mt. Olive Pickle Company, and the Carrotmob buycott of a liquor store. Mundo Yang et al. (2019) analyse Foodsharing, a German online platform for food reuse, focusing on its coverage in two leading German broadsheet newspapers. Santaoja and Jallinoja (2021) focus on a Finland-based vegan Facebook group and employ netography to provide a longitudinal analysis of the development of the group, including material published, digital media coverage of the group, as well as interviews with group moderators.

The majority of research cited in this chapter drew on ethnographic methods. Research in the UK, Finland, and Germany by Henninger et al. (2019) included interviews with clothes swappers, non-swappers and organizers, as well as six observations of swap-shop events. Similarly, Huddart Kennedy et al. (2018) conducted semi-structured interviews and participant observation of the eat-local movement in three Canadian cities. In their interrogation of green consumers and green parents in Canada, scholars employed interviews and focus groups (Cairns et al., 2013; MacKendrick and Stevens, 2016). Through consumer autobiographies by 16–19-year-old students, Autio et al. (2009) interrogated what they believe environmentally friendly consumption means and how they personally address environmental concerns. Finally, several scholars undertook interviews. For each of the 24 environmental protection and animal rights boycotts that he studied, Friedman undertook interviews with a representative of the boycott group and a representative of the targeted corporation. Wilén and Taipale (2018) interviewed individuals to explore the discursive construction of environmental awareness in relation to green identities and strongly sustainable consumption (environmentally conscious and decreased consumption). Studies of 'green' parenting also employed interviews (AbiGhannam and Atkinson, 2016; Auriffeille, 2020), allowing for complexity in relation to critiques of environmental consumer activism. Scholars find, for instance, that 'the market does not always provide consumers with satisfying answers to their ambivalence and uncertainties' (AbiGhannam and Atkinson, 2016: 469). Despite mass consumerism pushing expecting mothers towards abundance of commodities, '[e]nvironmentally conscious mothers defy this discourse when they choose to conduct their own research to find out what is good for their babies rather than abiding by a dominant societal perspective' (ibid.: 470). Consumption is a complex practice, one with multiple social layers and obvious environmental limits.

Case Study: The Environmental Politics of Smartphone Consumption

What's Behind the Screen? The Environmental Cost of Smartphones and Obsolescence Injustice

Scientists have attempted to answer this question, yielding interesting infographics where a chemist visually illustrates the chemical elements of smartphones,[17] or video animations where geologists conduct the 'smartphone in blender experiment'.[18] We know that, among other elements, smartphones typically contain microscopic portions of copper, silver, and gold (that are used to cover circuits as they are good conductors of electricity), as well as cobalt (to power lithium-ion batteries) and some of the rarest elements on earth (that produce the colours on smartphone screens). Tungsten (which makes smartphones vibrate) and cobalt are considered 'conflict minerals'.[19] When it comes to producing smartphones therefore, we are talking about mining precious, conflict and rare elements, all of which, as geologist Arjan Dijkstra reminds us, 'need to be mined by extracting high value ores, which is putting a significant strain on the planet'.[20] Additionally, a study by the Avfall Sverige (Swedish Waste Management and Recycling Association) on the waste footprint of products suggests that smartphone production generates an average of 86kg of 'invisible waste', which can be mining waste, slag and other types of waste produced during the extraction of minerals and the manufacturing of the product.[21] As Richard Maxwell and Toby Miller have written:

[m]obile telephony consumes us and the environment: it mixes sublime qualities into social conditions that make it indispensible; it is an exemplar of planned obsolescence; and it is an energy guzzler that brings hundreds of toxic compounds into the environment. (2012: 27)

Smartphones become obsolete the minute they are touched by consumers. Planned obsolescence is a grave reality for people and the planet. In the US, lawsuits over the past few years have resulted in Apple making million-dollar settlements and admissions that iPhone batteries were slowed down. As a result, consumers had no choice but to buy a newer model (Allyn, 2020; Greenfield, 2017). In the first quarter of 2021, global smartphone sales reached almost 378 million; this was a 26 per cent increase compared to the same time in the previous year.[22] In 2023, smartphone sales are expected to reach $1.85 billion per year, a 19 per cent increase from 2018.[23] What happens when a smartphone is replaced by a faster, newer model? It becomes e-waste and is discarded or recycled, with serious environmental health risks which call for environmental justice. Smartphones contribute to approximately 10% of global e-waste (Chatterji, 2021). E-waste has been sent to Asian and African countries where it is formally and informally sorted, posing serious threats to the health of (mostly informal) workers.[24] E-waste is 'a health and environmental hazard, containing toxic additives or hazardous substances such as mercury, which damages the human brain and/or coordination system'.[25] According to the *Global E-waste Monitor 2020*,[26] this is the fastest growing domestic waste stream, due to higher consumption rates of electrical and electronic devices, short life cycles, and few options for repair. There is increasing smartphone production and consumption, alongside limited opportunities for device recycling (which according to the same report, stood at approximately 17 per cent of all e-waste). This is obsolescence injustice: the structural configuration of the production, promotion, consumption, and discard of one of the most fundamental commodities for participation in the digital age.

Obsolescence injustice is global. A political economy of smartphones suggests an oligopoly between Samsung, Apple and Huawei capturing 50 per cent of the market, with Xiaomi rising fast as a popular contender.[27] In 2020, Apple launched its *Product Environmental Report*[28] for the iPhone 12, suggesting that it is the 'first smartphone with 100 percent recycled rare earth elements in all magnets', that it is made with better materials (99 per cent recycled tungsten, and 98 per cent recycled rare materials), that its packaging is responsible and that it is energy sufficient, with smarter chemistry and with 'Apple Trade In', their e-waste recycling service. Finally, Apple claimed to be 'tackling climate change 100 per cent'[29] through its commitment to transition to 100 per cent renewable electricity by 2030. Samsung has an ongoing pledge to developing environmentally conscious smartphones through their 'Eco-design Process'.[30] In addition, in August 2021, during the same week that the IPCC report[31] was published, it unveiled 'Galaxy for the Planet'[32] promising to deliver 'better environmental impact by 2025' by incorporating recycled material in all new mobile products, eliminating all plastics in mobile packaging, reducing standby power consumption (the power used after a smartphone is fully charged or disconnected, but the charger remains plugged-in) of all smartphone chargers below 0.005W and achieving zero waste to landfill (including a commitment to reducing e-waste globally).[33] Finally, in 2020, Xiaomi released its first sustainability report,[34] promising, among other things, that by the end of 2021, it would provide collection and recycling for Xiaomi products in China, India, and Europe. Whether minimally or maximally, all major corporate players make pledges towards sustainability. Yet none are suggesting slowing down production, even when estimates are that greenhouse gas emissions from computers, smartphones, and data centres could grow from 1 per cent of global emissions to over 14 per cent in 2040 with the footprint of smartphones surpassing the individual contribution of desktops, laptops, and displays (Belkhir and Elmeligi, 2018).

What Can Consumers Do? Environmental Consumer Activism and Smartphones

The smartphone is one of the most common and controversial commodities of our time. Its increasing production is inseparable from crucial issues related to labour, social and environmental justice. Jim McGuigan (2012) writes that this 'all-purpose communication device' calls for a 'multidimensional model of analysis' that exceeds disciplinary boundaries and takes into account production, consumption, and textual meaning (including promotional communication about the commodity and corporate ethics). Critical studies such as Jack Linchuan Qiu's (2016) *Goodbye iSlave* and Jenny Chan et al.'s (2020) *Dying for an iPhone* are significant works dedicated to unravelling labour injustice and centring fights for justice in cheap supply chains, mostly based in China. What can we do? In *How Green is Your Smartphone?*, Maxwell and Miller encourage us to 'outsmart [y]our smartphone' (2020: 53) by being informed about issues of health and safety related to smartphone addiction, accidents, and the emerging science that suggests radio frequency (RF) radiation[35] from our devices might be carcinogenic, in addition to their environmental costs. The advice coming from civil society and scholars is consistent: keep the smartphone you own for as long as you can, recycle it when you upgrade to a new one, and when you do make sure that it is as ethical as it gets (Belkhir and Elmeligi, 2018; Maxwell and Miller, 2020; Transform Together, 2018). If you are reading this, then like most people I know (though I know some who do not), including myself, you own a smartphone.

First, the obvious and best practice is buying fewer smartphones, thus engaging in 'anti-consumption' (Binkley and Littler, 2008). Reducing smartphone consumption is the most significant way in which consumers can engage in environmental consumer activism, so don't rush to get rid of your smartphone, but repair it if you can. As Maxwell and Miller (2020) posit, the greenest smartphone is the one we already own. Repairing one's phone or extending its lifespan as much as possible is key to reducing e-waste. In the USA, consumers replace their phones approximately every three years.[36] In Europe, consumers would like their products to last about five years but find that they last approximately two (European Environment Agency, 2020). According to the same report, extending the lifetime of all smartphones in the EU by one year would save 2.1 Mt CO2 per year by 2030 (the equivalent of taking over a million cars off the roads). To add to this, in 2019, each person in Norway created 26kg of e-waste, followed by the UK (23.9kg per person), the US (21kg) and China (20.2kg) (Global E-waste Monitor, 2020). Across the European Union, the right to repair certain electrical goods (as in the manufacturer needs to ensure that they can be repairable for 10 years) has been implemented, but legislation for smartphones is pending.[37] The case of France stands out, as since January 2021, a repair index on certain electrical and electronic devices (including smartphones) has been implemented; the score is calculated on the basis of ease of disassembly, price and availability of spare parts, and access to repair information, making Apple follow suit.[38] Recycling smartphones is also important at the very end of their lifecycle, but pressure your provider for transparency about the process.

Second, a new, niche and currently limited market for ethical (fair and sustainable) smartphones including examples such as the Dutch social enterprise Fairphone, US company Teracube and German small business Shift. The Fairphone ('the phone that cares for people and planet') launched in 2010 as a campaign for change in the electronics industry, particularly aiming to raise awareness about the use of child and forced labour. In 2013, it made its first phone and according to the UK-based magazine *Ethical Consumer*,[39] it now makes 'the most ethical smartphones in the world'.[40] Admittedly, Fairphone is 'as ethical as it gets'. Even the founder of the company acknowledged in an interview that developing a 100 per cent fair phone is not possible.[41] Aiming to destabilize the routine violence that occurs in legitimated sites of production, Julietta Hua reminds us that '[e]ven if we accept a consumer activist position, it seems disingenuous to think that production conditions at any electronics factory differ significantly from those at Foxconn' (2018: 320). In addition, there are serious limits to green consumerism, as change in the electronics industry will not come from consumers (although the packaging of Fairphone reassures that 'change is in your hands' and if you open it you are congratulated and told 'you're what progress looks like'). Change is more complex and requires the collaboration of consumers, but also industry, and, importantly, governments. Consumers are not uniform in their budgets and environmental identities. Advocates suggest that governments should promote and protect open repair cultures through regulation and that companies should scale up efforts to use recycled materials and metals in new phones (Transform Together, 2018). But, what about scaling back production? This is simply the reformist vision, and very much utopian. In any case, change is not going to come over night and it will certainly not come from buying more electronic devices without fully using and repairing, reusing or recycling old ones.

Questions for Future Case Studies

- What is environmentally conscious consumption and how can we study this? What are the possibilities and limits of green consumption for developing green identities?
- What development narratives frame consumption in relation to climate change and what are the connections with environmental and social justice movements?
- To what extent does environmentally conscious consumption connect with the environmental justice movement?
- How do consumers construct their views of environmentalism, sustainability, and green consumerism and what cultural resources do they employ in constructing such concepts?
- To what extent can methodologies such as consumer autobiographies be used to allow for reflection on sustainable consumption?
- What possibilities for degrowth do historical and contemporary examples of alternatives to mass consumerism present and to what extent can they be scaled up?
- What histories have social movements and NGOs told about mass consumerism? How can historical campaigning resources be used to highlight the consistency and urgency of the climate crisis?
- What is the role of media industries in relation to environmental politics?
- What narratives do media tell about sustainable consumption and green consumerism? How can media industries communicate sustainability in a fragmented media ecology?
- What are histories of public relations regarding environmental lobbying and campaigning?
- What is the relationship between consumption that seeks not to harm the environment and consumption that seeks not to harm the consumer?
- How do environmentally conscious citizens manage their wellbeing and how do they understand sustainable consumption in relation to that?
- How is environmental consumer activism relevant to the electronics industry?
- To what extent is sustainable consumption discussed in relation to specific industries (e.g. fashion) and how can the discussion expand to less highlighted industries (e.g. toys)?

Conclusion

Considering the role of consumer activism in the age of the climate crisis drives home points raised so far in the book about the limits of consumer activism, as well as its symbolic and material significance, and brings to centre stage the importance of regulation in intervening on advertising, curbing planned obsolescence, and protecting repair cultures. Economic growth that puts consumers behind the steering wheel of development and social change means growth of the climate crisis. Global media and cultural industries such as news and advertising foster a vision of no alternatives to development beyond a green economy, but a green economy is still underwired by the dogma of growth. A key debate within green consumerism research concerns the individualization of action and the depoliticization of environmentalism. Ideological alternatives to systems of provision and consumption such as degrowth and *buen vivir* offer a non-consumerist vision, but the challenges to such transitions are great.

Even when consumer culture addresses the issue of overconsumerism and embraces minimalist narratives, it still does so in an individualistic manner. What's more, green consumerism is not fully accessible to all. Individuals might long for an 'inverted quarantine' (Szasz, 2007) to shop themselves to safety, but there is a 'contingent boundary' (MacKendrick and Stevens, 2016) that separates their ability to safely control their consumer practices and total chaos. On the one hand, linked to a strong environmental identity and a commitment to 'anti-consumption' (Binkley and Littler, 2008) there is (strongly) sustainable consumption, which for Boström and Klintman 'will have to deviate extensively from a superficially eco-polished status quo' (2019b: 361) and, as Doyle puts forward, 'must appeal to our emotions, our ethics, our values and our rational selves in an attempt to change social norms about consumption' (2011: 143). On the other hand, linked to partial environmental awareness and market-friendly responsible consumerism, 'weak sustainability' can manifest as green consumerism which yields waste and maximizes greenhouse gas emissions through other forms of consumerism. In any case, scholars see various shades of grey in environmentally conscious consumption. Understanding the political potential of environmentally conscious consumption will need to regard this in relation to other practices of environmental publics (Eden, 2016).

This chapter has highlighted a number of critical issues. First, there is the often-invisible politics of justice and inequality: Who sources minerals and materials for smartphone production? Would they be able to afford what they are mining for? Where does e-waste end up? Where does domestic waste end up? Second, the politics of individualism is regarded in relation to the quest for wellbeing: Can I consume safe food? Can I drink clean water? Can my children play with non-toxic toys? Third, information and communication technologies are espousing environmentalism in a spectacular, blurry, and consumerist manner: Have you seen the latest sustainable fashion trend? Have you bought enough tote bags? Have you seen that climate change documentary on Netflix? Finally, the necessity of consuming less is perhaps the biggest challenge: How can people feel empowered beyond consumerism? How can consuming less be a rewarding experience in the age of consuming experiences? How can the rich be convinced to stop splurging first? Finally, when it comes to the green economy and green consumption, there has been abundant media attention in certain industries (especially food and fashion) but less in others (such as consumer electronics and toy markets).

To think about 'greening the media' (Maxwell and Miller, 2012) requires urgent attention, especially as e-waste is growing at an alarming rate and the global mobile phone penetration nears universal ownership. Obsolescence injustice is a persisting issue primarily for formal and informal workers in electronics sectors, then consumers who overpay for devices planned to fail, and governments that need to orchestrate translational agreements on how to curb this. When considering what this means for consumer activism at large, it is safe to say that it demonstrates the limits of individual or collective action through resistant practices in promotional culture.

Notes

1. www.un.org/sustainabledevelopment/blog/2019/06/michelle-yeoh-fashion/ (19 August 2021).
2. www.levistrauss.com/2018/01/25/no-dont-wash-jeans-really/ (31 August 2021).
3. www.peta.org/issues/animals-used-for-food/meat-environment/ (20 August 2021).
4. www.unep.org/explore-topics/resource-efficiency/what-we-do/sustainable-lifestyles/food-and-food-waste (20 August 2021).
5. The IPCC was created by the United Nations Environment Programme (UNEP) and the World Meteorological Organization (WMO) in 1988. It currently has 195 member countries and it is tasked with providing policymakers internationally with scientific assessment reports on climate change. In 1990, the first IPCC report suggested that increases in carbon dioxide and other GHG emissions from human activities enhance the greenhouse effect, and, subsequently, the temperature of the Earth. The IPCC suggests that we have up to 2030 to stop the irreversible effects of climate change, and that in order to do it global warming must be kept to a maximum of 1.5C. The 2021 report (www.ipcc.ch/srccl/), sixth of its kind, suggests that given current developments, we are on course to exceed 1.5C.
6. According to the UNEP (UN The 17 SDGs were universally adopted in 2015 as part of the agenda 'Transforming Our World: The 2030 Agenda for Sustainable Development' this is 'the transition to economies that are low carbon, resource efficient and socially inclusive.' (www.unep.org/explore-topics/green-economy) (2 September 2021).
7. In 1987, the United Nations Brundtland Commission defined sustainability as 'meeting the needs of the present without compromising the ability of future

generations to meet their own needs' (www.un.org/en/academic-impact/sustainability) (19 August 2021). Sustainability has three dimensions (economic, environmental, and social), the so-called 'triple bottom line' which forms the basis of several sustainability standards and certification systems.
8. The 17 SDGs were universally adopted in 2015 as part of the agenda 'Transforming Our World: The 2030 Agenda for Sustainable Development' (www.un.org.cn/info/6/620.html) (20 August 2021).
9. 'The Green Economy is an attempt to extend the reach of financial capitalism and to integrate all that remains in nature into the market. To do so, the Green Economy attributes a "value" or a "price" to biomass, biodiversity, and the functions of the ecosystems—such as carbon storage, crop pollination, and water filtration—with the intention of integrating these "services" as negotiable units in the financial market' (Another Future is Possible, 2012: 16).
10. These proposals include the application of the principle of a minimum and a maximum income, priority to the development of collective consumption of transportation, housing, education, health, energy, and culture to safeguard precarious populations, guarantee such goods and services by states and by grassroots communities within the framework of social and solidarity economy and define new rights to guarantee access to fundamental goods.
11. Radical Ecological Democracy based on self-rule including self-reliance.
12. www.un.org/sustainabledevelopment/sustainable-consumption-production/ (20 August 2021).
13. UNEP defines greenwashing as the mismatch between promoting sustainability through advertising and marketing 'than actually implementing business practices that minimise their environmental impact' (2010: 27).
14. Ecolabels are voluntary certification programs, such as the Global Organic Textile Standard (GOTS) and Cotton made in Africa (CmiA).
15. One example is Carbon Footprint Ltd, an environmental consultancy aiming to reduce emissions or render organisations carbon neutral, which also offers a free carbon calculator for individuals where one can calculate their carbon footprint through household energy consumption, flights, car, motorbike or public transport and secondary (food, pharmaceuticals, clothes, computers and electronics, banking etc). This then calculates and presents options for offsetting your carbon footprint by supporting certified carbon reduction programmes, tree planting programmes, reforestation or community projects from developing countries. (www.carbonfootprint.com/calculator.aspx) (26 August 2021).
16. www.ethicalconsumer.org/technology/shopping-guide/mobile-phones (12 December 2021).
17. www.compoundchem.com/2014/02/19/the-chemical-elements-of-a-smartphone/ (2 September 2021).
18. www.youtube.com/watch?v=bhuWmcDT05Q (2 September 2021).
19. The Democratic Republic of the Congo (DRC) is the world's largest producer of cobalt and holds more than 50 per cent of the global cobalt reserves. After campaigning from Global Witness (www.globalwitness.org/en/campaigns/conflict-minerals/#more), Amnesty International and AfreWatch www.amnesty.org/en/latest/news/2016/01/child-labour-behind-smart-phone-and-electric-car-batteries/) among others, attention has turned to cobalt. The Responsible Minerals Initiative has added cobalt as a dedicated focus area in 2017 and works

towards eliminating child and forced labour from the cobalt value chain (www.responsiblemineralsinitiative.org/minerals-due-diligence/cobalt/) (2 September 2020). According to a BBC article, concerns about 'conflict' cobalt is leading investors to seek mining in other countries (www.bbc.com/news/business-44732847) (3 September 2021).
20. www.plymouth.ac.uk/news/scientists-use-a-blender-to-reveal-whats-in-our-smartphones (2 September 2021).
21. www.avfallsverige.se/invisiblewaste/ (3 September 2021).
22. www.gartner.com/en/newsroom/press-releases/2021-06-07-1q21-smartphone-market-share (2 September 2021).
23. www2.deloitte.com/uk/en/pages/consumer-business/articles/the-future-of-the-smartphone.html (2 September 2021).
24. https://news.climate.columbia.edu/2018/08/27/growing-e-waste-problem/ (6 September 2021).
25. https://unu.edu/media-relations/releases/global-e-waste-surging-up-21-in-5-years.html (2 September 2021).
26. www.itu.int/en/ITU-D/Environment/Pages/Spotlight/Global-Ewaste-Monitor-2020.aspx (25 November 2021).
27. www.counterpointresearch.com/global-smartphone-share/ (2 September 2021).
28. www.apple.com/environment/pdf/products/iphone/iPhone_12_PER_Oct2020.pdf (2 September 2021).
29. ibid.
30. www.samsung.com/us/aboutsamsung/sustainability/environment/eco-conscious-products/ (2 September 2021).
31. www.ipcc.ch/report/ar6/wg1/ (2 September 2021).
32. https://news.samsung.com/global/samsung-electronics-announces-sustainability-vision-for-mobile-galaxy-for-the-planet (2 September 2021).
33. https://news.samsung.com/global/samsung-electronics-announces-sustainability-vision-for-mobile-galaxy-for-the-planet (2 September 2021).
34. www.mi.com/global/about/sustainability/ (2 September 2021).
35. 'Second-, third-, and fourth-generation cell phones (2G, 3G, 4G) emit radiofrequency in the frequency range of 0.7–2.7 GHz. Fifth-generation (5G) cell phones are anticipated to use the frequency spectrum up to 80 GHz'. (www.cancer.gov/about-cancer/causes-prevention/risk/radiation/cell-phones-fact-sheet) (3 September 2021).
36. www.statista.com/statistics/619788/average-smartphone-life/ (2 September 2021).
37. www.techrepublic.com/article/right-to-repair-moves-forward-for-your-broken-devices-but-campaigners-want-to-go-much-further/ (3 September 2021).
38. www.theverge.com/2021/2/26/22302664/apple-france-repairability-scores-index-law-right-to-repair (3 September 2021).
39. www.ethicalconsumer.org/company-profile/fairphone-bv (3 September 2021).
40. www.ethicalconsumer.org/company-profile/fairphone-bv (3 September 2021).
41. www.teamhuman.fm/episodes/ep-30-bas-van-abel-fingerprints-on-the-touchscreen/ (3 September 2021).

SIX
CELEBRITY ADVOCACY AND CONSUMER ACTIVISM

Introduction: Who Wants to be an… 'Activist'?

Reality TV has produced global entertainment based on competition for entrepreneurship, survival, knowledge, fame, and even romantic love, but never before on activism. In September 2021, CBS announced a new reality TV show co-produced with US-based non-profit organization Global Citizen[1] and hosted by musician–businessman Usher, actress-model Priyanka Chopra, and dancer–actress–musician Julianne Hough. In *The Activist*, three teams of activists were set to 'go head-to-head in challenges to promote their causes, with their success measured via online engagement, social metrics, and hosts' input'.[2] The activists would advocate hard all the way to the G20 summit in Italy to meet world leaders and raise funds and awareness for their causes. The series finale would celebrate the winning activist team that received the largest commitment and would 'also feature musical performances by some of the world's most passionate artists'.[3] Global Citizen, after all, had been in the business of organizing humanitarian concerts with compassionate celebrities throughout the COVID-19 pandemic. In April 2020, the World Health Organization and Global Citizen organized a virtual concert called One World: Together at Home, curated by musician–actress Lady Gaga, featuring a star-studded line-up raising funds in celebration and support to the healthcare workers on the frontlines of the COVID-19 crisis. A year later, another virtual global broadcast and socially distanced concert VAX LIVE: The Concert to Reunite the World, hosted by singer–actress Selena Gomez, took place in celebration of COVID-19 vaccines and an appeal for these to be universally accessible. Why should we care? This chapter questions the role of celebrities in processes of social change and the consequences for democratic politics.

CEO and co-founder of Global Citizen, Hugh Evans said:

> The Activist is a first-of-its-kind competition series that will inspire real change … [t]he audience will see the Activists' passion and commitment

for their causes tested as they petition world leaders to take urgent action to resolve the interconnected crises we face.[4]

Entertainment figureheads described the show as 'combining competition and compassion' and 'combining philanthropy and entertainment'. However, the premise of the show was widely pilloried on social media. A few days after the announcement of the reality TV series, CBS stated that it would be retooling the programme into an activism non-competition documentary, and Global Citizen issued an apology: 'Global activism centres on collaboration and cooperation, not competition. We apologize to the activists, hosts, and the larger activist community — we got it wrong'.[5] Yet while in *The Activist* the blending of celebrity entertainment and advocacy, as well as cause and compassion were off key, it serves as an uncomfortable case in point of how celebrity culture can intersect with global social change. Celebrities can become activists, humanitarians, environmentalists, while environmentalists, humanitarians, and activists become celebrities. Of course, not all celebrities become activists, or vice versa.

This chapter examines the role of celebrities as intermediaries between socially and environmentally progressive causes and consumer culture. Celebrities advocate against fast fashion, for conservation, against oil-drilling, for veganism, against climate change, for clean water, against flying, for planting trees, against human trafficking, for gender equality, against gender-based violence, for refugee rights and against poverty, among many emergencies of the 21st century. How has celebrity advocacy been implicated in consumer activism practices for charity and social change? To what extent does the relationship between celebrities and promotional culture condition their advocacy? What does a history of Northern humanitarianism suggest about the role of celebrities in advocating causes? What are key tensions in the mediation of celebrity advocacy? What types of stories and solutions do celebrities promote for development and social change? What legacies of development are being evoked and what are the global politics of celebrity advocacy? To what extent are critiques about celebrity humanitarianism in the North relevant in the South?

Next, this chapter discusses key concepts and key theories related to celebrity advocacy and celebrity humanitarianism, as well as critical issues arising, highlighting the importance of 1) a political economy of celebrity advocacy, 2) problematizing consumer-friendly simplifications, 3) understanding celebrity in relation to North/South relations, 4) the gender and racial politics of celebrity advocacy. Finally, I present methodological approaches and analyse a case of celebrity-driven youth advocacy for healthy eating in the UK. Through an appraisal of campaigning for advertising regulation of junk food by celebrity chef Jamie Oliver and the Bite Back 2030 youth-led campaign that he co-founded, we will explore issues relating to celebrity advocacy.

Key Concepts
Celebrity

What is a celebrity? Monarchs and models, socialites and sports stars, foodies and fashion vloggers, politicians and pranksters, environmentalists and entrepreneurs, activists and actors, all enjoy celebrity status from the elite to the ordinary, forever or for a day. As Crystal Abidin writes, celebrity culture emerges differently in different parts of the world and is shaped by 'cultural norms of the people, the social practices around media devices and personalities, and the structure of technological capabilities that mediate a population's access to content' (2018: 2). To paraphrase Graeme Turner (2010) and Olivier Driessens (2013), a celebrity is a manufactured and managed persona of fame that is embodied and communicated in their public and private proclamations (to the extent that publics can witness these). Celebrity is also an industry and its ideological formation influences culture. Where does celebrity come from? The source of celebrity status, as Chris Rojek (2001) suggests, can be familial ties (ascribed, as in the case of royals or the Kardashians), talent (achieved, as in the case of musicians, sports stars, actors or skilful influencers) or media exposure (attributed, as in the case of reality TV participants, or ordinary people whose sensational stories become newsworthy, such as senior citizen William Shakespeare, the first man who received the COVID-19 vaccine in the UK).

Importantly, celebrity is also an industry, as the political performances of celebrities are produced by institutions, interpreted by audiences, and meshed with political and corporate agendas (Brockington, 2014; Williamson, 2016; Richey and Brockington, 2020). Finally, celebrity capital's effects can lead to processes of 'celebrification' (the process of turning someone into a celebrity by association) and 'celebritization' (the process of turning a social field into a celebrity by association) (Driessens, 2013). The celebrification of Nature, for instance, has been constructed through celebrity involvement in the Conservation International campaign Nature Is Speaking, as celebrities give their voices to Nature (e.g. Penélope Cruz impersonates water) (Olausson and Uggla, 2021). The celebritization of indigenous activism, for example, through cases such as Tame Iti (a Tūhoe Māori activist in New Zealand) has been enabled by media convergence, elaboration of global indigenous mediascapes, and an expanding politics of decolonization (Cupples and Glynn, 2019).

Media, Celebrity, and Ordinary People

What is celebrity in the age of digital, social, and ubiquitous media? The shift from 'representational' to 'presentational' media and culture (typically, traditional media industries and platforms presented celebrity, while digital media technologies allow celebrities to represent themselves) has further produced a whole host of celebrities of attributed status such as DIY celebrities, micro-celebrities, and internet celebrities

(Abidin, 2018; Khamis et al., 2017; Marshall, 2010; Marwick, 2013; Senft, 2008; Turner, 2013). Social media platforms have catapulted the idea of '15 seconds of fame' into a matrix of apps, platforms and performances that make teenagers, workers, lovers, parents, and others into mass self-branded communicators that might enjoy or lament some degree of visibility and exposure. Today, the categories for celebrities are dumbfounding; according to an LA-based influencer–marketing agency, anyone who has between 1,000 and 10,000 followers is a nano-influencer, while the difference between celebrities and influencers is the 5 million followers mark.[6] As Graeme Turner has written, 'the opportunity of becoming a celebrity has spread beyond the various elites and into the expectations of the population in general' (2006: 156). While anyone can be a celebrity no matter what they have or have not done, celebrity status requires sustained public attention – without followers, the status is lost and the fame forgotten.

In the last few years, ordinary people around the world have been elevated to celebrity status, such as the young environmentalist turned eco-celebrity Greta Thunberg. The Fridays for Future school strikes built a critical mass of young environmentalists. Grown-up and younger people of celebrity or ordinary status can and do get involved in the arena of domestic and international politics. Particularly, there are influencers who promote ethical consumption or even anti-consumerist lifestyles, as well as digital communities of ethical influencers. While some engage with sustainability stories, promote thrift, and make cultures, most tend to engage with fast fashion promotion and practices. From 'haul' videos of (cost) conscious purchases (videos celebrating mass consumerism) to 'anti-haul' videos of (environmentally) conscious origins (videos challenging mass consumerism), influencers can potentially reinforce and challenge promotional culture within promotional media platforms. The example of a 'trash diving' influencer illustrates how ordinary people can bring into sharp focus unsustainable corporate practices and greenwashing. In her 'unboxing' video of luxury brand Coach bags and shoes (found in a dumpster-driving expedition), Anna Sacks shows that while the business has a repair programme where they promote their care for a circulate economy, they ask employees to slash unwanted merchandise to save on taxes (through a clause that secures the company if any products were accidentally destroyed).[7] Breaking from 'haul' and 'anti-haul', this example shows how individual influencers promote consumer activism and a critical interrogation of corporate policies. Further research is required to explore audience interest and practices in relation to influencer advocacy of ethical causes.

What we know from studies of audiences of celebrity culture is that the extent to which celebrities attain and maintain attention have power over our media diet is contested (Couldry and Markham, 2007; Thrall et al., 2008). Martin Scott's audience study (2015) highlights the point that celebrities do influence public perceptions of humanitarianism but are generally ineffective in cultivating cosmopolitan engagement with distant suffering. Finally, a study illustrated how (despite their newsworthiness) celebrity advocates appear to have limited effects on public engagement (Atkinson and DeWitt, 2019). Celebrity advocacy appears 'glossy' (Iqani, 2016) and significant in its intermediation of social change, but publics are not always moved to longer-lasting interest and investment in solidarity practices.

Celebrity Advocacy and Celebrity Humanitarianism: 'Charitainment' and Beyond

The website Look to the Stars (subtitled, The World of Celebrity Giving) documents celebrity philanthropy and advocacy. Are celebrities today entertainers, philanthropists, or both? A popular way in which celebrities participate in social change is through a mediated meshing of charity and entertainment, also known as 'charitainment'. Perhaps you have heard of the Band Aid phenomenon, orchestrated by musician Bob Geldof. In response to the 1983–5 famine in Ethiopia, Geldoff brought together a 'supergroup' of artists including Duran Duran, Phil Collins, U2, and Wham! to record a charity single for the Christmas market (the popular and problematic 'Do They Know It's Christmas?'[8]). Following the commercial success of the single, a rock concert to continue raising funds for Ethiopia took place on July 1985, at Wembley Stadium in London. Prince Charles and Princess Diana opened Live Aid. The televised concert continuously impressed upon viewers the phone number and address where they would call to donate or send cheques. This was a catalyst for more concerts to fundraise for poverty (Live 8) in 2005 and Ebola (Band Aid 30) in 2014, but also celebrities in action at large (for a brief history, see Richey and Ponte, 2011: 31–4). Just to name a few examples: rapper–comedian–actor Lil Dicky's charity single 'Earth'[9] has been described as 'Band Aid for the Internet' (Bote, 2019), and then there has been Red Nose Day in the UK since 1986[10] and one-off concerts such as One Love Manchester,[11] the (virtual) One World and the (socially distanced) VAX Live already mentioned.

Concepts such as celebrity advocacy and celebrity humanitarianism have been employed to discuss this phenomenon of 'charitainment'. Yet the concepts are not synonymous. For Brockington, celebrity advocacy broadly 'refers to any work by famous people in service of some cause other than themselves' (2014: xxii). The advocacy work of celebrities is also a process constituted by a network of actors, from individual celebrities and managing agencies to NGOs and policymakers. As Richey and Brockington clarify, celebrity advocacy is not the same as celebrity humanitarianism:

> [c]elebrity humanitarianism requires a needy 'Other'—it is something that one actor does for another person. Advocacy is taking up a cause and

amplifying it in the public discourse, which could be about issues across the political spectrum that engage the celebrity's own communities or those of Others. (2020: 45)

The United Nations has been using celebrity 'Goodwill Ambassadors' to promote its international development programmes since 1954, though the use of celebrities has been systematized since the 2000s (with celebrities such as actor Mia Farrow and footballer David Beckham attaining humanitarian status), and now it is common for NGOs to have in-house celebrity liaisons (Brockington, 2014). Celebrity advocacy is a broader term that includes all variations of celebrity involvement in social change and is considered a political form of engagement, while celebrity humanitarianism imagines social change in relation to specific suffering subjects and is not typically regarded in strong political terms.

Celebrity humanitarianism involves celebrities in humanitarian work at (their) home or abroad working to promote peace, health, education, gender equality, fair trade and sustainability, and to oppose poverty, conflict, slavery, and human trafficking. Celebrities have been discussed as a 'powerless elite' (Alberoni, 2006) in relation to fields beyond their stardom, but research has argued that celebrity advocacy indicates a new aspect of elite rule, which 'enhances the distributions of power and inequality that it purports to change' (Brockington, 2014: 159). Celebrities also get into political spaces and institutions and hold conversations with political persons. The following section addresses key debates and key issues emerging in research from international relations and international development to sociology, media, and cultural studies. It does so in order to examine celebrity advocacy and celebrity humanitarianism vis-à-vis consumption as a tool for change.

Key Theories: Celebrities, Causes, and Consumption
From Band Aid to Brand Aid

Celebrities, like ordinary people, care for peace, equality, and the environment but the way in which their care manifests as what Jo Littler calls the public fashioning of the celebrity soul in relation to 'a globalised sensibility and a cosmopolitan caring' (2008: 238) is contested. Arguably, celebrities come to operate as 'cultural intermediaries' (Piper, 2015) between publics and causes, and to study them as such requires a focus on 'the way that cultural information is moved around and how this information comes to shape contemporary tastes and consumption cultures' (ibid.: 248). Band Aid, as a form of marketized philanthropy, was one prominent example of how celebrity involvement in causes has been conditioned. The phenomenon fits into a longer history of British humanitarianism and charitable fundraising, 'co-opted within the dominant structures of capitalist culture and thus generally aligned with the New Right' (Jones, 2017: 191). As Jones argues, 'despite its lofty rhetoric, Band Aid was always more concerned with global spectacle and consumer gratification than it was with challenging the underlying political causes of African famine' (ibid.). What's more, Band Aid has influenced a problematic set of representations of Africa and Africans to come, capitalizing on a politics of pity and not drawing on a politics of justice (Franks, 2014; Müller, 2013). This context is important in understanding continuity and change in contemporary 'celebrity do-gooding' (Littler, 2008) in relation to what is presented as 'cosmopolitan caring consumption' (Littler, 2009).

In the global North, the legacy of Band Aid has materialized into myriads of opportunities to consume for global social change, often instigated or including one or more celebrities; this, for Lisa Ann Richey and Stefano Ponte (2011) is 'Brand Aid'. It refers to the holy trinity of celebrities, causes, and 'causumerism' (shopping to change the world), of which the most iconic (and analysed) case is product RED (Banet-Weiser and Lapsansky, 2008; Budabin, 2020; Ponte and Richey, 2014; Richey and Ponte, 2008, 2011). RED has a business model that connects consumption, trade, and aid. RED mobilizes the purchasing power of Northern consumers who go shopping for change and provides a percentage of profits from RED lines to the Global Fund to Fight AIDS, tuberculosis and malaria. The year 2021 marks the 15th anniversary of the campaign that was launched by musician Bono at Davos. Richey and Ponte argue that 'in RED the marriage of consumption and social causes has become one and indivisible… The primary goal of RED is not to push governments to do their part, but to push consumers to do theirs through exercising their choices' (2011: 33). For Ilan Kapoor, the form of celebrity advocacy typified by RED emphatically 'legitimates, and indeed promotes, neoliberal capitalism and global inequality' (2013: 1). Furthermore, critical studies on RED highlights that the roots of colonialism run deep; in the words of Zine Magubane, '[c]elebrities can be seen as modern day missionaries who are also engaged in a process of image building through philanthropy' (2008: 4). The promotional communication of the campaign commodifies humanitarianism, perpetuates the narrative of Africa as a 'problem child', and marginalizes social movements seeking to address structural dynamics in the continent (Bell 2011; Daley, 2013; Himmelman and Mupotsa, 2008). In their analysis of actor Ben Affleck's advocacy for the Democratic Republic of Congo (DRC), Alexandra Cosima Budabin and Lisa Ann Richey (2021) draw on the Brand Aid conceptual model to explore a new development in celebrity advocacy: celebrity strategic partnerships (with corporate partners) as 'neoliberal artifacts'. For instance, the Eastern Congo Initiative (set up by Affleck) collaborated with US business Theo Chocolate to connect producers in the DRC with consumers in the US. However, the promotion of this partnership is both gendered and racialized: '[a]way from the violent masculinity of an unexplained "Africa," American consumers can be alone with Ben Affleck, "good" business, and deserving Congolese women farmers, for whom chocolate is a main source of income' (Budabin and Richey, 2021: 111).

Appraising the relationship between celebrities, causes, and consumption thus necessitates a critical understanding of the politicized roles and tropes of celebrity, the range and modalities of causes advocated, and the types of consumer action evoked. In an early intervention on the politics of celebrity advocacy and humanitarianism, Littler (2008) identifies three critical problems: inequality of financial benefit; engagement with 'safe' or symptomatic (rather than systemic) problems; and celebrities being part of the problem of inequality as they so often embody the rich. Dan Brockington's extensive study similarly suggests that:

> Celebrity advocacy for development and humanitarian causes is at best an oxymoron and at worst an anathema for three reasons. First, that celebrity perpetrates damaging views of needy others and places (especially 'Africa'); second, that celebrity is part of an unjust humanitarian regime, and third, that celebrity is founded on, and implicated in, structural inequalities which it does not challenge. A variant of the last argument is that celebrity reproduces a violent and unjust capitalist global order. (2014: 42)

There remain considerable questions about the extent to which celebrities and their strategic partners benefit more from 'causumerist' sales than the causes and distant others they are advocating for, about the types of issues and solutions they advocate and about the contradiction of being part of the elites while trying to be part of the solution. To further develop these points in relation to the wealth of studies that have followed, we can think of three big themes to organize a critical appraisal of celebrity advocacy in relation to celebrities themselves (authenticity versus accountability), causes advocated (simplified causes and consumer-friendly solutions), and the global politics of celebrity advocacy (North/South relations).

Celebrity Authenticity vs Accountability

It might have crossed your mind that singer Madonna's post describing COVID-19 as 'a great equalizer' from the intimate comfort of a bathtub filled with rose petals in March 2020 makes her an 'inauthentic' celebrity, despite her donation of $1 million to the Coronavirus Global Response launched by the EU a couple of months later. The thought might be reaffirmed as you read that Madonna, the highest-selling solo artist in the music industry, had an estimated net worth of $850 million in 2021, so Madonna giving around 0.11 per cent of her net worth to 'the great equalizer' runs completely counter to this claim, rose petal bath aside. As Littler posits, celebrities are 'the embodiments of personalised wealth: a contradiction that makes this relationship [with poverty] to say the least, problematic' (2008: 243). Celebrity advocates perform authenticity through expert or experiential authority (knowledge and experience), affinity (similarity with others), empathy (shared emotions due to similar experiences), and sympathy (emotions evoked by the other's predicament) (Brockington, 2014). Perceived authenticity is key to the role of celebrities in development and social change (Chouliaraki, 2012; Doyle, 2016; Richey and Ponte, 2011; Scott, 2015). As Nathan Farrell suggests, 'a recognised authentic celebrity activist can use their authenticity to generate both economic and symbolic capital for themselves and to advance the activist cause' (2020: 6). Yet authenticity is better understood as a performance, one that is 'constructed, negotiated and mediated over time, and between people and institutions' (Brockington, 2014: 11). Furthermore, as Roopali Mukherjee states:

> Urging us against sweeping dismissals of commodified modes of social activism, these efforts are neither easily nor always written off as simply inauthentic or opportunistic. Instead, they reveal the ironic promise of political action borne out of neoliberalism itself. Highlighting the lurking constancy of contradiction within hegemonic discourses, these instances of activism allow us to trace how neoliberal citizens actualize their political subjectivities, not through rejections of commodity culture but, rather, from *within* circuits of consumption and exchange. (2012: 118, italics in original)

In addition, as Martin Scott argues in a study of audience perception of celebrity advocacy, despite perceived authenticity, 'celebrities with both credibility and legitimacy may still fail to connect spectators with distant suffering' (2015: 453). Still, authenticity is a process of negotiation of meaning about the validity or veracity of claims, and very much a key of the celebrity advocacy and humanitarianism industry.

Madonna's example is not unique. Contradictions and controversies often appear between celebrities and the causes they advocate. An example is celebrity environmentalists flying from one place in the world to another to discuss offsetting policies. A political economy of celebrity advocacy can generate insights into 'the relationships between the symbolic and the economic, between the cultural and the political, and how these relationships are articulated through the celebrity activist' (Farrell, 2020: 12). These relationships are undercut by the performance of the authentic, rather than the accountable, celebrity advocate, which is typical in Brand Aid initiatives (Richey and Ponte, 2011). In their study of tropes of celebrity humanitarianism, Lisa Ann Richey and Dan Brockington argue that:

> celebrity humanitarianism offers a politics that is based on *authenticity not accountability*... problems arise from the lack of accountability, or the

mechanisms by which accountability is diverted and distorted. Even if some forms of celebrity humanitarian performances can be considered 'legitimate' (by particular audiences), celebrities themselves are not formally accountable to anyone ... Celebrity humanitarianism exemplifies an underlying tension as it relies on the popularization of a crisis to enlist more 'caring,' yet more caring may not result in better practical care. (2020: 52, my italics)

There are also tensions in celebrities' strategic partnerships with for-profits. Budabin (2020) underlines the persistence of a lack of transparency in her study of actors George Clooney and Ben Affleck as celebrities promoting 'caffeinated solutions' for peace and development through partnerships with Nestlé and Starbucks respectively. For instance, Budabin asks, why did the Kivu Specialty Coffee project's support for farmers in the DRC last for only four years? Additionally, Joshua Gulam analyses the political economy tensions in Clooney's ambassadorship for Nestlé, which arguably 'helps mask a series of ecological issues relating to the Nespresso brand' (2020: 90) that the actor advertised. Why are possibilities for recycling individual aluminium pods used in Nespresso machines limited to only a handful of countries in relation to the global operations of the company? Performed authenticity of celebrity advocacy works to reiterate their 'globalised sensibility and ... cosmopolitan caring' (Littler, 2008: 238), while perceived authenticity is a complex negotiation within global audiences. For instance, calling celebrities to own up to their high-earning status, Chinese netizens published a list of celebrity donors, ranked in accordance with their donations to the COVID-19 response and overwhelmed the social media accounts of those who did not with accusatory messages (Xu and Jeffreys, 2020). It is, therefore, also possible for publics to hold celebrities accountable.

The key message behind celebrity advocacy remains a 'multiple-win' scenario (Budabin, 2020) whereby celebrities, their partners, and beneficiaries all benefit, though, importantly, not equally and not everlastingly. Of course, this is not always a seamless or enduring scenario. Take the case of actor Brad Pitt's Make It Right (MIR) charitable foundation to rebuild homes in the Lower Ninth Ward neighbourhood in New Orleans following Hurricane Katrina. Scholars have argued that the actor embodies neoliberalism and promotes neoliberal solutions (Fuqua, 2011; Gotham, 2012). Blurring the boundaries between entertainment and tragedy through charity galas and spectacular light events, Pitt's MIR partnership with global architecture brand Graft Architects committed to rebuilding energy-efficient and affordable houses, thus promoting individual innovation and fundraising as a means of addressing social problems that would otherwise fall within the realm of responsibilities of the state. Yet since its inception, the MIR project has encountered significant issues regarding the safety of rebuilt homes resulting in several lawsuits (from dwellers of MIR-constructed residencies against MIR for unsafe housing, from MIR against architects for flawed designs, and at least one more – MIR against their former executive director and former treasurer for mismanaging the project (MacCash, 2021; Nast, 2019). Yet the presentation and promotion of celebrity advocacy relies on a simplified narrative of both cause and solution. In the words of Brad Pitt, 'We went into it incredibly naïve ... just thinking we can build homes – how hard is that?' (MacCash, 2019). Quite hard, as it would turn out. While celebrity authenticity is professed from their stardom, accountability is deducted from their actions. Performances of celebrity humanitarianism can be inconsistent or ineffective. Yet their communication of change is typically exhausted in simplified, consumerist action.

Simplified Causes and Consumer-Friendly Solutions

Make 'it' right, End 'it', Shop till 'it' stops; these are just three of the promotional messages in the names or communication material of celebrity-driven campaigns for social change. 'It', in these cases, referred to rebuilding New Orleans, human trafficking and HIV/AIDS respectively. Making 'it' right or making 'it' stop is a simple enough message to rally the public or politicians or fellow celebrities to action, without necessarily having to go to great lengths to discuss why 'it' has been happening now or for such a long time. Whether 'it' is providing education and healthcare, or promoting fair trade and peace, celebrities proffer simplicity in the articulation and action on development or humanitarian causes. As Littler (2008) suggests, their engagement tends to be with symptomatic causes (poverty, education, or health crisis), rather than systemic causes (economic inequality, environmental injustice, globalized consumer capitalism). Research on celebrity advocacy repeatedly highlights this point (Biccum, 2011; Heynen and van der Meulen, 2021; Ponte and Richey, 2011). Patricia Daley argues that:

> celebrities, as branded commodities – in essence neoliberal subjectivities – and their advocacy, serve to enhance consumer capitalism – thus helping firstly to commodify humanitarianism as a largely privatised concern that sits easily with neoliberal imperialism and secondly to divert attention from the structural inequalities associated with such forms of domination. (2013: 376–7)

Chris Rojek further describes how 'celanthropy' (celebrity philanthropy) 'leaves the primary cultural, social and economic structures of invisible government intact' (2014: 127). Celebrities embody market and profit-based solutions and, thus, approach causes with simplified stories and solutions. As Budabin writes, '[i]n circulating narratives of business solutions, celebrity humanitarians conceal the complex nature of peace and development and the hazards of faulty interventions' (2020: 72). Sometimes, celebrity advocacy does not just obscure the complexity of context, but also advances problematic policies and interventions. Take, for example, a study of anti-trafficking groups supported by celebrities in the US. Heynen and van der Meulen (2021) demonstrate how consumer-friendly simplifications (the equation of trafficking and sex work) and consumerist solutions (the purchase of branded apparel sold by NGOs) have a negative impact on the cause. This is because they conflate sex work with victimhood, make simplistic connections between trafficking and slavery, and work to expand rather than limit 'the role of police and security agencies, along with their civil society partners, in anti-trafficking work' (ibid.: 5). Anti-trafficking groups are also contradictory as they are 'explicitly critiquing a particular kind of consumerism, the commodification of bodies and sex, while legitimating consumerist solutions to perceived social problems' (ibid.: 16). Such tensions are classic in neoliberal forms of market-based participation, decommodifying one aspect of a commodity, just to commodify the very action of buying it (Lekakis, 2012; Mukherjee, 2012).

From product RED vodka to anti-trafficking branded onesies for babies, consumerist action is the rule rather than the exception of what celebrities ask us to do (buy) in support of social change. This, of course, is by no means a new phenomenon, but one that has been intensified since the 2000s, alongside the institutionalization of celebrity advocacy. This was further intensified through the Brand Aid phenomenon, which draws upon aid celebrities to mobilize individual consumption as a mechanism for compassion (Richey and Ponte, 2011). For Richey and Ponte, '[i]n RED, the consumer is implicitly asked to consume more, not differently' (2011: 186). Calling this 'developmental consumption', Michael Goodman (2010) argues that it shifts the rhetoric and embodiment of free trade from the farmers that it is meant to be reaching to its celebrity advocates. This is the problem of individualized responses to global social issues as discussed in Chapter 2, where we witness further contradictions of celebrity advocacy as consumers are invited to tackle climate change and other environmental issues. As Patrick Murphy poignantly puts it, '[i]n essence, the public is encouraged to save the whales even as it is invited to eat all of the fish' (2021: 194). Additionally:

> environmental celebrity begins to replicate the very foundations of consumer capitalism through campaigns for voluntary donations, conservation programs, and sustainable consumption. Indeed, green, sustainable, and 'conscious' consumption figure large in many a celebrity environmentalist campaign: All we need is the right app to tell us which sustainable fish to buy, a barcode we can scan to find the most environmentally just household cleaner, or, at a larger scale, which hybrid/electric car to buy. (Abidin et al., 2020: 402)

Celebrities offer partial and frequently problematic solutions to complex problems. Just to name a few actors involved in green consumerism (see Chapter 5), Drew Barrymore owns an organic cosmetic line, Gwyneth Paltrow sells eco-friendly cosmetics and other things, Rosario Dawson has co-founded a sustainable fashion brand, and Woody Harrelson runs a paper company, selling paper made of 80 per cent wheat instead of trees. Alison Hearn (2012) analyses the way in which celebrity environmentalism coalesces with self-branding and conflates hyperconsumerism and promotionalism with social activism. Hearn further argues that the logic of self-branding is essentially connected to types of activism advocated by eco-entertainment websites, which are assuming 'the desire of individuals to self-brand as "activist" through the processes of active consumption and celebrity emulation' (ibid.: 30).

Similarly, influencers promoting ethical brands or alternative consumption practices (e.g. vegan products, zero waste) merge authenticity with self-promotion ('I care therefore I buy and promote ethical consumption'). Duffy and Pooley's (2019) study shows how influencers, as 'idols of promotion' signals the resonance of promotional culture across work and leisure, as well as the ongoing platformization of celebrity engagement. In other words, promotional intermediaries such as celebrities and influencers work to produce an authentic sense of self. This can be a self that cares for others and/or the environment, and in response to that promotes consumer-friendly advice to their fans and followers. Influencers impact consumer culture in novel ways, from the modes and messages of promotion to the ethics and actions advocated. 'Haul' videos of fast fashion are typical examples. Rachel Wood (2020) explores the phenomenon of 'anti-haul' videos in relation to their potential anti-consumerist politics. Acknowledging the ambivalent and contradictory politics of influencers who engage in 'anti-haul' communication, Wood demonstrates the concurrent risks of incorporation into consumer-centric solutions and the potentially hopeful and playful resistance for learning and transformation. Iqani's (2020) exploration of the case of 'Zero Trash Girl' as a typical case of middle-class self-regulation demonstrates the limitations of influencers advocating for broader social change. While further research on influencers and 21st century consumption is necessary (Matheson and Sedgwick, 2021), the legacy and recipe of Brand Aid is therefore present in the repertoire of humanitarian and environmental actions in the global North.

North/South Relations

An important intervention in the literature is the attempt to decentralize the Northern celebrity as an intermediary of humanitarianism and environmentalism, following the post-colonial critique of celebrity advocacy as intimately connected with white saviour complex where, typically, a white person attempts to 'save' a non-white person for self-serving purposes (Abidin et al., 2020; Bell, 2011; Daley, 2013; Magubane, 2008). Scholars argue that 'celebrity do-gooding' is a distraction from the deep-seated inequalities of neoliberal capitalism, which also works to reproduce these inequalities by rendering humanitarian crises as opportunities for public consumption and distant sufferers to rely on Northern audiences and consumers to be released from their predicament. This resonates with a critique of Brand Aid and developmental consumption as contemporary forms of the outdated one-dimensional and western-centric model of development (Richey, 2016a; Richey and Ponte, 2011). Specifically, 'Brand Aid brings modernization theory into postmodern times: consumption becomes the mechanism for compassion and creates new forms of value' (Richey and Ponte, 2011: 12). Modernization here refers to the modelling of development discourse and practices according to W.W. Rostow's 'stages of economic growth' where he charts a normative course for 'traditional' societies into the age of high mass consumption, one which is riddled with all the issues highlighted in this book so far. Rostow's 'non-communist manifesto' is to transform agricultural societies into highly industrialized urban societies where mass consumerism is widespread. Richey and Ponte continue, '[c]elebrities are the lubricant for this' (ibid.). Furthermore, as Daley argues, 'by promoting conspicuous consumption as "ethical" and the solution to poverty and dispossession, celebrity humanitarianism helps to further entrench Southern others in globally unequal relations' (2013: 390). This entrenchment involves the perpetuation of problematic North/South relations. As Richey suggests, '[t]here is no "North" as an empirical place, but rather "North" as a position in a hierarchy between North and South, across levels and geographies' (2016b: 10). The hierarchical relationship between North/South is not only evident in the media visibility of Northern celebrity humanitarianism, but also in the scholarly attention paid to their activities in Southern contexts, as well as to the activities of Southern celebrity humanitarians (Richey, 2016b).

Understanding the politics of celebrity humanitarianism as a form of North/South relations requires 'more attention to the Southern celebrities, Southern politics, and the consequences of humanitarianism in the South and the North/South relations that produce them' (Richey and Brockington, 2020: 44). In their analysis of tropes of celebrity humanitarianism in relation to humanitarian solutions promoted, Richey and Brockington (2020) appraise 'aid celebrities' (promoting technology), 'global mothers' (promoting love), 'strong men doing good' (promoting power), 'diplomats' (promoting institutions), 'entrepreneurs' (promoting money as a solution), and 'Afropolitans' (promoting awareness). They argue that all tropes provide in some way servitude to the 'mainstream and status quo of humanitarianism', as celebrity diplomats service institutions, 'global mothers infantilize, Afropolitans diminish contentious racial politics, and entrepreneurs equate more profit with better outcomes' (ibid.: 53). This further illustrates the tainted dynamics of race and gender in relation to celebrity advocacy. Yet analyses of celebrities in the South present nuanced approaches to the politics of celebrity advocacy and humanitarianism.

Celebrity Advocacy in the South

Celebrities in the South, and Asian stars particularly, have been taking part in advocacy and philanthropy at an intensifying rate (Kwon, 2019; Jeffreys, 2020; Xu et al., 2021). Examples are bountiful from basketball icon Yao Ming's Foundation to improve the lives of children in China and the US, to Goodwill Ambassadorships held by Japanese guitarist–singer–songwriter MIYAVI, South Korean actor Jung Woo-sung, Pakistani actress Mahira Khan, and K-pop girl group BLACKPINK, as well as singer Denise Ho's pro-democracy activism since the Umbrella Revolution in Hong Kong. Also, at the same time as Lady Gaga was putting on the eight-hour-long virtual concert One World: Together at Home, Chinese singer Han Hong (founder of the Han Hong Love Charity Foundation) also curated a star-studded fundraiser which raised over US$19 million for healthcare workers in Wuhan (Lau, 2021a). Turning our attention to the South requires a nuanced consideration of the politicized role of celebrity without the constraints of 'historicism' which, as Dipesh Chakrabarty (2000) argues, is a way of viewing history as something that happens 'first in the West, and then elsewhere' (cited in Jeffreys, 2020: 314). The following examples illustrate how 'a globalised sensibility and a cosmopolitan caring' (Littler, 2008: 238) appears in different contexts, and how the international spread of neoliberal politics influence the doing and undoing of celebrity advocacy.

Dorothy Wai Sim Lau (2021b) explores the case of Indian actor Aamir Khan's advocacy as a regional and cosmopolitan phenomenon. Analysing his celebrity advocacy within the country (through the TV show *Satyamev Jayate*, which dealt with social issues in the country and his Paani Foundation committed to the national drought problem), and juxtaposing it with his star currency in China, Lau argues that the celebrity 'works on the interstitial plane of commerce and benevolence' (2021b: 244). Lau further argues that the commercial success of Khan in China and his welcome acceptance by the government of the People's Republic of China (PRC) results in his involvement in the work of state-driven ideology, which is at odds with his 'people'-oriented advocacy in India. This tension in the construction of an 'authentic' cosmopolitan caring celebrity advocate highlights the importance of exploring the relationship between the 'symbolic' and the 'economic' in the political economy of celebrity advocacy.

In China, humanitarianism operates either through government-organized non-governmental organizations (GONGOs) or international non-governmental organizations (NGOs) which are approved by the PRC government, while 'philanthropy' and 'celebrity' appeared in China after 1978 and the market reforms spearheaded by the Chinese Communist Party (CCP). Elaine Jeffreys (2016) analyses former basketball player Yao Ming's celebrity advocacy for international NGO WildAid's campaign for shark-protection and argues that while the celebrity-endorsed campaign resonated with young people, the NGO's communication was culturally irrelevant in that it was advocating individual change for eating shark-fin that is considered a social event. Instead, Jeffreys argues, as the PRC government's austerity policies in 2012 included a reduction of extravagant spending, the state-driven 'authoritarian environmentalism' yields more possibilities for effective environmental protection policies. Jeffreys (2020) also argues that examples such as the Yao Ming's celebrity advocacy for shark-protection and celebrity-inspired but fan-driven philanthropy in China such as the case of the Li Yuchun Fans Charity Fund (which engaged in numerous activities beyond fundraising such as offline volunteering for a GONGO) present opportunities beyond a critique of celebrity philanthropy as elitist or depoliticizing. These examples illustrate the importance of the relationship between the cultural and the political and the appraisal of celebrity do-gooding within state-governed humanitarian structures.

Turning our attention to South Africa, we find a country that deals with a national context of post-apartheid transformation into global neoliberal politics and a continental context in which humanitarian imperialist imaginaries have been planted. Celebrities from the South (especially female celebrities) are exoticized and sexualized on the Northern stage and struggle with the global politics of racialized beauty (Iqani, 2016). As Mehita Iqani argues, 'racialized otherness has defined southern celebrities, as well as the colonial relationship that western celebrity culture has with the south' (2016: 172). Danai Mupotsa (2016) analyses Sophie Ndaba as a gendered celebrity commodity and argues that the post-apartheid narrative of neoliberal citizenship that celebrities in South Africa come to embody is infused with ideas of self-improvement and empowerment through entrepreneurship. In this context, Ndaba, the iconic soap opera actress of *Generations*, speaks to audiences as an equal, yet produces 'complicated identifications that are aspirational and at times disappointing' through a 'making Self while giving back' story and ratifies a mainstream approach to humanitarianism (Mupotsa, 2016: 102). This example highlights the importance of examining race and gender in relation to celebrity advocacy and celebrities' performances of neoliberal aspirations.

These are only three examples of celebrities from the South, and they testify to different issues in the performances of celebrity advocacy and humanitarianism beyond the North. What we see is an interlinked questioning of the power of celebrities and a grounded perspective in the specific transnational contexts in which they are operating. This is an important perspective that is often missing from research on Northern celebrities where the focus is placed on audiences in the North rather than on their operations and on perceptions in the South (Budabin and Richey, 2021). There are also exceptions, as celebrities struggle for democratic ends. Take the example of Cantonese pop idol Denise Ho and her pro-democracy activism since the Umbrella Revolution in Hong Kong. Lau writes:

> In 2019, Cantopop diva and prodemocracy activist, Denise Ho, spoke at the US Congress and the UN Human Rights Council in Geneva about the Chinese government's threat to Hong Kong's human rights. These celebrities' humanitarian work, which coincides with the rise of Global South rhetoric, have shifted the patterns of North-South relations and power politics as well as the regional imaginary. (2021b: 235)

The involvement of celebrities in democratic struggles illustrates an exception to the rule of celebrities as promotional intermediaries leaning towards simplified and consumer-friendly solutions.

Additionally, activists, celebrities, or ordinary people who become celebrities take up racial and environmental justice. In the US, celebrity involvement in Black Lives Matter illustrates higher risks. Furthermore, Duvall and Heckemeyer suggest that 'black celebrity involvement in #BLM is unique from other recent neoliberal celebrity activism because black celebrities are challenging deeply entrenched and racialized power structures that have defined the United States for centuries' (2018: 393). Duvall and Heckemeyer argue that the power of black celebrity activism lies in the discursive constructions of Black identity as collective identity, and the promotion of the BLM movement; '[b]lack celebrities … may further legitimise collective action that may otherwise be even more ignored or derided in news reports than it already is' (ibid.: 405). By keeping attention to issues of police violence, police shootings, and mass incarceration, celebrity activists can contribute to social change. Similarly, Patrick Murphy analyses Swedish environmental activist Greta Thunberg as different to celebrity environmentalists as 'she has developed an environmental politics of performance *for* the natural world, rather than *in* the natural world' (2021: 196, italics in original) by being consistent in her advocacy (through repeatedly advocating policy change and practising sustainable travel), and by centring young environmental justice activists from indigenous communities and the global South through the web series *Talks for Future*. Also, importantly Greta Thunberg is not sponsoring or branding any products. Celebrities can become activists and vice versa, and there are cases such as the above to prove that they do not always frame issues in self-interested terms.

Critical Issues

Celebrities are themselves commodities and sell commodities for themselves and for others. Celebrities promote their advocate status, as they promote their celebrity status, and, as Michael Goodman puts it:

[d]evelopment, at least in the UK, can be bought nearly everywhere. From the tried and true Oxfam shop, to the supermarket freezer case, sundry and spice isle, to the high street and mall, to the virtual spaces of the Internet. (2010: 105)

Yet while consumption is a key way in which they invite us to participate in processes of do-gooding, it is not the only one. Celebrities can and do get involved in more justice-oriented activism, though not as frequently as they do in consumer-oriented activism. Yet it is important to go into the study of celebrity advocacy or activism with the following key issues in mind.

1. *The importance of political economy*. Understanding how celebrities juggle their economic success with their humanitarian or environmental advocacy requires a careful appraisal of the relationship between (performed and perceived) authenticity and accountability.
2. *The importance of problematizing consumer-friendly simplifications*. From the Brand Aid model to the VAX Live concert, celebrities tend to promote consumer-friendly simplifications and consumer-based solutions to global challenges. These can lead to distraction and depoliticization, or even polarization. When celebrity advocacy focuses on neoliberal narratives and solutions, it distracts from the structural violence that exists within neoliberal capitalism. What's more, it provides a platform to non-expert celebrities to voice dangerous ideas that can find fertile ground in the age of misinformation. Think of cases of celebrities making anti-vaccination statements (Olutola, 2021) or promoting products with the phoney promise of health and wellness (Pardes, 2020).
3. *The importance of understanding celebrity in relation to North/South relations* (Richey, 2016b; Richey and Brockington, 2020). Celebrity advocacy is the stage of elites in the North (Brockington, 2014) and this stage is conditioned by colonial legacies, while politicians and publics in the North operate with the bias of 'historicism'. As Mupotsa argues, '[t]he celebrity is a figure produced through longer histories and technologies tied to colonialism, the spread of capitalism, and the processes broadly related to the "civilizing mission" of the various actors tied to the colonial enterprise' (2016: 92). We need to pay more attention to the Southern practices and perceptions of Northern celebrities, but also, importantly, to the Southern celebrities who perform care.
4. Celebrity advocacy is gendered and racialized. As mentioned above, celebrity culture operates within colonial legacies, and often serves to reinforce white saviour narratives. Celebrities embody many tropes of humanitarianism (Richey and Brockington, 2020) and environmentalism (Abidin et al, 2020), but are often gendered in relation to the types of performances and solutions

promoted, and are certainly racialized in their presence or absence from causes advocated.

Researching Celebrity Advocacy and Consumer Activism: Methodologies

Sociologists and media studies, cultural studies and literature scholars, as well as historians and political scientists have all studied celebrity advocacy and humanitarianism to appraise the extent to which celebrities mobilize publics, politicians, and business people in the struggle for a better world. Brockington's *Celebrity Advocacy and International Development* (2014) is the most comprehensive study of celebrity advocacy featuring over 50 interviews across the NGO sector, media and celebrity industries, large surveys of public opinion, newspaper and magazine analysis, and nine focus groups. Media and cultural studies scholars have produced arguments for the grounding of celebrity studies within social theory (Couldry, 2015). Littler (2008) conceptualizes the power of celebrity through the connection of debates on cosmopolitanism, distant suffering and Nietzsche's conception of 'the soul'. Driessens (2013) redefines celebrity as capital through Bourdieu's field theory and conceptualizes celebrity capital as productive of media effects, such as 'celebrification' and 'celebritization' mentioned earlier. Farrell's edited collection *The Political Economy of Celebrity Activism* (2020) highlights the importance of political economy in the study of celebrity advocacy. Conceptualizations of social, symbolic, and celebrity power are central in the study of celebrity advocacy.

A popular choice of methodology to study celebrity advocacy is the case study, which can be broad or narrow in scope. One of the earliest case studies is Richey and Ponte's (2011) Brand Aid that features broad analysis of product RED through publicly available information from the RED website, Facebook, and the 'joinred.com' community, combined with participant observation in shopping venues with RED products in the US and the UK. Focusing on Ben Affleck's advocacy as a case study, Budabin and Richey's (2021) *Batman Saves the Congo* is rich and informed by ethnographic methods (interviews and participant observation with humanitarian and development actors in Washington, New York, London, Kinshasa, and Eastern Congo), political economy analysis (of celebrity strategic partnerships), and narrative analysis of texts and visuals. Budabin (2020) also compares two case studies of Brand Aid involving fair trade coffee (orchestrated and endorsed by Ben Affleck and George Clooney respectively) through a political economy approach to the actors involved and a narrative analysis of their media coverage. Closely related is Gulam's (2020) case study of Clooney's Nespresso involvement through a political economy approach to the celebrity and the brand and an analysis of relevant promotions, film, and publicity texts. Further examples of case study approaches include Daley's (2013) study of Product RED, 50 Cent's SK drink, the Save Darfur Campaign (United to End Genocide), Kony2012, Raise Hope for the Congo, and the Eastern Congo Initiative to illustrate how celebrities frame humanitarian crises for public consumption. Furthermore, there is Mupotsa's (2016) study of Sophie Ndaba in relation to her performance as a black, female celebrity in post-apartheid South Africa. Heynen and van der Meulen (2021) study celebrity advocacy focused on anti-trafficking through social network and discourse analysis that examined 58 organizations in relation to communications, merchandising, and policy interventions. Finally, Lau (2021b) questions Aamir Khan's celebrity agency in relation to his goodwill within India and his popularity in China.

Textual/discursive approaches to celebrity advocacy are also common. Magubane (2008) examines two discursive moments related to the Product RED campaign (an October 2006 Oprah Winfrey Show and the 2007 *Vanity Fair* 'Africa' issue) to explore the way in which celebrities allude to their own history of oppression to authenticate their philanthropy. Bell (2011) analyses data (articles and videos) from the RED website, as well as newspaper and magazine articles, through a thematic textual analysis to examine racialized representations and the campaign's use of a consumer–celebrity fundraising model. Mukherjee (2012) presents an interpretive reading of the politics and aesthetics of West's song and music video 'Diamonds (Are from Sierra Leone)' to explore the racial politics of commodity activism. Duvall and Heckemeyer (2018) draw on qualitative textual analysis to identify dominant themes in black celebrity tweets about #BLM and racial justice. Murphy (2021) analyses English language news and current affairs media from around the world to illustrate how Greta Thunberg has achieved global celebrity status and how her example challenges critiques of celebrity activism as depoliticizing. Let us now turn our attention to the case of a celebrity chef and celebrity-supported youth-led organization whose activism targets advertising and presents an original approach to celebrity advocacy.

Case Study: Celebrity Chef Jamie Oliver and Youth-Led Advocacy for Healthy Eating in the UK

Celebrity Chef Jamie Oliver and Health Advocacy in the UK

Jamie Oliver is a British 'celebrity chef' who was awarded the MBE (Member of the Order of the British Empire) before he was 30 years old. He has created a transnational brand that spans lifestyle television (cooking programmes), cookbooks, social enterprises and corporate partnerships, as well as a business that went into administration in 2019, leading to the closure of most of his restaurants, and its comeback as a Certified B Corporation – a business that balances 'planet and profit' – in 2020. The Jamie Oliver Group is a team of people running media, products and licensing, restaurants, and campaigns, making his celebrity a part of an industry (Turner, 2010; Driessens, 2013).

Jamie Oliver has been an advocate for healthy food nationally and transnationally through lifestyle television and other media formats coupled with campaigns to improve the quality of food in British schools and in British society more broadly, as well as to regulate the junk food industry. His 'second career as a food activist' (Kjær, 2019: 334) begins with *Jamie's School Dinners* (2005), which featured a public health campaign and won him Channel 4's Most Inspiring Political Figure of 2005 award. *Jamie's School Meals* led to a relatively successful but highly contested campaign that needs to be viewed within the broader context of the governance of children and young people's health. A comprehensive study by Jo Pike and Peter Kelly argues that the Jamie Oliver phenomenon (an ambiguous celebrity chef) and effect (the chef that got Turkey Twizzlers[12] out of school menus in the UK) are part of a larger circuit of neoliberal governmentality. Beyond the glossiness and controversies of the celebrity chef, the cause of obesity is part of a larger history of nutritionists campaigning, but also government policies (e.g. the *Choosing Health* White Paper, 2004[13]) which created fertile ground for the cause to be 'celebritized' (Driessens, 2013) within lifestyle television and the Jamie Oliver brand.

Then, *Jamie's Ministry of Food* (2008) – a reference to the actual Ministry of Food (1939–54) – promoted 'a problem-solving television narrative', the food crisis of 'Broken Britain' (Hollows and Jones, 2010: 317). *Jamie's Food Revolution* (2010) lobbied for food reform in US schools and won the chef an Emmy Award for Outstanding Reality Programme and the TED Prize. Finally, the documentary *Jamie's Sugar Rush* (2015) campaigned for a reduction of sugar in soft drinks. In 2015, he appeared in front of the House of Commons Health Select Committee, urging then prime minister David Cameron to 'act like a parent' to the food and drink industry.[14] In 2018, the government enforced the 'sugar tax', and half of manufacturers reduced the sugar content of their drinks, while those that did not paid a levy to fund school breakfast clubs. Like many other British celebrities, Oliver has also participated in Red Nose Day to fundraise for Comic Relief.

A transnational celebrity with over 5 million subscribers and almost 800 million views on YouTube, Jamie Oliver is a controversial figure who has received popular criticism for numerous comments, recipes, and campaigns he has been involved in for his patronizing, insensitive, and sometimes offensive tone.[15] Studies have produced critical arguments about the celebrity chef's problematic convergence of information and consumption and naturalizing brand culture for social change (Lewis, 2010); performance of 'moral entrepreneurship' (Hollows and Jones 2010; Jackson, 2016); linking of moral discourses to the individual problem of personal choice (Gibson and Dempsey, 2015); reproduction of ethical consumerism as a distinction between 'ethical' and 'unethical' subjects (Lewis, 2008; Bell and Hollows, 2011); creation of intimacies through style and commodities which 'ultimately serve to obfuscate the multiple ways that this relationship remains premised on industry and commercial gain' (Abbots, 2015: 240); affirmation of his social hierarchy in framing encounters with other culinary cultures (Leer and Kjær, 2015); promotion of the moral dimensions of neoliberal governmentalities (Pike and Kelly, 2014); management of ideas about 'eating well' in an austerity culture (Hollows, 2022).

Appraising Jamie Oliver's Celebrity Advocacy

To apply key issues from the discussion so far, we can observe that, first, a political economy approach to the celebrity chef unveils a series of celebrity strategic partnerships (Budabin and Richey, 2021) that characterize the relationship between the commercial and the symbolic aspects of his status. For example, Jamie Oliver had been a brand ambassador for British supermarket chain Sainsbury's (2000–11), and in 2018 he partnered with Tesco's. Furthermore, the Jamie Oliver Group has created partnerships with corporations such as Royal Caribbean Cruises (since 2014) and Shell (since 2019), raising particular concerns about the incongruity between the latter's lack of action on climate change and Oliver's health advocacy. Second, Jamie Oliver's simplification of food poverty and the health crisis in Britain is evident in the 'problem-solving narratives' of his programmes. For Slocum et al., his 'food revolution' approach is 'one in which the hero (Oliver) simplifies complex food environments through win–lose narratives in which he dramatically provokes and then wins over collaborators he construes as "foes"' (2011: 186). Third, while Jamie Oliver's advocacy does not primarily engage with a Southern context (the chef mostly travels between the UK, Italy, the US, and Australia) he does not fail to adapt world cuisines into his national brand, raising criticism over cultural appropriation of Jamaican and Bengali cuisine. The unequal power dynamics between the celebrity chef and the 'others' that he is trying to help are observable. The celebrity chef falls into the category of elite people whose advocacy puts them at stark odds with the realities faced by the very people they are trying to help (the first episode of *Jamie's School Dinners* discusses the challenges of cooking with a meagre budget of 37 pence per child – this coming from a millionaire). The added antithesis is that in advocating certain food practices and ethics, Oliver, like other celebrity chefs, embodies 'branded identities [which] are often ironically embedded in the very marketized and corporatized foodways that their own food practices and ethics would seem to eschew' (Lewis and Huber, 2015: 290). It is also important to note that when the Jamie Oliver Restaurant Group went into administration in 2019, over 1,000 jobs were lost,[16] the celebrity took a £5.2m pay-out.[17] Furthermore, the way in which he projects 'ideas of authenticity on territories, food and people' (Leer and Kjær, 2015: 313) in *Jamie's Italian Escape* (2005) is indicative in his attempts to 'fix' an 'authentic' (Italian) cuisine, so that he can 'fuse' it; hence, the celebrity chef remains 'within a discursive framework that is reminiscent of a colonial mindset, which fetishizes the strange encounter as a gateway to an affective experience of authenticity' (ibid.: 324). Finally, celebrity advocacy is gendered and racialized. Joanne Hollows (2003) discusses Oliver's 'domestic masculinity', promoting a narrative that the gendered labour of cooking can be seen as leisure, a position that is uncomfortably classed and gendered. As Warin argues, it is important to explore 'the cultural politics of power and resistance at play ... and in particular the possibilities that give rise to allow a young, wealthy, white man to come to an English [poorer] northern town and save it from obesity' (2011: 25). Yet as Hollows (2022) argues, we cannot just see celebrity chefs who campaign as expressive of neoliberal ideologies, but also promoters of the responsibilization of retail and of state action. While this critical appraisal is justified, it is important to explore how the celebrity chef influences the 'celebritization' of anti-obesity activism and demands state regulation for public health. The Bite Back 2030 campaign which the celebrity co-founded is an example of this.

Bite Back 2030: Celebrity-Backed, Youth-Led, and Health-Related Advocacy Organization

In 2019, Jamie Oliver and Nicolai Tangen founded the youth-led organization Bite Back 2030 with a ten-year plan to improve children's health by halving child obesity in the UK. Bite Back 2030 is a celebrity-backed organization with a Youth Board leading the campaign: 12 teenage activists fighting for health rights, change in the systems of food provision, and public action. The organization is run in three parts. In addition to the Youth Board, there is a board chaired by a food policy professor and comprising food, policy, and health experts, as well as journalists and young people. A managing team consists of professionals with experience in the news and PR industries, in education and health advocacy or charity organizations, as well as in youth work and environmental campaigning. Bite Back 2030 is presented as 'a movement fighting for a fairer system'.[18] It runs campaigns for free school meals, affordable healthy cooking (through the provision of the free *Cook with Jack* cookbook which 'helps pupils and their families get cooking from a £15 weekly shopping list'), the youth coalition Feed Britain Better, #SaveOurStandards, a post-Brexit campaign to avoid unhealthy food trade alliances, and the 9pm TV Watershed (on junk food advertising). Here, I focus on the campaign to curb junk food (high fat, sugar, and salt or HFSS foods) advertising.

Celebrity Chef and Bite Back 2030 Campaign for Advertising Regulation and against Obesity

There is consistent evidence suggesting that children's exposure to HFSS product advertising can affect what and when they eat (WHO, 2013); that children in more deprived communities are more likely to spend more time online (Ofcom, 2017) and also to be living with childhood and adult obesity (NHS, 2018); that HFSS products are prominent on almost half of children's websites in the UK and 71 per cent of YouTube channels aimed at children (ASA, 2019[19]).

Before Bite Back 2030, Jamie Oliver had launched the #AdEnough campaign to lobby the government for advertising regulation in 2018. It started with the celebrity chef's wife posting a photo of their children covering their eyes (because they've 'ad enough of junk food ads). Celebrities such as Fearne Cotton, Richard Branson, Paloma Faith, Claudia Schiffer, Laura Whitmore, Kate Thornton, and Amanda Holden participated in the hashtag campaign.

Following the founding of Bite Back 2030, Jamie Oliver took a more behind-the-scenes stance to anti-obesity campaigning, demonstrating how once celebrities establish elite connections they no longer need to be in front of the camera. Campaigning by the youth-led organization has been thorough, timely, and poignant, directly targeting the prime minister Boris Johnson. In the process, they have gathered support from their peers and publics, but also celebrity chefs such as Hugh Fearnley-Whittingstall, as well as Bite Back 2030 ambassador and male fashion model David Gandy, and media attention. In February 2021, Bite Back 2030 published a report – a 'junk food marketing exposé', which explored online advertising strategies that target children and young people. The report raised concerns about the volume of junk food advertising that children in the UK see online and the complicity of platforms such as YouTube and influencers in heavily promoting unhealthy branded items.

In April 2021, Bite Back 2030 co-signed a letter to Boris Johnson initiated by the Obesity Health Alliance with 97 UK health and children's organizations, academic experts, and individual campaigners, requesting progress with the removal of junk food advertising from online platforms and social media. In May 2021, Bite Back 2030 posted a video of young people asking the prime minister to regulate the advertising of HFSS foods: 'Hey Boris Johnson! We kept our promise to protect the health of others – staying home, missing exams, birthdays and seeing our friends. Now, will you keep your promise to protect our health?'[20]

Campaign Impact

In the summer of 2021, the British government published legislation to restrict unhealthy food and drink promotions in shops in England. In response, the Cancer Research UK Policy Team Twitter account posted a cartoon representation of Boris

Johnson in a panoply of armour (minus the helmet, so that his iconic hairstyle is apparent), sword in hand, and ready to slay a dragon-resembling monstrosity made of onion rings, doughnuts, cakes, chips, sugary drinks, crisps, and pizza which is coming out of a tablet that a child is holding.[21] Cancer Research also used the hashtag #AdEnough in the post, to urge that legislation on junk food advertising restrictions not be stalled. Interestingly, the same cartoon was used in the Bite Back 2030 webpage that notified of the success of the campaign for 'tough new measures on how and when junk food can be advertised'. This is a heroic representation of the prime minister, who was also commended by Bite Back 2030 ambassador David Gandy 'for listening and for the measure to include online advertising'.[22] Following wide public support, the government also announced regulations to introduce a 9pm watershed for advertisements of HFSS foods on TV and on-demand programmes, as well as restrictions in online advertising to apply from the end of 2022. In September 2021, the UK was selected to head the World Health Organization's (WHO) Sugar and Calorie Reduction Network in Europe.

What this case tells us is that celebrity advocacy can result in policy change. Jamie Oliver, in his own celebrity campaigning chef persona, and Bite Back 2030, the youth advocacy organization which he co-founded (with a hedge fund manager and philanthropist, who is mostly mentioned in his second capacity only), are significant forces in the promotion of advertising regulation, and this is an important step nationally, but also internationally. But the case is more complex than this. First, the celebrity embodies wealth and unavoidably (willingly or unwillingly) becomes embroiled in struggles for justice, such as when the restaurant group went bankrupt and employees were fired without consultation. Second, the celebrity performs authenticity, but that is often manufactured in simplistic terms (the Mediterranean where people are healthy is an ignorant framework of understanding in relation to food poverty in post-austerity Southern Europe) and is exercised as social or moral entrepreneurship and authority (which can offend and alienate rather than involve and empower audiences). Finally, what we see is that celebrity brands and celebrity advocacy can morph (Bite Back 2030's campaigning is commendable for its focus on health as connected to justice and for often speaking from the contexts that they are campaigning to see change) what they call 'food deserts'. Yet the focus on advertising and promotion does not resolve the structural poverty that means that children from poorer backgrounds are more likely to eat HFSS foods in the first place. Furthermore, in their promotional communication (which is produced by a well-structured and managed organization that supports the Youth Board) we also see the politics of neoliberalism, in the reproduction of the heroic prime minister who slays the advertising dragon. This is the same prime minister whose country had one of the highest fatality counts in the European continent and who posts short videos of himself vigorously eating a portion of fish and chips saying 'build back better'.[23]

Questions for Future Case Studies

- What are key issues in the performance and practice of celebrity advocacy?
- How can we study North/South and other power relations through celebrity advocacy?
- How does celebrity advocacy appear in Southern contexts and how does it connect with local and transnational contexts?
- What issues and are hidden from the limelight due to the high visibility of 'charitainment' and high-status celebrity advocacy?
- How do celebrities mobilize consumption and consumers for social and environmental justice and to what effect?
- To what extent does celebrity (consumer) activism matter to publics?
- To what extent can 'causumerism' be a vehicle for policy change? What are some successful examples and lessons learnt?
- To what extent is 'causumerism' similar or different to 'green consumerism'?
- In what ways does commercial work carried out by celebrities complicate or consolidate their humanitarian work?
- To what extent is a political economy approach complemented by an analysis of the politics of representation in celebrity advocacy?
- How is celebrity advocacy framed in media discourses?
- How successful is celebrity advocacy in spearheading causes?
- To what extent does internet celebrity replicate or resist critiques of celebrity advocacy as simplifying and depoliticizing?
- How does the 'celebrification' of ordinary people impact their involvement in processes of social change?
- What activist fields have undergone 'celebritization' and what are the political ramifications of this process for the causes advocated?

Conclusion

Celebrity involvement in social change has a long history, rooted in philanthropy and indeed extending into philanthropy today; while other modalities of celebrity politics have also appeared, such as celebrity activism, celebrity advocacy, celebrity humanitarianism, and celebrity environmentalism. Celebrities sing, dance, and generally entertain for social change, and invite us to drink, eat, and generally consume for causes. This 'causumerism' (Richey and Ponte, 2011) or 'developmental consumption' (Goodman, 2010) is a persistent phenomenon. This chapter has mostly focused on celebrities and not ordinary people as intermediaries of 'causumerism', though this phenomenon is evident among conscious influencers. The industry that is celebrity has been mobilizing publics through consumption from the era of Band Aid (of the New Right) that continues into the era of Brand Aid (of neoliberal politics). The dominant narrative is that celebrities, causes, and consumers in the North can drive social change in the South; in the promotional communication of the narrative, the South is represented as a pitiful and helpless place. This reproduces North/South relations rooted in capitalist colonialism and permeated by celebrity humanitarianism (Iqani, 2016; Richey, 2016a).

In the period following the COVID-19 pandemic, it is important that appraisals of celebrity involvement in causes remain more than ever 'fraught with tensions and contradictions' (Gotham, 2012: 109). Some of these contradictions include first, the performance and perception of authenticity versus accountability. Celebrities attempt to charm audiences through performances of authentic attachment to causes, without transparency in relation to the impact of their involvement, or, for instance, the contradictions between their humanitarianism and environmentalism. Second, there is a simplification of causes and promotion of consumer-friendly solutions, as celebrities tend to draw on 'celanthropy' and brand culture to simplify complex causes and promote easy fixes through 'causumerism'. Third, there is a promotion of development as a one-dimensional and western-centric model, which is reminiscent of modernization, where it was believed that the aspiration of developing nations is to reach high mass consumption. Fourth, there are significant questions about the role of celebrity advocacy in the South. It is important to understand the involvement of Northern celebrities in the South, as well as the advocacy of Southern celebrities. Fifth, the racial and gender politics of celebrity advocacy need to be questioned in relation to the white saviour model, as well as the positionalities of celebrity and the social hierarchies that they resist or reinforce. Finally, a key tension is that celebrities embody the rich and reinforce neoliberal politics (Budabin, 2020; Littler, 2008). Yet we need to analyse the texture of celebrity advocacy and humanitarianism through the critical issues outlined in this chapter.

An examination of celebrity chef Jamie Oliver highlights the relevance of these key issues in relation to his health campaigning, and in particular campaigning for junk food advertising regulation in the UK. Aware of the tensions involved in a white middle-class man who has a polarizing effect on the public, the team behind the Oliver industry centred on a youth-led advocacy organization that has garnered much media and public support and has re-oriented the narrative from a politics of pity towards a politics of justice (Chouliaraki, 2013). The campaign that Oliver started over three years before the advertising regulation was implemented presents an engaging case. As discussed in this chapter, celebrities tend to target consumer culture for the enactment of social change, but this case targeted advertising and mobilized celebrities and consumers to campaign for restrictions on junk food advertising, in support of the health of children and young people.

The politics of advertising intersects with consumer activism in crucial ways. From boycotts and buycotts to commodity activism at large, advertising is a contested topic as the following chapter demonstrates.

Notes

1. Global Citizen is an international non-profit organisation headquartered in the US and co-founded by Hugh Evans, Simon Moss, and Wei Soo in 2008. In its own words, 'Global Citizen is a movement of engaged citizens who are using their collective voice to end extreme poverty by 2030' (www.globalcitizen.org/en/content/topics/frequently-asked-questions/) and Hugh Evans has given a TED talk of nearly 2 million views on its origins (www.ted.com/talks/hugh_evans_what_does_it_mean_to_be_a_citizen_of_the_world) (16 September 2021).
2. https://deadline.com/2021/09/usher-priyanka-chopra-julianne-hough-the-activist-cbs-1234829647/ (16 September 2021).
3. ibid.
4. ibid.
5. www.bbc.com/news/newsbeat-58587699 (16 September 2021).
6. According to Mediakix, the influencer marketing industry sets the following marketing standards to categorise influencers based on the number of followers; Nano-influencers: 1,000–10,000 followers; Micro-influencers: 10,000–50,000 followers; Mid-tier influencers: 50,000–500,000 followers; Macro-influencers: 500,000–1,000,000 followers; Mega-influencers: 1,000,000–5,000,000 followers; Celebrities: over 5 million (https://mediakix.com/influencer-marketing-resources/influencer-tiers/) (20 September 2021).
7. www.buzzfeednews.com/article/tanyachen/a-viral-tiktok-can-be-the-first-step-of-real-policy-changes (20 November 2021).
8. For one of several critiques on the problematic representations of Africa in the song, see Adewunmi (2014).
9. 'Earth' is a star-studded 2019 charity single by Lil Dicky's (aka David Andrew Burd) including appearances by Sia, Justin Bieber, Ariana Grande, Katy Perry, Ed Sheeran, Leonardo DiCaprio, Snoop Dogg, Miley Cyrus. Lil Dicky also launched a website to give fans further information on climate change: http://welovetheearth.org/ (14 September 2021).
10. Like Band Aid, Red Nose Day too is a result of the Comic Relief British charity's foundation in response to the famine in Ethiopia. Red Nose Day has since raised over £1 billion in 30 years of operation (https://fundraising.co.uk/2015/03/16/comic-reliefs-total-over-30-years-passes-1-billion-mark/) (2 September 2021).
11. Justin Bieber, Miley Cyrus, Katy Perry, Take That, Robbie Williams, and Coldplay were among the bands that performed at One Love Manchester, a 2017 benefit concert for the We Love Manchester Emergency Fund and British television special organised by Ariana Grande and others, in response to the bombing after her concert at Manchester Arena two weeks earlier.
12. The Turkey Twizzler was a food product in the form of corkscrew strips of processed meat that contained 34 per cent turkey, water, pork fat, rusk and coating, as well as additives, sweeteners, and flavourings. It was a staple on food

menus until it was banned following a campaign led by Jamie Oliver. Following negative publicity, the manufacturer Bernard Matthews stopped making them in 2005. In 2020, Bernard Matthews announced the return of the product, this time with a 67 to 70 per cent turkey content.

13. https://webarchive.nationalarchives.gov.uk/ukgwa/20120509221640/www.dh.gov.uk/en/Publicationsandstatistics/Publications/PublicationsPolicyAndGuidance/DH_4094550 (2 September 2021).
14. www.theguardian.com/society/2015/oct/19/jamie-oliver-david-cameron-has-not-written-off-sugar-tax (28 September 2021).
15. Jamie Oliver has made derogatory statements on a number of occasions in his shows. In Ministry of Food, for instance, he called one of the mothers who passed burgers, chips and crisps to their children through the school fence a 'big scrubber', a highly derogatory term, suggesting promiscuity.
16. In 2020, a court found that Jamie Oliver's restaurant group broke labour laws by failing to consult employees prior to redundancies and ordered three restaurants to award 56 days' wages (https://london.eater.com/2020/7/20/21330893/jamie-oliver-restaurants-jamies-italian-staff-unpaid-wages-unite-union) (12 September 2021).
17. www.theguardian.com/business/2019/sep/30/jamie-oliver-restaurant-closures (12 September 2021).
18. www.jamieolivergroup.com/campaigning/bite-back-2030/ (13 September 2021).
19. www.asa.org.uk/resource/asa-monitoring-report-on-hfss-ads-appearing-around-children-s-media.html (2 October 2021).
20. www.youtube.com/watch?v=2cjHEmGqm6I&t=59s (1 October 2021).
21. https://twitter.com/CRUK_Policy/status/1417905671341809668 (4 October 2021)
22. https://biteback2030.com/real-story/today-we-celebrate-announcement-9pm-watershed (4 October 2021).
23. https://twitter.com/BorisJohnson/status/1445104926431006722 (2 October 2021).

SEVEN
SUBVERTISING AS ANTI-CONSUMERISM

Introduction: Can We Protest Consumerism through Advertising?

During the summer of the 2012 London Olympics, while the city was loudly remodelled to welcome transnational athletes, audiences, and capital, a quieter coordination of events was taking place. In five cities, 36 large-format advertising billboards (aka '48 sheets') were taken over by artworks, commenting on the global event but also on how consumerism and advertising saturation create or hide social ills, degrade public dignity and wellbeing as well as pollute the visual and actual environment. This '48 sheet' project (publicly accessible, visually strong, and ephemerally interventionist) gained media attention and marked the inauguration of a movement of artists and activists, known as Brandalism.[1] The anti-consumerist ideology of the project and movement was clear (Figure 7.1). Such forms of anti-consumerist resistance have typically been subcultural, niche, and associated with anarchism, dissidence, and anti-capitalism more broadly. Yet in the ephemeral interventions of the Brandalism project, they momentarily disrupted promotional culture and became public and sometimes difficult to disagree with. Who has not felt the similarities between zombie movies when observing people moving in commercial spaces?

So began the story of Brandalism. Two years later, Brandalism scaled up their operations by doubling the number of cities and multiplying the number of interventions by ten. In 2015, one day before the launch of the UN's 21st Conference of Parties (aka COP21), the movement of artists and activists claimed to have installed 600 artworks in ad spaces across Paris, criticizing corporate sponsorship and delayed and disinterested political governance concerning the climate crisis. In 2016, the 'Advertisers Anonymous' programme presented workers in advertising industries with an invitation to a London event on 'How to Switch Sides'. Joining invitees, I was introduced to stories of escape from the advertising industry, and was encouraged to connect, exchange knowledge, and imagine alternatives. The accompanying

Figure 7.1

Source: http://brandalism.ch/wp-content/uploads/2017/03/Leo_Murray_1_web-1.jpg (16 April 2020).

takeovers of advertising spaces near key businesses featured messages such as 'Work for TBWA? You're shaping desire. You've got power and a moral responsibility. We'd love to talk to you'. 2017 saw the rise of the transnational social movement Subvertisers International, where Brandalism and advertising adversaries from around the world formed a network and inaugurated annual coordinated actions. Since 2018, Brandalism have been campaigning for the environment against corporate greenwashing: by taking over advertising panels on bus stop shelters protesting Shell's Make the Future festival and their use of celebrities in what Brandalism called 'pop start PR'; the 'unsanctioned art campaign #BushfireBrandalism' in Sydney, Melbourne, and Brisbane in 2020 projecting alternative narratives about the fossil fuel industry, the bravery of local firefighters and the destruction of Australia's ecosystem; the #BanFossilAds campaign in France, Belgium, and the UK targeting advertising agencies over their role in the climate crisis; and the '#CarbonOffsets' campaign in the UK in 2021, in response to banks sponsoring the #COP26 summit. This chapter presents practices by anti-consumerist intermediaries such as Brandalism in relation to how they protest against promotional culture.

Brandalism is part of the transnational resistance to consumer capitalism that uses the texts and spaces of advertising to invoke alternative discourses and actions. The story of Brandalism requires our reflection, in terms of the tools, tensions, and targets involved in contemporary anti-consumerist resistance. There is a history of creative resistance to consider, a close contextualization of anti-consumerism, culture jamming, and subvertising, as well as a theorization of the terms in relation to anti-consumerism and ideology, society of the spectacle (see pp. 156–158) and creative resistance through play, politics, and law. This chapter does so by introducing key concepts (anti-consumerism, culture jamming, and subvertising), before introducing key theories, discussing specific examples and drawing out critical issues. It then maps out key arguments from relevant research, reflects on the methods, and discusses the subvertising campaign Resistance is Female in New York City before presenting key questions for future cases. It argues for the importance of recognizing, analysing, and critically appraising each case based on specific considerations: 1) history, 2) ideology, 3) agency, and 4) justice. The aim of this chapter is to examine activism through and against advertising in order to reflect on its operations within promotional culture and its possibilities for progressive political change.

Key Concepts

What do art, street art, graphic design, punk bands, media education foundations, media pranks, performance artists, artists undertaking other paid work, and former advertisers all have in common? For one, they are forces 'coalescing to create a climate of semiotic Robin Hoodism' (Klein, 2005: 280). The phrase 'semiotic Robin Hoodism' is about how activists are taking away the symbolism of mainstream (corporate and consumer) culture and giving it back to people through the redistribution of its meaning. There are many examples to illustrate this, such as the iconic media education foundation Adbusters whose creative approach to anti-consumerism remixed corporate logos to bust the myth of the brand. Adbusters launched campaigns urging people to switch off their TV or stop buying for a day. Up to the time of writing, it continues to publish a magazine, featuring artworks and lengthier pieces that provide polemic responses to global political developments. Such attempts to change, disrupt, and slow down excessive consumption of media and commodities are part of a larger field of ephemeral or continuous practices known as anti-consumerism (for a non-exhaustive list of documentaries on anti-consumerism, see the Appendix). I discuss culture jamming and subvertising as key variants of 'discursive political consumerism' (Stolle and Micheletti, 2015), exemplary of what Kim Humphery calls the 'cultural politics' of consumption, which is 'focused on challenging the ideology of consumerism purveyed through advertising' (2010: 50).

Culture Jamming

> Part artistic terrorists, part vernacular critics, culture jammers, like Eco's 'communications guerrillas', introduce noise into the signal as it passes from transmitter to receiver, encouraging idiosyncratic, unintended interpretations. (Dery, 1993)[2]

Culture jamming is about subversion, semiotics, and counter-culture. Umberto Eco's 1967 essay 'Towards a Semiological Guerrilla Warfare'[3] drew attention to the importance of consuming messages. Audiences are encouraged to critically interpret and interact with information they receive; these guerrilla tactics of critical reading and learning to challenge the hegemony of mediated messages gave rise to theorizations of culture jamming. In 1984, in their album *JamCon'84*, the US-based experimental music band Negativland coined the term 'culture jamming' and talked about 'billboard artists' who repurposed corporate messaging. Almost a decade later, Mark Dery published a pamphlet, drawing on a similar critique of (US) media in terms of corporate ownership and commercialized information, and regarding culture jamming as 'directed against an ever more intrusive, instrumental technoculture whose operant mode is the manufacture of consent through the manipulation of symbols' (1993). This manipulation happens by using 'the images, ideas, and discourse of popular culture and commerce to critique and subvert that culture' (Lievrouw, 2011: 215). Culture jamming subversively speaks back to promotional communication. Within the research on political consumerism, it is conceptualized as 'discursive political consumerism' (Micheletti 2010), given its focus on discourse rather than the practice of anti-consumerism.

Culture jamming employs tactics such as 'media pranks, advertising parodies, textual poaching, billboard appropriation, street performance, and the reclamation of urban spaces for noncommercial use' (DeLaure and Fink, 2017: 6). For instance, Canada-based Adbusters and (for a limited time) its France-based sister organization Casseurs de pub have been creating and distributing advertising parodies, aka subvertisements (subverted advertisements). Then there is the US-based Billboard Liberation Front and Australia-based B.U.G.A. U.P. (Billboard Utilising Graffitists against Unhealthy Promotions) which have been reclaiming urban spaces and appropriating billboards in their pursuit for 'the joyful demolition of oppressive ideologies' (1993[4]). There are the US-based Yes Men, who have been engaging in media hoaxes and pranks since the early 2000s, pretending to be corporate spokespersons and apologizing publicly for social or environmental catastrophes or creating video games such as 'Angry Bergs' where you have to destroy the angry icebergs before they defeat your off-shore oil rig.[5] Then there is US-based Reverend Billy and the French-based L'Eglise de la Très Sainte Consommation (The Church of the Most Holy Consumption) who engage in street performances and religion-infused stunts such as ATM exorcisms and anti-consumerist choirs to bring public attention to the cause.

Subvertising

> One of the brilliant things about putting a subversive message in what is now a very comfortable space – people are so familiar, sadly they're comfortable with corporate messaging and advertising – when you mess with that it can be a very powerful tool, send a bit of a jolt down into the brain. (Special Patrol Group, interviewed in Subvertisers for London, 2019)

Subvertising is similar to culture jamming, but refers to its more recent manifestations such as ad takeovers or 'adbusting' (e.g. Brandalism, Special Patrol Group, and Protest Stencil in the UK, Dies Irae in Germany), advocacy and awareness-raising (e.g. Résistance à l'agression publicitaire in France), workshops and exhibitions (e.g. Proyecto Squatters in Argentina and Consume Hasta Morir in Spain) or civil disobedience (e.g. Le Collectif des Déboulonneurs in France and Democratic Media Please in Australia). In 2017, several of these groups coalesced into the transnational movement entitled Subvertisers International and started organizing annual coordinated actions (Lekakis, 2021). Subvertising is the act of subverting advertising to correct, distort, or completely replace its meaning. Subvertising mobilizes various practices ranging from the momentary to the monumental, from removing and replacing advertisements to providing an alternative education about advertising and lobbying for advertising regulation. Subvertising is different to culture jamming in that it goes beyond the creation of resistant rhetoric to subverting promotional communication and includes the practices mentioned above.

Key Theories
Anti-Consumerism and Ideology

Anti-consumerism is an ideological position, as the term suggests in opposition to the cultural enchantment, social stratification, and environmental damage of unbridled consumerism. Kozinets and Handelman (2004) wrote a much-cited paper entitled 'Adversaries of Consumption' where they foreground the question of ideology and representation among anti-consumerist groups. In later work, they reinstated the view that anti-consumerism 'must be an act of ideological extravagance – wandering beyond the accepted limits of cultural acceptance' and that its acts 'must be purposeful, mindful acts of ideological protest' (Kozinets et al., 2010: 226–7). But what ideology exactly does anti-consumerism protest against? Part of the answer lies in the concept of the 'culture-ideology of consumerism' posited by Leslie Sklair (2002) to discuss the operations of neoliberal globalization at the turn of the century. The term referred to the mass broadcasting and acceptance of consumerist lifestyles across the developed world, but also to newly industrializing countries and cities in the developing world since the mid-20th century. Two consumer 'revolutions' spearheaded the spread of the culture–ideology of consumerism: the shopping mall and the credit card. In addition, the culture–ideology of consumerism is related to cultural imperialism and the idea of Americanization through Hollywood and Madison Avenue from where producers, advertisers, and marketers launched their propaganda of 'Consumer America' both within and beyond the country. It is against the backdrop of this historical period and ideological conceptualization that theories of anti-consumerism emerge.

For or against? The key issue with approaches of this kind is that the relationship between consumerism and anti-consumerism is theorized as a binary relationship between 'for' and 'against'. Kozinets and Handelman (2004) argue that their analysis of three campaigns (anti-corporate, anti-advertising and anti-genetically engineered) suggests that anti-consumerism can be represented through binaries. If, for example, you recognize the culture–ideology of consumerism in popular culture, social media, and trending topics, then you are 'woke', and if you practise anti-consumerism in any way, you are trying to 'awaken' the masses. Writing particularly of 'revelation' as typical among anti-advertising activists, they view the metaphor of 'awakening' as reminiscent of an evangelical religious identity, which activists embrace. Such a binary approach to anti-consumerism recreates a moral binary, which can be problematic in its simplification, as the practice of anti-consumerism is sometimes more about identity and community-building than about absolute abstinence from global consumer capitalism. As Laura Portwood-Stacer (2012) demonstrates in her research with anarchists in the USA, a purist approach to anti-consumerism is neither universally accepted nor practised. Chatzidakis and Lee (2012) also directly challenge the study of anti-consumerism through the binary of 'reasons for' and 'reasons against', arguing that it conceals a complex continuum of resistant practices. Sam Binkley and Jo Littler (2008) break with the binary in reasserting the role of cultural studies in providing a critical yet multidimensional approach to anti-consumerism. The ideological binary (awakened vs asleep) is also evident in much of the critique of culture jamming as an exclusionary medium, which addresses the enlightened but patronizes the politically aloof (Carducci, 2006). However, as this chapter shows, subvertising can illustrate a sophisticated approach to public engagement.

Society of the Spectacle Past and Present: Ethical, Fascist, Commercial Spectacles

The work of contemporary culture jammers does not exist in a vacuum. It goes back to historical moments of resistance to the rise of modern consumerism. For instance, the Situationist International (Internationale Situationiste or IS) was a

European intellectual and artistic collective (1957–72) which developed a critique of capitalism by engaging Marxist theory with surrealist art. IS advocated the creation of 'situations' as a remedy to the pacification and alienation of society under the 'spectacle'. One of its key intellectual figures, Guy Debord, discussed consumer society in his book *The Society of the Spectacle* (1967/1994), which describes the 'spectacle' as the total takeover of the cultural environment, which leads to the pacification and alienation of societies. As a remedy, he offers the 'situation' and specifically the practice of détournement as a suggestion for the 'awakening' of the dazed sleepwalking spectator; détournement is a mode of disruption to the spectacle-as-usual (hence the insistence on 'awakening' in later theorizations of anti-consumerism and ideology). Détournement is a tactic of culture jamming and subvertising practice.

Contrary to the Situationist International's distinction between 'situation' and 'spectacle', in *Dream*, Stephen Duncombe (2007) proposes the concept of the 'ethical spectacle' to reclaim the allure of the society of the spectacle and put it to the service of progressive political activism. Duncombe specifies that the ethical spectacle is the work of progressive activists, those aiming for social and environmental justice goals, and differentiates it from the fascist or commercial spectacles, which 'appear to have cornered the market on the political use of fantasy and the mobilization of desire' (ibid.: 124). Duncombe sets up a set of beliefs that can create and facilitate ethical spectacles: belief in democracy (as in *for* universal suffrage in representational government and *against* hierarchy of privilege), belief in interconnectedness and interdependedness of life (care for community, value of individual expression, inclusion, and discussion among different voices), and a 'strong belief in the essentiality of the real' (and a belief in progress and hope for the future). Several studies have taken up the concept of the ethical spectacle to connect it to forms of anti-consumerist action. Paul Routledge (2012) further expands on the concept of ethical spectacles, which can mirror, appropriate, and thus open spectacles up for examination through the cultural activism of the Clandestine Insurgent Rebel Clown Army (CIRCA) in the G8 meeting in Gleneagles, Scotland. I have also argued that the ethical spectacle is a powerful catalyst for the way in which a cultural politics of consumption intersects with a systemic politics of consumption in an analysis of Brandalism's COP21 action (Lekakis, 2017c). How effective is an ephemeral act of anti-consumerism? What happens when an activist buries themselves under several kilograms of prospectus in Place Felix Poulat in Grenoble to highlight the environmental costs of their production, while a clown army goes around the city inviting citizens to question advertising?[6] Anti-consumerist activism opens up critical questions as to the potential of the ethical spectacle in competing with commercial or fascist spectacles.

At different moments in history, in alignment with certain socioeconomic circumstances, the ethical spectacle can come up against the allure of the fascist or commercial spectacle. Stephen Duncombe writes that 'fascism and commercialism appear to have cornered the market on the political use of fantasy and the mobilization of desire' (2007: 124). On the one hand, the aesthetics of totalitarian power in different myths (of creation, revolution, and nation) and rituals (of dress, speech, and behaviour) have historically been significant in giving rise to and maintaining fascist regimes. Whether through the myth and cult of the leader (Mussolini as The Duce or Hitler as The Führer), the promotion of and access to cultural events, or the new advertising ethos of Nazi Germany, public spectacles have facilitated the rise of fascism (Falasca-Zamponi, 1997; Swett, 2014). More recently, the existence of spectacles for authoritarian regimes is noticeable in, for instance, the spectacles of Hosni Mubarak and Abdel Fattah Al-Sisi dominating the aesthetic order of modern Egypt (Othman, 2020). The politics of symbolism has also been mobilized by Narendra Modi since his election campaign with spectacular stunts such as his simultaneous speech in 26 cities through hologram technology (Sen, 2016). Donald Trump, 'a successful creator and manipulator of the spectacle' (Kellner, 2016: 5) of US politics, has similarly drawn on his promotional experience of selling buildings, golf courses and casinos, steaks, chocolates and vodka, reality TV shows, publishing, and beauty pageants to sell his brand of politics. In this sense, the 45th US presidency is a clear example of authoritarian spectacle meeting commercial spectacle.

The commercial spectacle is sparked by promotional industries (advertising, branding, and marketing), which create and cross-promote a series of desires, fantasies, and aspirations. The commercial spectacle no longer relies on loud declarations of the amazing values of a product, or the amazing identity it bestows on the consumer, but quietly beckons attention through minimalistic logos or even by pretending to disrupt the spectacle itself (Serazio, 2013). The way in which the society of the spectacle pre-empts its critique poses a key barrier to the potential of the ethical spectacle. This is especially true for culture jamming. Richard Gilman-Opalsky discusses the need to expand culture jamming beyond media savvy activism as then it 'risks becoming a liberal fantasy that gives good news to capitalism: Is this all the Left has left?' (2013: 3).

Culture Jamming: Incorporation, Play, Participation and Pedagogy, Law

DeLaure and Fink (2017: 12–24) qualify culture jamming in terms of what it is and what it does through the following: appropriates, is artful, is often playful, is often anonymous, is participatory, is political, operates serially, and is transgressive. Here I draw attention to four key areas to summarize academic debates on culture jamming and bring in interdisciplinary approaches to the topic: incorporation, play, participation, and law.

Incorporation

Incorporation is a key concern or reason for dismissal of the potential of culture jamming to stoke the flames of progressive political change. Accounting for the transformations in advertising as mentioned at the end of the above section, but also in relation to the totalizing power of the spectacle, critics have noted that even anti-consumerist activists sell products; Heath and Potter have noted the ways in which '"alternative" is, and always has been, good business' (2005, 131). Revolutions within culture, communities, or society have been mirrored by revolutions in the cultural industries, as their economic motive have led them to seek for sources of innovation, ingenuity, and, ultimately, profit. Thomas Frank's (1997) iconic study of the 'business revolution' in the US of the 1960s sold consumption as rebellion, as a break from mass consumer culture and the conformist advertising of the 1950s. This 'revolution' dominates consumer capitalism for the following four decades and presents an annexe into the new selfhood gained by exceptional products that are unforgivingly hip. Two decades later, Bradshaw and Scott (2018) write the story of another 'advertising revolution', that of a song (The Beatles' 'Revolution') cajoled into advertising for Nike (and later, in 2016, as the song in Trump's inauguration). How a song about the global political struggles of the 1960s comes to be credited for the multinational corporation's rise to the top of global sports brands is not a matter of irony, as they explain, but one of creative and commercial intentions.

Market actors and creative agencies often engage in the 'rebel sell' of their products, making the ideological red lines of the 'guerilla tactics' (Klein, 2005) of culture jamming succumb to 'guerilla marketing' (Serazio, 2013). Serazio notes that 'while culture jamming may have set out to issue symbolic challenges to destabilize the corporate communication that clutters our contemporary environment, it seems to have also rejuvenated the industry it meant to parody' (2017: 238). Similar are challenges brought forward by the shift towards branded content, as it manifests through native advertising and content marketing (Einstein, 2016). Such 'revolutions' condition our ability to imagine and aspire to a better future. Several authors have noted the dangers of incorporation of culture jamming into the fold of advertising (Carducci, 2006, 2021; Stolle and Micheletti, 2015). The fact that *Advertising Age* named Kalle Lasn[7] among the ten most influential players in marketing in 2011 for 'branding' the Occupy Movement[8] serves as evidence to such arguments.[9] It is important to note, however, that this push of incorporation into commercial messages and activities co-exists with the pull of alternative messages and activities propagated by progressive activists (Lekakis, 2017c). Resistance in promotional culture is not static, but constantly shifting from the visibility of activists to that of market actors.

Play

> On some level, it's making a public statement, saying this is not ok. As difficult as it is to change people's minds I think it's important to try, but it's also important to reassure the people who believe in things such as social justice and rolling back some of the extremes of capitalism at the very least. So if you can make them laugh, especially about one of these kinds of issues, then you've kind of got them to agree with you that at least there's something absurd about what you're pointing out. (Darren Cullen, interview in Subvertisers for London, 2019)

Culture jamming is undoubtedly playful. It plays with art and rhetoric, typically in a humorous manner. It 'injects art into everyday spaces and routines, reclaiming them for the imagination' (DeLaure and Fink, 2017: 15). Artists such as New York-based Jordan Seilor (Public Ad Campaign[10]), London-based Robert Montgomery, and Berlin-based Vermibus often feature in subvertising campaigns. In 2018, activists glued bubble speech stickers to outdoors advertising across Madrid, and members of the public took to spelling out their ideas of the real thoughts of models depicted. Some of their thoughts included, 'they removed my hair through Photoshop!', 'happiness is not to be found in this announcement', 'size 38 squeezes my genitals'.[11] As Cammaerts suggests, 'cultural/political jamming also embodies the de-elitization of art and allows the citizen/activist to voice dissent and challenge dominant discourses in society' (2007: 86). There is a wealth of research on artistic activism, discussing the difference between institutional 'Art' and grassroots 'art' and noting the significant role that art plays in stirring, supporting, and spreading social movement action (Kraidy, 2016; McKee, 2016; Reed, 2019; Werbner et al., 2014). Critical approaches to artistic activism have noted the importance of embodied action (Serafini, 2018), as well as the overlooked parameters of labour (Serafini et al., 2018) and of law (Finchett-Maddock and Lekakis, 2020).

Culture jamming mobilizes rhetorical tactics of sabotage, appropriation, and intensification/augmentation in its engagement with commercial messages (Harold, 2009). Sabotage refers to the direct interruption of commercial messages. Appropriation is about subverting by editing commercial messages. Intensification is another case of tampering with the commercial message, this time to bust the myth of the ad. Humour is often a key driver of resistance narratives in culture jamming (Reilly, 2018; Sørensen, 2016). A philosophy of laughter, which draws on Plato's *Republic*, regards three types of ethics of humour: relief theory, superiority theory, and incongruity theory (Morreall, 1987). Wettergren problematizes how 'fun and humor as part of protest in culture jamming can be understood as "utopian"' (2009: 6) as it demonstrates ambivalence in relation to irony; humour, in other words, can be incorporated too, into an apathetic disposition. According to relief theory, for instance, humour is intended as a therapeutic medium, which remedies a difficult situation. A subvertisement joke about climate change, for instance, can provide temporary relief, but can also appease anger. Similarly, a subvertisement that is not immediately obvious to all, but to some who are 'in' on the joke, can be an example of superiority theory where the recipient recognizes the joke, feels better about themselves, and moves on with their daily lives. Incongruity theory forms the basis of many subvertisements, as they are usually not expected and there is a 'double-take'. Still, the audience might continue passing them by, mistaking them for 'guerilla marketing' tactics. For Wettergren (2009), the resolution of the ambivalence and the claiming of the 'real fun' that can be had in pursuing social change is production; in other words, we need to be makers, not consumers, of culture jamming and its messages. Hence, the playfulness, artfulness, and humour of culture jamming are not to be regarded as utopian characteristics but as processes of involvement, of immersion in terms of embodiment and production that can also carry risks.

Participation and Pedagogy

> The motivation for subvertising is certainly to challenge the dominance of outdoor advertising, of corporate messaging in public space. That's always a beautiful side effect of taking down an advert and putting up a political message or a piece of artwork. By doing so you challenge the dominance and you start to have a conversation about the legitimacy of corporate messaging in public space. (Special Patrol Group interview in Subvertisers for London, 2019)

Traditionally, Adbusters and iconic culture jamming collectives took the risks that come with reclaiming public spaces, repurposing commercial messages and spreading them across information networks for broad reach. Much has changed with interactive and social media platforms. MyDavidCameron.com was a meme-generating platform launched prior to the UK's general election in 2010 by a former web designer. When someone visited the website, they could customize the message on the Conservative politician's banner, effectively generating a political culture jam. Political culture jams are effectively culture jams which directly address party and parliamentary politics rather than consumer culture (Phillips, 2015). MyDavidCameron.com offered citizens political expression by providing an opportunity to poke fun at the Conservative leader rather than observe political culture jams installed around London (see Figures 7.2 and 7.3).

Seven years later, Theresa May ran as leader of the the Conservative party and Jeremy Corbyn as leader of the Labour party in the general election of June 2017. I encountered political culture jams such as those depicted here near Queens Park

Figure 7.2 London, 11 June 2017
Photograph taken by author.

London Overground station, and they serve the purpose of discussing the relationship between culture jamming and participation. Figures 7.2 and 7.3 appear as an alternative political campaign, anti-May and pro-Corbyn, connecting the first to lies (Figure 7.2 reads 'Stop the lies and U-turns. Vote the Tories out at all odds') and the second to the attempt to save the national healthcare system from the Conservatives' gradual attempts to privatize the NHS ('save the NHS. For the many, not for the few' reads Figure 7.3). Whether one agrees or not with the politics of the alternative campaigns, one thing is clear: the two political culture jamming campaigns are radically different in terms of offering participation.

Figure 7.3 London, 11 June 2017
Photograph taken by author.

Whether culture jamming can shift public perceptions away from the spectacle and towards the ethical spectacle remains the topic of debate. For some, culture jamming can be a revolutionary tactic in terms of teaching and pedagogy more broadly (Sandlin, 2010). Sandlin and Milam (2008) analyse Adbusters, Reverend Billy, and the Church of Stop Shopping in terms to how they use culture jamming as a means of resisting consumerism. They argue that, in those cases, culture jamming involves practices as critical public pedagogy as it fosters participatory, resistant cultural production, engages learners corporeally, creates a community politic and opens transitional spaces through détournement. For Sandlin and Milam, culture jammers become both producers and consumers and culture jamming a space where audiences can partake freely, as the former demonstrate 'how popular culture is a field of contestation' (ibid.: 332). Others disagree and suggest that 'AdBusters' public pedagogy is not simply inadequate to confront the cultural hegemony of neoliberalism, but in some ways complicit with it' (Haiven, 2007: 86). Furthermore, developing the participatory aspect of culture jamming against the threat of incorporation discussed above, Milstein and Pulos argue that its power is 'experiencing conscious reappropriation by creators and educators who use participatory communication strategies to bring the act of jamming back into the realm of questioning and relocating culture' (2015: 396). There is something utopic and deterministic in culture jammers' belief that the society of the spectacle has distorted the 'authentic' lives that people used to live (Lasn, 2000) suggests that the 'authenticity' of culture jamming can correct that. Sarah Banet-Weiser's (2012a) work on 'authenticity' brings the concept of 'ambivalence' to the heart of both brand culture and consumer resistance.

Culture jamming is openly accessible through the concepts of participation and pedagogy. Sandlin and Milam (2008) claim that culture jamming is participatory as culture jammers are able to participate in remixing popular culture – but they don't consider the audiences of culture jams and how they are only participating by consuming. Wettergren reminds us that audiences are more likely to engage with the cause and escape the temptation of merely consuming culture jams when they are able to participate in the making of such culture jams. Sandlin and McLaren, in *Critical Pedagogies of Consumption*, bring 'educators to not only consider consumption as a space of education and learning, but also to critically analyze what it might mean to *resist* consumerism and overconsumption' (2010: 2, italics in original). Their approach to 'a critical pedagogy of consumption' reminds us that 'in focusing almost exclusively on the realm of consumption, culture jamming has, in effect, precluded any discussion of a class politics that would speak to the level of capitalist production' (Scatamburlo-D'Annibale, 2010: 230). Similarly, Gilman-Opalsky (2013) argues that culture jamming is not a revolutionary tactic of grassroots social movements, as it falls on liberal complacency and that revolt is the only way of unjamming the insurrectionary imagination. Yet subvertising, a loosely defined and promiscuously practised practice can include both physical and digital actions ranging from ad takeovers, civil disobedience, détournement, and artivism workshops, to online petitions and crowdfunding. There is a difference between The Citizens Advertising Takeover Service set up by Glimpse, a London-based collective that crowdfunded to legally replace advertisements on Clapham Common tube station with pictures of cats over a day, and Le Collectif des Déboulonneurs in France which has been organizing advertising takeovers on a monthly basis since 2005 aiming to 'to unbolt and debunk advertising, remove it from its pedestal and destroy its prestige'.[12] Ephemerality or sustained action play a role in the analysis of participation and impact of action, as does the law.

Law: Copyright and Civil Disobedience

The book *Subvertising: The Piracy of Outdoors Advertising* (Hogre, 2017), featuring the work of subvertiser Hogre, defines the term as the unsolicited reaction to the visual pollution of advertising; 'removing, replacing and defacing advertising is an act of civil disobedience that is both legally and morally defensible'. Subvertisers can often come up against the law. Whether through accusations of vandalism or infringement on corporate copyright, subvertisers can be at risk. It is not the point of this section to debate whether subvertising is or is not legally defensible, and there is even recognition among legal professionals that there is a 'greyness' and a 'blurriness' (Lydia Dagostino, solicitor, interviewed in Subvertisers for London, 2019) on the matter. The point is to recognize, without dismissing, the various practices of subvertisers in relation to the law. One of the obvious ways in which subvertising comes up against the law is in relation to copyright issues. Isidro Jiménez-Gómez and Mariola Olcina Alvarado (2020) reflect on Consume Hasta Morir's legal battles against companies whose logos and copyrighted material they have tampered with, and draw key lessons for the relationship between artivism and the law. They note the indirect ways in which companies have sent them faxes, letters, and emails, demanding not that they do not appropriate their logos, but to withdraw content that directly refers to them from the activists' website. Others have previously also noted that advertisers often avoid direct legal confrontation with subvertisers (Smith-Anthony and Groom, 2015), possibly as the publicity generated from such legal battles could raise negative attention to the former and positive to the latter. Yet facing the law does not only happen at the level of content creation and online dissemination, but mostly at the street level, where subvertisers use keys to do their adbusting (removing and replacing advertising panels).

Out of 24 subvertisers in seven countries who I inteviewed,[13] several had spent at least a night in prison, while some had exit restrictions and could not leave the country. The majority had consciously decided to put their names and faces forward in support of their activism. This logic of 'bearing witness' (della Porta and Diani, 2006: 170), where activists engage in public performances and civil disobedience, comes with a conscious decision to use the attention paid to the activists themselves by the law (and media) to raise public awareness of the issues they are being arrested for. In his booklet *what the f*#k do you do that for*, kyle magee,[14] Australian citizen and adversary of advertising who aims for maximum exposure, responds to the question of why he is risking ending up in jail when he will not change anything:

the only reason i'll be in jail will be because i have done/changed something. even though the temporary physical change to the advertising itself is deliberately trivial, the important change is that i'm now a person who openly and unashamedly acts against the anti-democratic for-profit media-advertising system. (2016: 68)

kyle's case is similar to cases such as Berlin-based artist Vermibus and the French collective Le Collectif des Déboulonneurs who also engage in acts of civil disobedience.

Civil disobedience is following one's conscience and acting non-violently to change what is considered by the public an unfair policy or law. The civil disobedience of Australian group B.U.G.A. U.P. against smoking advertisements on hoardings is considered to have had 'an outstanding role in politicising tobacco control' (Chapman, 1996: 179). Civil disobedience is also broadly connected to a history of consumer activism, as evident in the case of the civil rights movement. In this present-day case, kyle refuses to accept that advertising cannot be abolished: 'i do honestly think for-profit advertising can be abolished — there is every reason to abolish it, and the practice is only allowed by the laws of our society, which we have the power to change' (magee, 2016: 69). Civil disobedience can also offer some wins; on 25 March 2013, members of Le Collectif des Déboulonneurs arrested for appropriating outdoors advertising were acquitted as the judge ruled that they were protecting their freedom of expression and acting out of necessity.[15] In 2014, the United Nations Office of the High Commissioner for Human Rights recognized the right of citizens to consent to forms of advertising:

> The issue of consent needs to be included in discussions about the impact of advertising and marketing strategies on human rights. For example, some people claim a right not to receive advertising, while others call for provisions to opt out from exposure to advertising and for the development of software to block online advertising. (UN Report of the Special Rapporteur in the field of cultural rights, III A 33).[16]

Civil disobedience, thus, can be in some cases justified in a court of law, as in the case of France.

Many subvertisers do not take the legal risk. Cautious of the possibility that it might result in legal action or threaten their work life, citizens operating under monikers undertake subvertising covertly. Still, they highlight the legal ambivalence that advertisers enjoy. In an interview with a Parisian who goes by the moniker Fabien Tipon & Co, he spoke of the unacceptability of advertising companies finding ways to circumvent legislation which limits them from public spaces in the city of Paris.[17] Specifically, he mentioned Biodegr'AD, a company that uses 'clean tag' (a method of advertising which uses a stencil placed on the street and pumped with a pressure washer so that the advertisement is formed on the parts where the stencil cleans the street) to introduce advertising on the streets (see also Chapter 8) and how infuriating this new practice was to him. Hence, it is particularly important to think about the agency of subvertisers: who they are and the capacity in which they act is crucial to their ideological standpoints, as well as their practice and exposure to risk. The section below summarizes critical issues that have emerged so far.

Critical Issues

To theorize anti-consumerism through culture jamming and subvertising is to acknowledge the dynamic relationship of advertising power between those who reinforce and those who resist it (Dekeyser, 2019). As has been evident so far, ambivalence characterizes the relationship between advertising and subvertising. Core critical issues for future studies of culture jamming and subvertising emerging in scholarly debates concern history, ideology, agency, and justice.

1. *The importance of history.* If we are not able to explore the context and historical roots of an action, we are missing half of the picture. Consuming subverted advertisements can trigger political consciousness as well as cynicism and apathy. Engaging in the production of culture jams is a process that requires further engagement with a cause, and hence its context allows for public pedagogy beyond the surface level of political consciousness. Attention to history can also help disentangle the ambiguity of our multifaceted society of the spectacle, where the fascist and commercial spectacle have merged. The ethical spectacle is dedicated to contextualization of its causes and engagement of its participants.
2. *The importance of ideology.* Culture jammers rebel against the 'culture-ideology of consumerism' (Sklair, 2002) but a 'for or against' binary between 'consumerism' and 'anti-consumerism' is not productive. Similarly, to search for 'authenticity' in the marketplace one has to ignore the constant presence of ambivalence in brand culture. Neoliberalism has produced culture as ambivalence, and sensibilities as crafted through consumer choice. Similarly, we cannot assume that 'adversaries of consumption' are 'outsiders' in a system of consumer capitalism through anti-consumerist choices. This would make invisible the multiple ways in which consumer capitalism structures our lives. Yet at the same time there is a big difference between those who engage in subvertising for political purposes and those engage in it for commercial purposes. Since the 1960s, advertisers have been working on incorporate dissent through their appropriation of countercultural songs and prose, or punk aesthetics and revolutionary aspirations. Subvertisers have tried to expose that. Again, engaging audiences in the deconstruction of the

commercial spectacle is a clear way through which the deliberate ambivalence of advertising ideology (Wernick, 1991) can be exposed.

3. *The importance of agency.* The line is drawn on the question of who is engaged in culture jamming or subvertising. Is it one or more individuals or a local or transnational institution? Scholars have noted that agencies in culture jamming can range from citizens to governments and from news shows to NGOs and social movements (Cammaerts, 2007; Philipps, 2015; Warner, 2007). We have also seen cases where NGOs (for instance, Greenpeace) collaborate with activists (here, the Yes Men) to appropriate Shell's drilling in the Arctic (Davis et al., 2016). The question of whether subvertising is a social movement also produces various answers. For some, the answer is a definite yes. Adbusters founder Kalle Lasn has called culture jammers 'a loose global network of media activists who see [themselves] as the advance shock troops of the most significant social movement of the next twenty years' (2000: xi), although he later saw culture jamming as part of 'an "occupy" movement' (Lasn and McLauchlan, 2013); and, in the early 2000s, some scholars also tended to agree (Carty, 2002; Kozinets and Handelman, 2004). Most arguments, however, agree that culture jamming is more a form of political participation and an activist tactic (Balsinger, 2010; Colli, 2020; Stolle and Micheletti, 2015). In order to evaluate the practice of subvertising, one first has to evaluate the agent who is partaking in it. In that case, when companies such as Coca Cola engage in their own subvertising, it is apparent that subvertising is not an activist practice anymore but rather corporate practice. It is also apparent when a social movement emerges to join transnational subvertisers' forces and organise annual coordinated actions (Lekakis, 2021).

4. *The importance of justice.* This concerns the way in which advertising and subvertising traverse the thin lines of legality and illegality in various national contexts. Recognizing that subvertising is not just another meme circulating on the web, but usually a process that involves embodied action and bodies at risk is important. It is also important to recognize that whether through copyright infringements or adbusting, activists take risks because they want to challenge the normalization of advertising through the lack of appropriate legal frameworks. The United Nations Office for Human Rights 'is concerned about the confusion that can result concerning the hierarchy of norms, where and how to file complaints and who has the authority to penalize violations. While States' responses indicate that a number of bodies have monitoring or disciplinary powers, whether those bodies can impartially address complaints is unclear. The number of cases addressed seems minimal.' (UN Report of the Special Rapporteur in the field of cultural rights, II D 23[18])

Civil disobedience is for those who choose it the only appropriate way to fight for the right to regulate or abolish advertising.

Researching Anti-Consumerism and Subvertising: Methodologies

Culture jamming remains a topic of much academic and activist engagement – and much cultural, counter-cultural, and commercial activity. Given its historical precedence and continued influence in the world of culture jammers, it is understandable that Adbusters, its magazine and its founder's book *Culture Jam* (Lasn, 2000) have featured prominently among the material analysed by researchers (Cherrier, 2009; Rumbo, 2002; Wettergren, 2009). Yet the attempts of several other groups, many of which have continued their operations, but even more so those who have not, remain underexplored. Given the western dominance of the English language, accessing knowledge about *contrapublicidad* or *antipublicitaire* is not always possible. Within English-speaking academia, there is limited research specifically focusing on subvertising (Dekeyser, 2019; Lekakis, 2017c, 2021).

Regarding specific methodologies, several studies engage with cultural studies through a theoretical approach (Cammaerts, 2007; Carducci, 2006; Binkley and Littler, 2008). Carducci (2006) employs a sociological approach to culture jamming and contextualizes it through the 18th century 'expressivist' tradition and how that has influenced the development of consumer society through 'expressive' individualistic consumption. This allows Carducci to argue that, as the expression of political will against expressive consumerism in late modernity, culture jamming is more prone to the incorporation of consumer society than its appropriation. Cammaerts (2007) applies a rhizomatic approach of communication to challenge the divides between civil society activism and the market and proposes a theory of culture jamming that 'jams the political' and includes identical practices which are not necessarily counter-hegemonic. Such an approach is informed by Deleuze and Guattari's (1987) concept of the 'rhizome', a metaphor for connecting a point of a network to any other point and developed by Carpentier et al. (2003) in their approach to community media where one node of the network can move in and through the public sphere and counter-public sphere, thus challenging hegemony. Finally, offering a cultural studies approach, Binkley and Littler (2008) untangle the reluctance to engage with a polemic politics of consumer culture and engage cultural studies with the critique of commodities in a special issue, ranging from the difficulties encountered by cultural studies scholars to consumerism and environmentalism and the cultural continuum of anti-consumerism (as in consuming differently).

There is research that draws on a case study approach. Harold draws on three contemporary examples of culture jamming to argue that 'pranking repatterns commercial rhetoric less by protesting a disciplinary mode of power (clogging the machinery of the image factory) than by strategically augmenting and utilizing the precious resources the contemporary media ecology affords' (2004: 208). Farrar and Warner (2008) focus on Billionaires for Bush to explore their work at the level of representation, and the way they use the spectacle as a boomerang to challenge audiences' perceptions of what they are watching. Routledge (2012) focuses on the Clandestine Insurgent Rebel Clown Army to explore the performative turn of artistic activism through ethical spectacles. Day (2018) explores Yes Men's subversion of Chevron's 2010 ad campaign, which responded to consumer concerns about corporate social responsibility through 'ventriloquism'. Madden and colleagues (2018) analyse the feminist activist organization FORCE's response to Victoria's Secret's advertisement through the creation of a website inviting users to 'join the consent revolution'.

Most often one comes across studies focusing on culture jams as texts, engaging in a visual or rhetorical analysis of the discourses it puts forward. Christine Harold's (2009) book *Our Space* undertakes a rhetorical analysis of strategies used by culture jammers. Bringing 'cultural economy and consumer culture into dialogue with contemporary anti-consumerist discourses' (Littler, 2005: 248), Littler appraises anti-consumerism in light of cultural studies, beyond its material manifestations (e.g. boycotts and buycotts). Connecting to research on identity and culture in anti-corporate resistance, scholars have explored the 'constitutive aspect of narrative' (Atkinson, 2003: 164) put forward by subvertisers. Connecting it to studies on environmental communication activism, scholars explore the way in which culture jammers appropriate corporate discourses through irony, humour, and artful intervention (Davis et al., 2016; Kaylor, 2013; Lekakis, 2017c) or how the media frame the performances of culture jammers such as the Yes Men (Robinson and Bell, 2013). Focusing on culture jams as texts has been a frequent and standard practice among scholars, although there are several who have undertaken combined methodological approaches.

Scholars who appraise culture jamming from a mixed methods perspective tend to combine textual with ethnographic approaches. Ian Reilly's book *Media Hoaxing* (2018) draws from interviews, media archives, and local and international media discourses from 1996 to contextualize the Yes Men and evaluate their failures and successes. A classic piece by Kozinets and Handelman (2004) analyses online data from activist newsgroups and interviews with 13 activists in three different anti-consumerist campaigns (anti-advertising, anti-Nike, anti-genetically engineered food and crops). Similarly, Cherrier (2009) examines three types of anti-consumerist discourses through two anti-consumerist books, two voluntary simplicity websites, and 11 interviews with voluntary simplifiers and culture jammers. Wettergren (2009) engages in textual and visual analysis (of material from the websites of Adbusters, RtMark, The Institute of Applied Autonomy, the Bureau of Inverse Technology and The Church of Stop Shopping), participant observations (of a Reverend Billy performance and a Surveillance Camera Players Manhattan city walk), interviews (with members of The French Adbusters, the RtMark, the IAA, the BIT, the SCP, Reverend Billy and an individual jammer), and with the book *Culture Jam*. Exploring the Brazilian protests of 2013 from an anti-consumerist perspective, Fontenelle and Pozzebon (2019) engage with netography and participant observation of the protests to illustrate how culture jamming targeted the government instead of corporations.

Finally, as of the time of writing, there are only a couple of studies that engage subvertisers directly through ethnographic methods, whether it is through full immersion or interviews. I have analysed interviews with 24 subvertisers in seven countries to identify the social movement frames they use to identify the problem and solutions associated with subvertising. Thomas Dekeyser's (2019) ethnographic research addresses the dialectics of advertising and subvertising and the production of advertising power through a collaborative ethnography, reflections on the author's past advertising career and interviews with advertising professionals. Such work traverses the thin red line between legality and illegality and exposes the opportunities and challenges of subvertising beyond the text. The case study below illustrates some of the complexities in analysing contemporary subvertising activism and allows us to draw a key design for further research.

Case Study: Resistance is Female

To provide some context, in 2017, the New York based collective Resistance is Female started working with artists to replace old phone booth panels with original works by female and queer artists around the world, alarmed by Trump's comments and actions against women. The collective includes street artists, as well as other artists, graphic designers, and photographers. With the exception of Abe Lincoln Jr, none of the other members had previously been involved in subvertising or political activism. Their involvement in subvertising grew in response to sexism and gender-related oppression in both institutional and everyday settings. Within its first year, the Trump administration had promoted gender injustice in four major ways. First, through an attack on Obama's equal pay data collection. This had revealed a general gender pay gap for full-time, year-round workers of 19.5 per cent, according to the 2016 annual report of the Institute for Women's Policy Research.[19] Second, by reducing women's control over their bodies. In April 2017, the Trump administration proposed the Pain-Capable Unborn Child Protection Act, amending the criminal code to make it a crime, with some caveats, for any person to perform or attempt to perform abortion if the foetus is 20 weeks old or more. Third, through more strict measures to prove sexual assault. In September 2017, then Education Secretary Betsy DeVos rejected a key part of government policy on campus sexual assault giving schools a choice on standard of proof and appeals. The new guidance now allows schools to choose between a 'preponderance of the evidence' standard of proof and a higher 'clear and convincing' standard when determining guilt. Finally, through an attack on trans rights. Anti-transgender activist Bethany Kozma was appointed as Senior Advisor to the Office of Gender Equality and Women's Empowerment at the US Agency for International Development. This was followed by the launch of a 'United We Stand' campaign against Obama's 'Dear Colleague Letter' that allowed transgender students access to facilities (restrooms/locker rooms) consistent with their gender identity.

To such gender-based attacks, Resistance is Female responded through the promotion of visual narratives of gender empowerment to make intersectional feminism, queer and trans empowerment visible in public spaces (Figures 7.4, 7.5, and 7.6). Their influences include subvertisers such as Public Ad Campaign and the Art in Ad Places campaign, street art, punk subcultures, as well as other grassroots anti-Trump activism. I interviewed five key members of the collective who had formed shortly after the Women's March on 21 January 2017, the day of the inauguration of the 45th US president. Two years later, the campaign concluded, and some of its members became involved with a new campaign, Keep Fighting, run by Abe Lincoln Jr.

Figure 7.4

Copyright Dusty Rebel, permission granted.

Figure 7.5
Copyright: Dusty Rebel, permission granted.

Figure 7.6
Copyright: Dusty Rebel, permission granted.

Analysing Resistance Is Female through Anti-Consumerism and Culture Jamming

We can gain a closer understanding of this movement by questioning it in relation to anti-consumerism and culture jamming, as well as to speculate on its impact in terms of those involved and those witnessing the campaign. Resistance is Female is less of an anti-consumerist campaign and more of a campaign to highlight gender politics and the problematic way in which they have become particularly controversial in the spectacle of the Trump administration:

> The personal is political. I don't know if I'm outdated, no, I don't think I am outdated. I guess because I'm a queer person, identity politics is the core of how I understand… because it's hard for me to even articulate because I'm shocked by this weird thing that identity politics is controversial. Oftentimes I think that people who are pushing that are usually white straight people because of most of my friends or most of the thinkers who I follow who are Muslim or black or gay or women, feminists, it's like no, I mean that's the core of what some of those issues are. To somehow ignore that, I don't know how you can ignore that. (Dusty Rebel)

Members of Resistance is Female do not always rebel against advertising, but instead promote gender empowerment through advertising spaces. Yet a member of the collective says that while he is personally not against advertising, there is a tipping point when it comes to gender and representation:

> I'm not inherently against advertising but I'm all about fucking with it as much as possible. It's just good to fuck with shit, you know, call things to question. On the subway, they have these ads on the subway cars and there are these ones in particular that are really fucking horrible plastic surgery ads and you know they had one ad where there's a woman holding like a pair of limes against her chest and sad and then in the next – before and after – she was holding cantaloupes and she was smiling. So that kind of shit? Fuck them. That pisses me off so bad. ... Advertising in general, they're putting it up there, it's gonna get fucked with. (Abe Lincoln Jr)

Here, as argued earlier, it is apparent that Abe's non-binary approach to advertising and subvertising as ideological enemies challenges the binary opposition between for and against consumerism. As is illustrated below, the campaign became anti-consumerist when it came to gender politics.

The campaign engaged in culture jamming. Through the takeover of advertising spaces and promotion of narratives of gender empowerment Resistance is Female used creativity for social justice. This combination of strategic appropriation of advertising spaces and rhetorical appropriation of advertising messages aims to propagate intersectional feminism. Rhetorical appropriation of visual content related to female, queer, and trans resistance invite a consideration of oppressive constructions of gender and a dialogue about preconceptions, policies, and actions for equality and empowerment. Consumer activism found its way in the discourse of a like-minded campaign, A Presidential Parody, through a culture jam which targeted Ivanka Trump's clothing brand (Figure 7.7).

Figure 7.7
Copyright: Luna Park, permission granted.

This employs what Christine Harold (2009) identifies as the rhetorical strategy of appropriation where the message is reworked to expose the hidden sweatshop labour behind the fast fashion brand and the likes of it. In this case, we can observe culture jamming's original aim of 'truth in advertising' (Klein, 2005: 286). Mostly, however, the campaign engaged in the production and distribution of visual materials that aimed to make counter-hegemonic narratives of gender equality and empowerment visually present and verbally affirmed in public spaces. The campaign name stands as 'visual signposts that just encourage people to keep fighting' (Abe Lincoln Jr). As another member suggests:

> the message is for everyday women who are just going by, having their day, whatever, and for them to be caught off guard in a way that is like 'oh wow this is actually women coming together to share this message'… you know, just to give them a little push and inspire them, you know? (Sara Erenthal).

Finally, for Dusty Rebel, the aim is for the campaign to add to the toolkit of political resistance:

> I hope that it would maybe motivate people, I hope it would inspire people, keep them activated, that's sort of my hope that it would just keep that energy going in all different ways. ... One of those tools is using visual media, art, to inspire people keep them going in that way, as well as calling congress people and keeping pressure. It's a multi-pronged thing.

The Impact of Resistance Is Female

We can speculate on the campaign's impact in relation to those involved in the project and those who have witnessed the project on the street. Through the campaign, artists participated in (sometimes) embodied culture jamming and adbusting for the first time. Coming from an ultra-Orthodox Jewish background and having left ultra-orthodoxy behind at the age of 17, artist and collective member Sara Erenthal told me why she got involved with the campaign:

> I thought about what it meant for me to come from where I came from and how I actually fought as a female, I created my own path against all odds and I said no to an arranged marriage and I just took my own path and made my own life, despite basically men controlling us, men are always the ones deciding on everything and that was something I didn't like, I didn't want, and now with this recent election and this shitty president – I'm not even gonna say his name – I felt that I was again facing the same issues where men are trying to control women and I said fuck no and it's made me even more motivated.

Gigi Chen, reflecting on her Asian-American background, the everyday racism she has experienced growing up and being part of the US where certain freedoms are constitutionally protected (though certain rights are also challenged), talked about the way in which the campaign made her rethink what it means to be a feminist:

> this project specifically it's made me think a lot about it because there's so much talk about diversity, about stereotypes, about who we are as a people and who we want to be and what are our aspirations now and what does it mean to go backwards?

The politicization of artists such as Sara and Gigi speaks to the effects participation on this campaign has had on them.

To speculate on the effects the campaign has had on members of the public would require research on the kinds of responses members of the collective have received during adbusting as well as an analysis of their social media profile. Yet even that would not capture the subtle effects of people walking by and faced by incongruity. Photographer Maha Al-Asaker says:

> People in the street are used to walk and ad ad ad, you know? But then replacing them, having something like an art form they will start asking 'where is the ad'? There is no ad, there is just a hashtag. And then there's the 'ah! ah!' moment and they figure it out and they take a picture and they post it and that's the message, it's there, question what you see. Not everything you see is what it looks like.

Resistance is Female is a temporary campaign, which morphed into the Keep Fighting subverting campaign run by one of its members and is specific to the context of New York and its concentrated creative capital. Its members remain connected with a broader network of subvertisers and socially motivated artists within and beyond the city and country who continue to coalesce in ephemeral interventions on the street. The impact of such ephemeral campaigns is difficult to measure, but can be elaborated in relation to their inspirations, collaborations, and contributions to the broader fight against social injustice.

Going back to the four key debates in culture jamming (incorporation, play, participation, and law), a few observations follow. The end of the campaign and the beginning of its sequel suggest that incorporation of Resistance is Female did not take place. Both campaigns remain run by grassroots members and do not engage with commercial entities or messages. The campaign was playful, engaging with various messages of intersectional feminism and ranging from visual reminders of gender empowerment to consent declarations, iconic representations of female fighters, surreal images of warrior women, mournful depictions of protesters, as well as graphic designs of girl characters. As discussed above, the campaign engaged artists and street artists in the production and distribution of political artworks in public space for the first time. Finally, regarding the fine lines of the law, the choice of phone booths offered the campaign a grey area. In defining what they do as civil disobedience, Abe told me:

> All this stuff to get into the phone booths is readily available at a hardware store so it's a grey area. Do I think I'm doing something not legal? Eh, there's no law in the books that says I can't do it. But generally what I like to do, as a crew what we like to do is there's a lot of booths that don't have ads in them and we'll hit those up first because we're not taking money out of anyone's pockets or making trouble for them in that sense. Whether they're going to be like 'we're going after those guys, they're fucking up our cash flow'. That's one thing I'm trying to be clear consciousness of. I mean, there are times when that does happen, when it's like a really good spot, you know? But those really good spots actually don't last very long.

Up to the time of interviews, Abe and other subvertisers running the campaign had never been interrogated by the police during an adbusting expedition. Yet the possibility is always there, and the risk is taken.

Questions for Future Case Studies

Deciding to explore anti-consumerism, one is faced with a fluid and fluctuating field of ideologies and practices and should thus proceed with caution: first, identifying the agents stirring the action, as the kinds of opportunities and challenges will change accordingly and second, identifying the targets of the action, in order to explore the direct and indirect potential aims and consequences of the action. More specifically, we can question:

- How can we locate specific histories of anti-consumerism in different national contexts?
- What are the anti-consumerist discourses emerging across media platforms?
- What agencies are involved in resistance through culture jamming? Who is doing the jamming? Who are they targeting?
- How do incorporation, play, participation, and the law play out in a specific culture jamming campaign?
- How are targets of culture jamming responding?
- What kind of rhetorical strategies are being used by culture jammers?
- To what extent can anti-consumerist agents set the news agenda? How are acts of culture jamming framed in media discourses?
- How can humour be a useful strategy for subverting hegemonic discourses or propagating counter-hegemonic ones?
- To what extent can opportunities for participation in culture jamming engage citizens in further campaigning?
- How does civil disobedience appear in contemporary subvertising activism and what are the arguments for a legal defence based on UN guidance and the national context?

Conclusion

Anti-consumerism started as a response to mass consumerism enabled by post-Fordism in advanced western capitalist societies. It rebels against the 'culture-ideology of consumerism' (Sklair, 2002), which normalizes the freedom of transnational corporations and the rise of the transnational capitalist class at the expense of the unfreedom of outsourced labour and the rise of further global underclasses. Anti-consumerist activism is not the only force in the fight for equality. Anti-corporate activism, financial justice movements focusing on debt and tax, as well as environmental activism all coalesce in the defence of economic, social, and environmental justice. Over the past few decades, anti-consumerist resistance practices have been variant, from individuals refraining from branded consumption for a day or a year to collectives working to promote alternative economic practices and counter-hegemonic narratives.

Broadly speaking, culture jamming is a genre of creative activism characterized by subversive tactics, alternative cultures, and an anti-consumerist ethos. 'Semiological guerillas', 'semiotic Robin Hoods' and culture jammers protest against advertising and mass consumerism. For Adbusters founder Kalle Lasn (2000), advertising is a form of visual or mental pollution. Culture jamming is a response to promotional culture, 'an elastic category' that 'accommodates a multitude of subcultural practices' (Dery, 1993). Whether through individual acts or organized group activities, citizens in urban centres of several countries have been protesting against advertising on street walls, bus stops, and underground transport advertising panels, but also lobbying their mayors and governments to take regulatory action. As playful protest, subvertising engages in rhetorical appropriation of advertising to articulate a critique of its power through the interweaving of humour and justice.

In the early 1980s, Negativland coined the term 'culture jamming'. Almost four decades later, band member Mark Hosler expresses concerns with the present state of the phenomenon in an interview with a local alternative newsweekly:

> 'The whole idea of culture-jamming was to demonstrate things like "The media lies!" and "This is fake news,"' says (Mark) Hosler. 'But what we were really doing was punching up – speaking truth to power, as they say – trying to get people to look at things in a different way, trying to create a more educated, thoughtful, compassionate, kinder, better world. In our own weird-ass way... I think a lot of the people who use culture-jamming techniques now are ... doing things to manipulate people, not enlighten them. And I think, "My god, that's not what Negativland was doing."' (Moyer, 2019)

Hosler talks about the way in which culture jamming has been diverted from its original counter-hegemonic target of speaking back to corporate (US) media and into myriad directions, including towards hegemonic ends. This is a common concern among academics too who for over a decade have continued to bring attention to the possible folding of creative anti-consumerist resistance within the dough of neoliberal capitalism – the way in which counterculture is recuperated within consumer culture is now obvious from the commodification of Frida Kahlo to strategies of corporate greenwashing.

Yet the ideological oscillation between hegemony and counter-hegemony plays out differently in different contexts, with different scenarios and players. To embrace or dismiss culture jamming as neoliberal child's play is to assume that consumerism and anti-consumerism are absolute opposites; this position does not allow for a reflexive look into the cultural economy of anti-consumerism, as Littler (2005) reminds us. It also does not bode well for the realities and ambivalences of everyday lives of anarchists that Portwood-Stacer (2012) brings to our attention. Subvertising is similarly susceptible to the dynamics of ambivalence in promotional culture. Yet to point to its incorporation into promotional culture is to ignore the fact that every so often, for a few minutes, activists put their bodies and freedoms on the line to reach into that bus stop advertising panel, remove the advertisement, and replace it with a subvertisement before walking away. Subvertising often draws on humour, but that does not always mean that it is a joke lightly taken. There are different ethics of humour and different audience responses to that. So that the joke is not lightly taken, some scholars propose engaging audiences in the production of culture jams. Being part of the process of producing anti-consumerist discourses can empower audiences, enhance their participation, and engage them in critical pedagogy. To conclude, to inquire into anti-consumerism is to accept the ambivalence of neoliberal culture, but struggle to find productive alternatives by teasing out historical and ideological frameworks of a phenomenon, inquire into its agency and question its approach to justice.

Notes

1. This term is possibly coined by Banksy whose exhibition Turf War in 2003 included the following: 'Our culture is obsessed with brands and branding. I'm taking the idea of branding back to its original roots, which is cattle branding. I call it Brandalism' (quoted in Ellsworth-Jones, 2012: 93).
2. https://markdery.com/books/culture-jamming-hacking-slashing-and-sniping-in-the-empire-of-signs-2/ (22 April 2020).
3. www.disruptnow.org/wp-content/uploads/2021/04/UmbertoEco_Towards-a-Semiological-Guerrilla-Warfare.pdf (22 April 2020).
4. https://markdery.com/books/culture-jamming-hacking-slashing-and-sniping-in-the-empire-of-signs-2/ (17 April 2020).
5. www.mobygames.com/game/angry-bergs (22 April 2020).
6. https://subvertisers-international.net/2017/03/rap-grenoble-burying-of-prospectus-covering-of-ads-and-wandering-of-clowns-grenoble-france/ (29 April 2020).
7. https://adage.com/article/special-report-book-of-tens-2011/influential-players-marketing/231511 (4 May 2020).
8. Adbusters created a poster, which in an early oral history of the Occupy movement is considered to have launched the movement to the public on Twitter through the hashtag #OccupyWallStreet. (www.vanityfair.com/news/2012/02/occupy-wall-street-201202, 4 May 2020).

9. https://adage.com/article/special-report-book-of-tens-2011/influential-players-marketing/231511 (4 May 2020).
10. Public Ad Campaign is the project under which Jordan Seiler works on writing, artwork, organising, lectures, and through which he generally advocates for a more democratic use of public space by challenging outdoor advertising and creating opportunities for public communication (http://daily.publicadcampaign.com/ accessed 17 May 2020).
11. https://subvertisers-international.net/2018/03/madrid-sticker-attack/ (5 May 2020).
12. www.deboulonneurs.org/ (7 May 2020).
13. I interviewed subvertisers in the UK, US, Germany, France, Spain, Australia, and Brazil between 2016–18 with regards to their personal histories, motivations, practices, connections and opinions on advertising and its transformations.
14. kyle prefers to avoid writing conventions and does not capitalize his name, as he explains in a section called 'note on style': 'i just write how i want to write—i'm trying to express myself after all, not a set of grammatical expectations' (magee, 2016: 16). In respect to his choice, I also do not capitalize his name.
15. https://antipub.org/mobilisations/journee-contre-la-pub/ (11 May 2020).
16. https://ap.ohchr.org/documents/dpage_e.aspx?si=A/69/286 (11 May 2020).
17. In 2011, authorities decided to decrease the amount of advertising in the streets of Paris by 1/3 and to ban all advertising within 50 meters of school gates (www.theguardian.com/world/2011/jun/22/paris) (10 May 2020).
18. https://ap.ohchr.org/documents/dpage_e.aspx?si=A/69/286 (11 May 2020).
19. The Gender Wage Gap 2016: Earnings Differences by Gender, Race, and Ethnicity. Available: https://iwpr.org/publications/gender-wage-gap-2016-earnings-differences-gender-race-ethnicity/ (20 May 2020).

EIGHT
CONCLUSION

So What?

What constitutes activism through consumption? In order to reclaim any possibilities of resistance and change within promotional culture, I have defined consumer activism as a set of practices that extends beyond ethical consumerism, beyond boycotts, and beyond culture jams. It includes buying or not buying products for ethical, environmental, or religious reasons, participating in alternative economic practices, holding businesses accountable, advocating for social and environmental justice, and practising minimal or mindful consumption, or anti-consumerism. How has research previously captured such an intricate set of interconnected and disparate everyday practices? How has consumer activism been analysed in relation to media activism? How has it been conceptualized within studies of promotional culture? This book has provided responses to these questions and illustrated the disconnections and gaps through an interdisciplinary review of the literature, a reflection on methodologies, and discussion of original case studies.

Consumer Activism argues against narratives of 'consumer activist solutionism' which suggest that all political action can be mediated by the marketplace. Specifically focusing on nationalism in relation to race and ethnicity, gender in relation to feminism, and environmentalism, I present a plethora of perspectives to question the affordances and limitations of consumer activism as perceived across disciplines. What we see are persisting contradictions. In relation to nationalism, there are campaigns aiming to regulate citizens ('buy national'), at the same time as there are campaigns to represent communities ('buy black') and resist oppression ('yellow economic circle'). Connected to gender, there are consumer activism campaigns fighting against sexism (#GrabYourWallet), as there are advertising campaigns promoting feminism and LGBTQ justice (#ActForLove). Stemming from environmental concerns, there are myriads of examples of green consumerism (from recycled underwear to recently launched iPhones powered by recycled earth elements) while e-waste is becoming the fastest growing form of domestic waste. There are no easy conclusions or solutions when it comes to consumer activism. Yet while promotional culture makes its possibilities swing like a pendulum from the direction of recursion to that of resistance, I suggest that we do not rush to dismiss practices of consumer activism. That being said, it is important to underscore again that while I call it 'consumer' activism I do not centre or privilege 'the consumer', but I aim to acknowledge and appraise the centrality and impact of consumer practices in contemporary culture.

Practices of consumer activism are mobilized for social justice struggles and can play important roles in raising awareness for causes, raising funds for social movements, as well as promoting more just and sustainable uses of the marketplace. Furthermore, including actions that target advertising to the realm of consumer activism allows for its comprehensive conceptualization. As advertising has seeped further into societies and self-branding is increasingly encouraged across our communicative practices, we cannot ignore the power of promotional culture. Hence, to make sense of practices that constitute activism through consumption, it is imperative to include practices that question advertising as a culture that promotes consumption. The battle over meaning is also a battle for our futures. If advertising sells 'wokeness', 'feminism', and 'sustainability', what is the role of consumers beyond subscribing to that ideology? Their role is to remain critical of simplified solutions to social change. Emergent movements targeting advertising draw on consumer activism for change. Stop Funding Hate in the UK is a campaign 'to make hate unprofitable' by mobilizing consumers to call out advertisers who fund newspapers that promote hate speech. Stop Funding Hate listed 'five reasons to be hopeful in 2021'; among these, they write that 'the movement for ethical advertising is gaining momentum'.[1] Of course, this is not the result of individual consumer action, but rather orchestrated campaigns from collectives and organizations. Yet consumers have a part to play.

Why do we need to make sense of consumer activism urgently? Primarily, because of the state of the environment, and then because of the increasing centrality of promotional culture in all aspects of social life from gender and race relations to childhood and public wellbeing. Paying particular attention to history, ideology, agency, and justice, case studies of consumer activism can illustrate productive pathways to social and environmental change. Before commencing such explorations, one should question what one knows, what remains underexplored, and how to take to the task. Balancing optimism with analyses of the power of promotional culture requires critical methodological design, focusing on practices, but recognizing and analysing structures and contextual dynamics. It also involves questioning existing knowledge as produced within hierarchies that privilege global North agents and narratives. In this chapter, I outline a summary of debates in relation to markets, consumers, and media technologies, as well as the location of resistance within promotional culture, before concluding this book with some final reflections.

Summary of Debates: Markets, Consumers, and Media Technologies

Within promotional culture, there is more celebration and less criticism regarding the political potential of markets, consumers, and media technologies. Within studies in the social sciences and humanities, there is more critical appraisal (a balance of theory and evidence that evaluates the extent to which consumer activism is powerful), suggesting that consumer activism is susceptible to individual action, corporate takeover of social change, and simplification of causes. Of course, there are significant qualitative differences among interdisciplinary approaches, many of which specifically suggest that we do not rush to label contemporary consumer activism as apolitical (Heldman, 2017; Mukherjee and Banet-Weiser, 2012; Stolle and Micheletti, 2015). Its politics are there, but they depend on context. This section provides a sketch of the broad debates and arguments of the book.

First, some background for inspiration. As Phaedra Pezzullo suggests, we have to make 'a leap of faith and to try to bring about a more sustainable future … no solution can be pure and … inaction is the only response that will guarantee further loss and devastation from global ecological disasters' (2011: 137). Similarly, Julie Doyle argues that we need collective efforts to reduce consumption, that '[t]he energy and carbon intensive practices of consumerist societies, and the commodity chains which mask these processes … need to be made more visible, and actively reduced, by individuals, societies, businesses and governments' (2011: 142). Finally, as Kim Humphery argues, '[i]n interpreting and reinterpreting what consumerism is and how it is maintained over time, we in fact make and remake our understanding of the individual and collective action needed to reinvent current forms of economic and social life' (2010: 156). These three statements capture the rationale behind this book and its main argument. Considering consumer activism across time and space allows us to trace continuity and change in the histories of our societies. It allows us to remember that consumption within promotional culture will always seem like not enough, and, as Patrick Murphy succinctly put it, we will always be 'encouraged to save the whales even as … [we are] invited to eat all of the fish' (2021: 194). The alternative, as Miriam Meissner imagines it, is that 'narratives would need to account for the ways in which "too much" correlates with capital accumulation' (2019: 197). We have to account for practices that are working towards more inclusive, sustainable, and just futures, and it cannot be disputed that consumer activism includes practices that do precisely that.

To what extent are markets arenas for change? The market, as Margaret Willis and Juliet Schor write, is 'similar to all other sites of social practice, is a space of contestation and change, where there may be structural imbalances of power but not preordained outcomes' (2012: 168). We see this all the time. Promotional industries play a key part in the direction of narratives of change towards the market. Whether it is race or gender equality or environmental sustainability, advertisers promote change as an integral part of corporate practice. Yet 'carewashing' in the post-pandemic age, alongside 'wokewashing', 'pinkwashing', and 'greenwashing', persist as corporate communication remains removed (and often disconnected) from corporate practice. The example of Coach slashing unwanted products unveiled by an influencer while advocating for sustainability illustrates this.[2] Chapter 4 problematizes the involvement of advertisers in issues of gender equality and highlights tensions in relation to definitions of feminist subjects, histories, and struggles. We also see market actors taking a stand against consumer holidays such as Black Friday with businesses in the UK ranging from independent retailers[3] to large high street staples like Next and Marks & Spencer[4] deciding to boycott this in 2021.[5] Chapter 5 discusses the paradox of green consumption in relation to smartphones where the only truly sustainable solution is repairing existing commodities and reducing consumption, rather than choosing an ethical option (though there are some). Chapter 7 discusses the ideological ambivalence of culture jamming and subvertising. We constantly come up against advertising outdoors and in digital spaces. In outdoor spaces particularly, advertising tends to emulate subvertising practices. Here is an example. One autumn during an afternoon walk in London, I came across an advertisement for a pizza restaurant chain that was stencilled on the pavement through water pressure (Figure 8.1).

Figure 8.1 London, 28 October 2018

Photograph taken by author.

Such forms of temporary advertising fight for our attention. Whether through communication campaigns or actions resembling consumer activism, market actors are promotional agents with an interest in social and environmental change. As Keith Brown (2019) suggests, we cannot abandon the idea that markets are potential arenas for change, and that we should pay attention to the supply chains of markets for ethically labelled goods and to the emotional processes that connect consumers to these ethical markets. Consumers are typically the key agents of change within of the literature on consumer activism.

To what extent are consumers agents of change? One important contribution of this book is the identification of agents of consumer activism beyond consumers. Corporations, as outlined above, but also promotional intermediaries such as celebrities, anti-consumerist intermediaries such as subvertisers, and collectives working around alternative consumption as well as alternatives to advertising practices are all agents of consumer activism. Consumers engaging in politics through the marketplace have been called 'caring' (Littler, 2009), 'compassionate' (Richey and Ponte, 2011), 'conscious' (Willis and Schor, 2012), and 'contentious' (Minocher, 2019). The choice of terms always signals the politics undertaken by consumers as understood by these scholars. 'Caring' and 'compassionate' consumers care for others while caring for themselves, thus the politics behind the causes they support are often blurred or simplified. This is highlighted in Chapter 6, as it is often observed in celebrity advocacy and humanitarianism appeals where consumers are called upon to 'save' distant others through 'simple' ways such as shopping. 'Conscious' consumers tend to be politically active within and beyond the marketplace. Finally, 'contentious' consumers are increasingly becoming more prominent within what Douglas Holt (2016) identifies as 'crowdcultures' which seek to influence the ideologies and practices of brands. 'Contentious' consumers can collectively rebel both for and against progressive political aims in support of social movements. Chapter 3 demonstrates how consumer activism can be a two-sided coin, flipped for social justice aims (e.g. 'buy black' to support Black Lives Matter or 'buy yellow' to support Hong Kong businesses that supported the Anti-Extradition Law Amendment Bill movement) or against them (e.g. 'buy blue' to support Blue Lives Matter or 'buy blue' to support businesses which supported the police and suppression of the Hong Kong uprisings). Beyond consumers, collectives are also significant players in contemporary consumer activism. Chapter 7 discusses how subvertisers operate both as individuals and as collectives. There are emergent examples of collective action online (e.g. Sleeping Giants) and offline (e.g. AdFree Cities) that raise attention to the centrality of how advertising and promotional culture impact citizens in relation to social change.

To what extent do media technologies enhance consumer activism? This question deserves further interrogation, particularly in relation to the growth of the digital economy (Jordan, 2020). Connecting with relevant research on media activism, this book recognizes and reinforces the importance of practice within explorations of resistance in promotional culture. Chapter 2 provides a theoretical framework for analysing the relationship between consumer activism and media technologies, based on ecologies, publicities, and algorithms. Chapter 3 discusses how the Yellow Economic Circle in support of the Anti-Extradition Law Amendment Bill Movement relied on digitally enabled consumer activism. As Francis Lee and Ivy Fong (2021) argue, the idea of this form of consumer activism was co-developed by movement participants. Without movement participants, the Yellow Economic Circle would have been a contentious and ephemeral marketing campaign that would yield under the financial pressure of mainland China. This is not to suggest that the Yellow Economic Circle can be separated from the outcomes of the broader movement that did not manage to curb China's law making to police Hong Kong through Beijing. Yet the way in which digital media were used by Hong Kong people for protest purposes highlights a complex interplay between people, consumption, and technology in the shaping of social change. Chapter 5 highlights the environmental footprint of smartphones and the largely limited sustainable options available, where planned obsolescence and even ethical alternatives are all destined to become e-waste. Yet media technologies can and do play a part in the information, communication, and organization of social struggles and their potential can be measured in relation to media ecologies (changes in the media and communications environment), publicities (ideological information and communication), and responsibilities (appeals to individual, collective, or corporate action).

So how can we recognize consumer activism practices towards inclusive, sustainable, and just futures? First, we need to identify the agents and the practices they advocate and consider their communication and actions historically and in context. Second, we need to interrogate consumer activism ideologically in relation to its politics and promotional culture. To do so, we can draw from an extensive toolkit of methodological approaches from qualitative to mixed methods and be inspired by studies that have previously engaged with various strategical perspectives to respond to the ever-changing phenomenon of consumer activism. Every chapter includes a methodological review of the interdisciplinary literature presented and invites scholars to undertake new research on relevant topics. To highlight the possibilities of resistance within promotional culture, the next section reiterates the definition, urgency, and practices of consumer activism practices.

Consumer Activism and Beyond: Resistance Practices in Promotional Culture

How does a broad definition of consumer activism fare in relation to the powers of promotional culture? Consumer activism practices can be limited in the wake of 'woke' advertising or when considering the volume of 'green' consumerism. It can also be limited in the face of hybrid promotional culture that takes cues from subvertising practices and further infuses public spaces with advertising messages. The definition of consumer activism that this book presents is wide-ranging and includes practices such as boycotting, 'buycotting', engaging in alternative economic practices, lobbying businesses or governments, practising minimal or mindful consumption, and targeting advertising. This might sound like an optimistic stance in the face of hypercommercialism and chameleon-style promotional culture. For example, can we consider Mancunians' responses to 86 grey advertising boxes installed in the city in the autumn of 2021 a form of consumer activism? Manchester residents photographed, fly-posted and drew on the advertising boxes that they found invasive.[6] Why call pedestrians who rebelled against advertising 'consumer activists'? My aim is not to argue that agency (capacity to change things) is only within the realm of consumption and promotional culture. I believe that considering ourselves citizens first is the only way to claim and exercise political agency. However, in a world where consumption is increasingly inseparable from everyday life, connecting forms of practices that resist mass consumerism and omnipresent advertising can help illustrate the connections between these and create a space for broader dialogue about the pervasiveness of promotional culture.

The urgency of making these connections also lies in the establishment of the 'digital' in the realms of work, play, and (mostly due to the COVID-19 pandemic) everything else in between. Digital environments are largely unregulated and increasingly susceptible to overt and covert advertising. Undercover or 'stealth' marketing is not a new phenomenon (e.g. product placement on media programmes is a traditional form of this), but it has bloomed in the age of digital media. Mara Einstein (2016) discusses 'native advertising' (advertising hidden within publishers' websites where publishers become advertisers), 'content marketing' (advertising made to look like something other than advertising where advertisers are publishers), and the rise of 'programmatic advertising' (the automated buying and selling of online advertising). In this context, Einstein revisits the myth of consumer empowerment in relation to 'brand evangelism' (the myth that brands repeat: consumers own and control the brand). The myth of 'brand evangelism' is powerful and limits the intention, imagination, and action that consumers take in response to social change. Similarly, Veronica Barassi (2020) talks about the 'data reductionism' of computer systems and algorithms, where human experience is denigrated and simplified, stereotyped, and exposed; Barassi identifies the experience of everyday (family) life through targeted advertising. The political distractions of 'brand evangelism' and the emotional harms of 'data reductionism' are only some of the exposed symptoms of promotional culture in digital environments. Yet the potential of resistance should not be obliterated.

When considering the state of the environment, it is obvious that the push to mass consumerism persists and the COVID-19 pandemic has further intensified the production and discard of waste, particularly plastic (Adyel, 2020). Mehita Iqani (2020) focuses on the representation of waste within popular culture and argues that we need to see and comprehend wasteful consumption not as individual choice and responsibility, but as part of a larger ecology of individuals, collectives, consumer goods, the environment, the economy, and culture. Perhaps the most challenging case discussed in this book is that of the smartphone. There are two key modes of consumer activism in response to the environmental and social cost of smartphones; reduce your consumption by repairing (and recycling), or buy an ethical smartphone. Individual consumption is limited. This will not change the world. Reducing consumption is a step towards less waste. This is particularly true for e-waste (the fastest growing form of consumer waste), which, as Iqani writes, ends up becoming 'a public problem, as well as an individual problem for the worker tasked with burning away the plastic to get to the copper wire' (2020: 25). While mass consumerism is a well-established ideology and one that is difficult to escape, we must continue trying to imagine alternatives. We need to keep asking what we can do as critical individuals, collectives, neighbourhoods, and organizations: less screen time, more slow time, less plastic, more discussion? There can be no quick fixes when it comes to defending democracy, human rights, and social and environmental justice. However, a number of practices can be recommended.

First, it is important to reframe contemporary consumer activism as connected to advertising and promotional culture. By connecting resistance to consumption and advertising, we can respond to the dominance of the digital and its embrace of promotional culture, as well as to address the direct and indirect effects of advertising through a human rights framework. *At What Cost?* (Harrop, 2021) cites a number of rights (e.g. freedom of expression, freedom of information, right to privacy) and corresponding international human rights treaty articles (e.g. UN Convention on the Rights of the Child, 1989,[7] Articles 12, 13, and 17; International Covenant on Civil and Political Rights, 1966,[8] Article 17). Within this context, citizens can raise attention to violations of their human rights, market actors can be responsible for upholding ethical practice, and governments are responsible for complying with international human law treaties.

Second, it is important to consider our spending practices (particularly in global North and highly industrialized countries). Big tech behemoths such as Amazon shape promotional culture, preach 'brand evangelism' (you can choose whatever you want at the cheapest price on the market and get it delivered as soon as possible on your doorstep), and reproduce 'data reductionism' (if you like this, you will also like this, and while you are here buy this, because you need all these, and then you need some more). Alternatives to Amazon exist, and can be preferred on considerations of labour (Amazon workers have been trying to unionize against ongoing pressures and precarity[9]) and environmental justice (workers have been trying to convince Amazon to reduce its greenhouse gas emissions and take a more active stance against the climate crisis[10]). Considering how our spending can be used for social and environmental change also extends beyond consumption. The majority of social movements witness scarcity in funding, especially when they are not endorsed by philanthropists, celebrities, or brands. Financially supporting movements that matter to us (when possible) is another form of using economic practices for resistance. The same applies to media outlets. There are examples of cooperative journalism that offer clear and nuanced approaches to complex issues, but which rely on foundation or independent funding.

Overall, in addition to examples already mentioned in this book, resisting promotions, becoming acquainted with waste, financially endorsing selected markets, media, and movements are some of the ways in which consumer activism can shape resistance in promotional culture. Acknowledging context, agents, histories, and the targets of such resistant practices is what can separate potentially impactful change from ambiguous, diverted, and distracting actions susceptible to the push of promotional culture.

Activism and Consumption: Possibilities, Limitations, and Ambiguities

For some, activism and consumption are antonyms. For others, they are perfect partners. For citizens, they are a recurrent convergence in everyday life. Some are doing it unconsciously through purchases of products whose companies have propounded ethical commitments to people and planet, as well as profit. Some are doing it conscientiously, subscribing to ethical magazines, blogs, and influencers and developing their own habits in a manner that they consider as sustainable as their politics and pockets allow. For celebrities, the marriage of activism and consumption is a means to an end, a direct way of engaging consumers in processes of development and social change and advocating their way through celebrity status and industries. Some are doing it for the poor, for the suffering, for women, for children, for the environment. Routinely, they are doing it through simplifying causes and inviting consumers into social change in the arena of promotional culture. For market actors, consumption is activism par excellence; why not place your politics where your pocket is and pick your struggles? How can we make sense of such a complex ecology of consumer activism?

This book has built on work that questions the constitution of activism through consumption to locate the phenomenon within the contemporary context, to conceptualize it more broadly within promotional culture, and to provide a set of theoretical and methodological guidelines for future research. It has identified pockets of possibilities, limitations, and ambiguities in the manifestation of consumer activism as a set of sometimes-interconnected practices that focus on advertising and consumer culture to express and impact politics. Research has previously captured consumer activism in the presence or absence of connected political participation, in the commodification of care for distant others, in the tensions and distinctions it can produce, and in its ambivalence within neoliberal culture. Connecting these debates, I have provided a thorough conceptualization and contextualization of consumer activism in relation to nationalism (particularly race and ethnicity), gender (particularly feminism), and the environment. I have also provided an analysis of intermediaries of consumerism (celebrities) and anti-consumerism (subverisers). It is possible to practise consumer activism individually, collectively, digitally, discursively, and physically. Drawing on a media practice approach, I have suggested that we can explore ecologies (changes in the media and communications environment), publicities (ideological information and communication), and responsibilities (appeals to individual, collective, or corporate action) to make sense of consumer activism.

We know that contemporary digitally connected societies are inevitably societies of consumption. We know that the historical transformations have been variant and that consumerism has been experienced differently in different places. We know that our identities are gendered and racialized, and often inform our political and consumption decisions. We can draw some final thoughts from the discussions that have preceded. First, consumer activism remains a central phenomenon and practice of everyday and organizational politics and has accelerated in the context of the pandemic. COVID-19 has increased inequalities and polarization within societies and forced us further within promotional cultures increasingly experienced in a mediated manner. Second, consumer activism is typically located and analysed within the context of the global North, but it is important to question what it is and where it is beyond this in the global South too. This is not to find something 'fixed' and familiar to the western context, but to make visible the injustices at the level of production, distribution, and discard of commodities. It is also to analyse the aspirational narratives of mass consumerism and question the role of advertising within those. Third, there is a tendency to conceptualize consumer activism within progressive causes, but it is important to locate and unpack its complex interplay with regressive causes (e.g. those targeting women or minorities). This is particularly important in the context of backlash politics and increasing polarization. Fourth, consumer activism goes beyond an individualistic politics. Consumer activism is a range of individual and collective practices related to consumption and consumer culture that stem from a social, political, or environmental concern and begin with questioning processes of production, distribution, and discard of consumer products or services, or questioning the values of promotional communication. Consumer activism takes on a plethora of issues connected to social or environmental justice, ranging from trade and labour justice, corporate transparency, political accountability, identity politics, and commercially free lives.

This is not the first book about consumer culture and its politics, and it is probably not going to be the last. In advanced capitalist societies and societies that are underway to reach advanced consumer capitalism, consumer activism is offering an easy solution, a small step, an ordinary means to a larger political end. Consumer activism will continue to feature prominently within promotional culture. Its role within social and environmental struggles will also continue to carve out possibilities for a progressive politics. However, celebrations of 'consumer solutionism' are also likely to persist. We need to work against easy solutions and nuance consumption as practice. From buying local produce to support fragile economies to buying national to support post-pandemic economies and buying distantly produced goods to support fragile communities, the politics of consumption is significant in the consideration of contemporary forms of being political.

Notes

1. https://stopfundinghate.info/2020/12/31/five-reasons-to-be-hopeful-in-2021/ (24 November 2021).
2. www.buzzfeednews.com/article/tanyachen/a-viral-tiktok-can-be-the-first-step-of-real-policy-changes (20 November 2021).
3. www.theguardian.com/business/2021/nov/21/black-friday-largest-boycott-planned-by-independent-retailers (25 November 2021).
4. www.theguardian.com/business/2021/nov/20/black-friday-uk-john-lewis-asda-currys-deals-shortages (25 November 2021).
5. www.theguardian.com/business/2021/nov/21/black-friday-largest-boycott-planned-by-independent-retailers (25 November 2021).
6. www.theguardian.com/uk-news/2021/nov/24/theyre-in-the-way-manchester-rebels-against-grey-advertising-boxes (29 November 2021).
7. www.unicef.org.uk/what-we-do/un-convention-child-rights/ (6 June 2022).
8. www.ohchr.org/en/instruments-mechanisms/instruments/international-covenant-civil-and-political-rights (29 November 2021).
9. www.reuters.com/article/health-coronavirus-amazon-com-workers-in/how-big-unions-smooth-the-way-for-amazon-worker-protests-idINKBN22Y0AW?edition-redirect=in (29 November 2021).
10. https://amazonemployees4climatejustice.medium.com/ (29 November 2021).

APPENDIX

Anti-Consumerism in Documentaries

- *Advertising and the End of the World* (1998) Directed by Sut Jhally [Documentary]. USA: Media Education Foundation.
- *Advertising at the Edge of the Apocalypse* (2017) Directed by Sut Jhally [Documentary]. USA: Media Education Foundation.
- *Affluenza* (1997) Directed by John de Graaf [Documentary]. USA: KCTS Seattle and Oregon Public Broadcasting.
- *Bag It* (2010) Directed by Suzan Beraza [Documentary]. USA: Reel Thing.
- *Black Gold* (2006) Directed by Nick Francis and Marc Francis [Documentary] UK: Fulcrum Productions.
- *Consumed: Inside the Belly of the Beast* (2011) Directed by Richard Heap [TV movie]. UK: Slackjaw Film.
- *Consumerism and the Limits to Imagination* (2011) Directed by Sut Jhally [Documentary]. USA: Media Education Foundation.
- *Consuming Kids: The Commercialization of Childhood* (2008) Directed by Adriana Barbaro and Jeremy Earp [Documentary]. USA: Media Education Foundation.
- *Culture Jam: Hijacking Commercial Culture* (2001) Directed by Jill Sharpe [Documentary]. Canada/USA: Right to Jam Productions.
- *Czech Dream* (2004) Directed by Vít Klusák and Filip Remunda [Documentary, Comedy]. Czech Republic: Ceská Televize and others.
- *Exit through the Gift Shop: A Banksy Film* (2010) Directed by Banksy [Documentary]. UK: Paranoid Pictures.
- *Fault Lines: Made in Bangladesh* (2013) [Documentary]. USA: Al Jazeera.
- *Generation Wealth* (2018) Directed by Lauren Greenfield [Documentary]. USA: Evergreen Pictures.
- *Gran Superficie* (2005) Directed by ConsumeHastaMorir [Documentary]. Spain: Independent.
- *Just Eat It: A Food Waste Story* (2014) Directed by Grant Baldwin [Documentary]. Canada/UK/USA: Peg Leg Films.
- *Knock Off. Revenge on the Logo* (2004) Directed by Anette Baldauf and Katharina Weingartner [Documentary]. USA: First Run and Icarus Films.
- *Lightbulb Conspiracy* (2010) Directed by Cosima Dannoritzer [Documentary]. France/Spain: ARTE and others.
- *Logorama* (2009) Directed by François Alaux, Hervé de Crécy and Ludovic Houplain [Animation/ Short]. France: Autour de Minuit.

- *Mardi Gras: Made in China* (2005) Directed by David Redmon [Documentary]. USA: Carnivalesque Films.
- *Minimalism: A Documentary about the Important Things* (2015) Directed by Matt D'Avella [Documentary]. UK: Catalyst.
- *No Impact Man* (2009) Directed by Laura Gabbert and Justin Schein [Documentary]. USA: Eden Wurmfeld Films and Shadowbox Films Inc.
- *No Logo: Brands, Globalization & Resistance* (2003) Directed by Sut Jhally [Documentary]. USA: Media Education Foundation.
- *Reverend Billy and the Church of Stop Shopping* (2002) Directed by Dietmar Post and Lucía Palacios [Documentary]. Germany/USA/Spain: Play loud! Productions.
- *Shop'Til You Drop: The Crisis of Consumerism* (2009) Directed by Gene Brockhoff [Documentary]. USA: Media Education Foundation.
- *Skoros: Anti-Consumption in Crisis* (2016) Directed by Athina Souli [Documentary]. Greece: Independent production partly funded by Royal Holloway, University of London.
- *Subvertisers for London* (2019) Directed by Dog Section Press [Documentary]. Published under Creative Commons Attribution-NonCommercial 4.0 International Public Licence. Available: www.youtube.com/watch?v=zunPa9rGndg (12 March 2020).
- *The Overspent American: Why We Want What We Don't Need* (2004) Directed by Sut Jhally and Loretta Alper [Documentary]. USA: Media Education Foundation.
- *The Society of the Spectacle* (1974) Directed by Guy Debord [Documentary]. France: Simar Films.
- *The Story of Stuff* (2007) Directed by Louis Fox [Animation]. USA: Free Range Studios and others.
- *The True Cost* (2015) Directed by Andrew Morgan [Documentary]. Various: Life Is My Movie Entertainment Company in association with Untold Creative.
- *The Yes Men* (2003) Directed by Dan Ollman, Sarah Price and Chris Smith [Documentary]. USA: MGM.
- *The Yes Men Are Revolting* (2014) Directed by Andy Bichlbaum, Mike Bonanno and Laura Nix [Documentary]. Netherlands, Denmark, France, Germany, USA: Gebrueder Beetz Filmproduktion and others.
- *The Yes Men Fix the World* (2009) Directed by Andy Bichlbaum, Mike Bonanno and Kurt Engfehr [Documentary]. France, UK, USA: ARTE and others.
- *What Would Jesus Buy?* (2007) Directed by Rob VanAlkemade [Documentary]. USA: Palisades Pictures and others.

REFERENCES

Abbots, Emma-Jayne. 2015. 'The Intimacies of Industry'. *Food, Culture & Society* 18 (2): 223–43.

Abidin, Crystal. 2018. *Internet Celebrity: Understanding Fame Online*. Bingley: Emerald Publishing.

Abidin, Crystal, Dan Brockington, Michael K. Goodman, Mary Mostafanezhad, and Lisa Ann Richey. 2020. 'The Tropes of Celebrity Environmentalism'. *Annual Review of Environment and Resources* 45 (1): 387–410.

AbiGhannam, Niveen and Lucy Atkinson. 2016. 'Good Green Mothers Consuming Their Way through Pregnancy: Roles of Environmental Identities and Information Seeking in Coping with the Transition'. *Consumption Markets & Culture* 19 (5): 451–74.

Adams, Matthew and Jayne Raisborough. 2008. 'What Can Sociology Say About Fair Trade? Class, Reflexivity and Ethical Consumption'. *Sociology* 42 (6): 1165–82.

Adams, Matthew and Jayne Raisborough. 2010. 'Making a Difference: Ethical Consumption and the Everyday: Making a Difference'. *The British Journal of Sociology* 61 (2): 256–74.

Adewunmi, Bim. 2014. 'Band Aid 30: Clumsy, Patronising and Wrong in So Many Ways'. *The Guardian*, 11 November 2014. www.theguardian.com/world/2014/nov/11/band-aid-30-patronising-bob-geldof-ebola-do-they-know-its-christmas

Adyel, Tanveer M. 2020. 'Accumulation of Plastic Waste during COVID-19'. *Science* 369 (6509): 1314–15.

Ahmed, Sara. 2017. *Living A Feminist Life*. Durham, NC: Duke University Press.

Alberoni, Francesco. 2006. 'The Powerless "Elite": Theory and Sociological Research on the Phenomenon of the Stars'. In P. David Marshall (ed.) *The Celebrity Culture Reader*, 108–23. New York, NY: Routledge.

Albert. 2021 'Subtitles to Save the World'. Available: https://wearealbert.org/editorial/wp-content/uploads/sites/6/2021/09/albert-subtitle-report-2021.pdf

Alfredsson, Eva, Magnus Bengtsson, Halina Szejnwald Brown, Cindy Isenhour, Sylvia Lorek, Dimitris Stevis, and Philip Vergragt. 2018. 'Why Achieving the Paris Agreement Requires Reduced Overall Consumption and Production'. *Sustainability: Science, Practice and Policy* 14 (1): 1–5.

Allyn, Bobby. 2020. 'Apple Agrees To Pay $113 Million To Settle "Batterygate" Case Over iPhone Slowdowns'. *NPR*, 18 November.

Alter, Karen J and Michael Zürn. 2020. 'Conceptualising Backlash Politics'. *The British Journal of Politics and International Relations* 22 (4): 563–84.

Anderson, Benedict. 1991. *Imagined Communities*, 2nd ed. London: Verso Books.

Another Future is Possible. 2012. Available: http://rio20.net/wp-content/uploads/2012/02/Another-Future-is-Possible_english_web.pdf

Ariztia, Tomas, Dorothea Kleine, Roberto Bartholo, Graca Brightwell, Nurjk Agloni, and Rita Afonso. 2016. 'Beyond the "Deficit Discourse": Mapping Ethical Consumption Discourses in Chile and Brazil'. *Environment and Planning A: Economy and Space* 48 (5): 891–909.

Aronczyk, Melissa. 2013. 'Market(ing) Activism: Lush Cosmetics, Ethical Oil, and the Self-Mediation of Protest'. *JOMEC Journal* (4). http://doi.org/10.18573/j.2013.10256

Aronczyk, Melissa. 2021. 'Annals of Promotional Culture'. *Canadian Journal of Communication* 46 (1). https://doi.org/10.22230/cjc.2021v46n1a3923

Aronczyk, Melissa and Devon Powers. (eds.) 2010. *Blowing up the Brand: Critical Perspectives on Promotional Culture*. New York, NY: Peter Lang.

Aronczyk, Melissa, Lee Edwards, and Anu Kantola. 2017. 'Apprehending Public Relations as a Promotional Industry'. *Public Relations Inquiry* 6 (2): 139–55.

Atkinson, Joshua. 2003. 'Thumbing Their Noses at "The Man": An Analysis of Resistance Narratives about Multinational Corporations'. *Popular Communication* 1 (3): 163–80.

Atkinson, Lucy. 2014. 'Green Moms: The Social Construction of a Green Mothering Identity via Environmental Advertising Appeals'. *Consumption Markets & Culture* 17 (6): 553–72.

Atkinson, Matthew D. and Darin DeWitt. 2019. 'Does Celebrity Issue Advocacy Mobilize Issue Publics?' *Political Studies* 67 (1): 83–99.

Auriffeille, Deborah McCarthy. 2020. '"Before She Was Born, I Ate Cheerios and Beer for Dinner": A Qualitative Examination of Green Parenting in Lowcountry South Carolina'. *Humanity & Society* August, 0160597620943195.

Austin, Regina. 1994. '"A Nation of Thieves": Consumption, Commerce, and the Black Public Sphere', *Public Culture*, 7: 225–48.

Autio, Minna, Eva Heiskanen, and Visa Heinonen. 2009. 'Narratives of "Green" Consumers – the Antihero, the Environmental Hero and the Anarchist'. *Journal of Consumer Behaviour* 8 (1): 40–53.

Balsiger, Philip. 2010. 'Making Political Consumers: The Tactical Action Repertoire of a Campaign for Clean Clothes'. *Social Movement Studies* 9 (3): 311–29.

Banet-Weiser, Sarah. 2012a. *Authentic™: The Politics of Ambivalence in a Brand Culture*. New York, NY: New York University Press.

Banet-Weiser, Sarah. 2012b. '"Free Self Esteem Tools?": Brand Culture, Gender, and the Dove Real Beauty Campaign', in R. Mukherjee and S. Banet-Weiser (eds) *Commodity Activism: Cultural Resistance in Neoliberal Times*, 39–56. New York, NY: New York University Press.

Banet-Weiser, Sarah. 2018. *Empowered: Popular Feminism and Popular Misogyny*. Durham, NC: Duke University Press.

Banet-Weiser, Sarah, and Charlotte Lapsansky. 2008. 'RED Is the New Black: Brand Culture, Consumer Citizenship and Political Possibility'. *International Journal of Communication* 2: 1248–68.

Banet-Weiser, Sarah and Roopali Mukherjee. 2012. 'Introduction: Commodity Activism in Neoliberal Times', in Roopali Mukherjee and Sarah Banet-Weiser (eds.), *Commodity Activism: Cultural Resistance in Neoliberal Times*. New York, NY: New York University Press. pp. 1–22.

Barassi, Veronica. 2015. *Activism on the Web: Everyday Struggles against Digital Capitalism*. Oxon: Routledge.

Barassi, Veronica. 2020. *Child Data Citizen: How Tech Companies Are Profiling Us from before Birth*. Cambridge, MA: MIT Press.

Barnett, Clive, Paul Cloke, Nick Clarke, and Alice Malpass. 2011. *Globalizing Responsibility: The Political Rationalities of Ethical Consumption*. Chichester: Wiley-Blackwell.

Bay, Mia. 2015. 'Traveling Black/Buying Black: Retail and Roadside Accommodations during the Segregation Era'. In M. Bay and A. Fabian (eds) *Race and Retail: Consumption across the Color Line*, 15–33. New Brunswick, NJ: Rutgers University Press.

Bay, Mia and Ann Fabian. (eds) 2015. *Race and Retail: Consumption across the Color Line*. New Brunswick, NJ: Rutgers University Press.

Beck, Ulrich. 2004. 'Cosmopolitan Realism: On the Distinction between Cosmopolitanism in Philosophy and the Social Sciences'. *Global Networks*, 4 (2): 131–56.

Belkhir, Lotfi and Ahmed Elmeligi. 2018. 'Assessing ICT Global Emissions Footprint: Trends to 2040 & Recommendations'. *Journal of Cleaner Production* 177 (March): 448–63.

Bell, David and Joanne Hollows. 2011. 'From River Cottage to Chicken Run: Hugh Fearnley-Whittingstall and the Class Politics of Ethical Consumption'. *Celebrity Studies* 2 (2): 178–91.

Bell, Katherine. 2011. '"A Delicious Way to Help Save Lives": Race, Commodification, and Celebrity in Product (RED)'. *Journal of International and Intercultural Communication* 4 (3): 163–80.

Bennett, Elizabeth A. 2021. 'Consumer Activism, Sustainable Supply Chains, and the Cannabis Market'. In D. Corva and J. Meisel (eds) *The Routledge Handbook of Interdisciplinary Cannabis Research*, 192–200. London: Routledge.

Biccum, April. 2011. 'Marketing Development: Celebrity Politics and the "New" Development Advocacy'. *Third World Quarterly* 32 (7): 1331–46.

Billig, Michael. 1995. *Banal Nationalism*. London: Sage.

Billig, Michael. 2017. 'Banal Nationalism and the Imagining of Politics'. In M. Skey and M. Antonsich (eds) *Everyday Nationhood: Theorising Culture, Identity and Belonging after Banal Nationalism*, 307–12. Basingstoke: Palgrave.

Binkley, Sam and Jo Littler. 2008. 'Introduction: Cultural Studies and Anti-Consumerism: A Critical Encounter'. *Cultural Studies* 22 (5): 519–30.

Bite Back 2030. 2021. *Junk Food Marketing Exposé*. Available: https://biteback2030.com/sites/default/files/2021-02/Bite Back - Junk Food Marketing Expose (1).pdf (last accessed 4 October 2021).

Boström, Magnus and Mikael Klintman. 2019a. 'Mass Consumption and Political Consumerism', in Magnus Boström, Michele Micheletti, and Peter Oosterveer (eds.), *The Oxford Handbook of Political Consumerism*. Oxford: Oxford University Press. pp. 855–78

Boström, Magnus and Mikael Klintman. 2019b. 'Can We Rely on "Climate-Friendly" Consumption?' *Journal of Consumer Culture* 19 (3): 359–78.

Boström, Magnus, Michele Micheletti, and Peter Oosterveer (eds). 2019. *The Oxford Handbook of Political Consumerism*. Oxford: Oxford University Press.

Bote, Joshua. 2019. 'Lil Dicky's "Earth" Video Is Band Aid for the Internet'. *NPR*, 19 April 2019. Available: www.npr.org/2019/04/19/715140398/lil-dickys-earth-video-is-band-aid-for-the-internet?t_=%201574948680182 (last accessed 24 March 2022).

Bradshaw, Alan and Linda Scott. 2018. *Advertising Revolution: The Story of a Song, from Beatles Hit to Nike Slogan*. London: Repeater Books.

Braun, Joshua A., John D. Coakley, and Emily West. 2019. 'Activism, Advertising, and Far-Right Media: The Case of Sleeping Giants'. *Media and Communication* 7 (4): 68–79.

Brockington, Dan. 2014. *Celebrity Advocacy and International Development*. London: Routledge.

Brown, Keith. 2019. 'Ethical Consumption', in Frederick F. Wherry and Ian Woodward (eds.), *The Oxford Handbook of Consumption*. Oxford: Oxford University Press. pp , 541–59.

Brown, Nicole Marie. 2015. 'Freedom's Stock: Political Consumerism, Transnational Blackness and the Black Star Line'. *Critical Sociology* 41 (2): 237–48.

Brown, Nicole Marie. 2017. 'Bridge Leadership: Gendered Consumerism and Black Women's Political Power within Early 20th Century "Don't Buy" Campaigns'. *Sociological Focus* 50 (3): 244–60.

Brubaker, Rogers. 2020. 'Populism and Nationalism'. *Nations and Nationalism* 26 (1): 44–66.

Budabin, Alexandra Cosima. 2020. 'Caffeinated Solutions as Neoliberal Politics: How Celebrities Create and Promote Partnerships for Peace and Development'. *Perspectives on Politics* 18 (1): 60–75.

Budabin, Alexandra Cosima and Lisa Ann Richey. 2021. *Batman Saves the Congo: How Celebrities Disrupt the Politics of Development*. Minneapolis, MN: University of Minnesota Press.

Bulakh, Tetiana. 2017. 'Made in Ukraine: Consumer Citizenship during EuroMaidan Transformations'. In Abel Polese, Jeremy Morris, Emilia Pawłusz, and Oleksandra Seliverstova (eds) *Identity and Nation Building in Everyday Post-Socialist Life*, 73–90. London: Routledge.

Cairns, Kate, Josée Johnston, and Norah MacKendrick. 2013. 'Feeding the "Organic Child": Mothering through Ethical Consumption'. *Journal of Consumer Culture* 13 (2): 97–118.

Cammaerts, Bart. 2007. 'Jamming the Political: Beyond Counter-Hegemonic Practices'. *Continuum* 21 (1): 71–90.

Carby, Hazel V. (2019) *Imperial Intimacies: A Tale of Two Islands*. London: Verso.

Carducci, Vince. 2006. 'Culture Jamming: A Sociological Perspective', *Journal of Consumer Culture*, 6 (1): 116–38.

Carducci, Vince. 2021. 'Culture Jamming', in M. Baker, B.B. Blaagaard, H. Jones and L. Pérez-González (eds.), *The Routledge Encyclopaedia of Citizen Media*. Oxon: Routledge.

Carfagna, Lindsey B, Emilie A. Dubois, Connor Fitzmaurice, Monique Y. Ouimette, Juliet B. Schor, Margaret Willis, and Thomas Laidley. 2014. 'An Emerging Eco-Habitus: The Reconfiguration of High Cultural Capital Practices among Ethical Consumers'. *Journal of Consumer Culture* 14 (2): 158–78.

Carpentier, Nico, Rico Lie, and Jan Servaes. 2003. 'Community Media: Muting the Democratic Media Discourse?' *Continuum: Journal of Media & Cultural Studies* 17 (1): 51–68.

Carty, Victoria. 2002. 'Technology and Counter-Hegemonic Movements: The Case of Nike Corporation'. *Social Movement Studies* 1, 129–46.

Castelló, Enric and Sabina Mihelj. 2018. 'Selling and Consuming the Nation: Understanding Consumer Nationalism'. *Journal of Consumer Culture* 18 (4): 558–76.

Castells, Manuel, João Caraça, and Gustavo Cardoso (eds.). 2012. *Aftermath: The Cultures of the Economic Crisis*. Oxford: Oxford University Press.

Chakrabarty, Dipesh. 2000. *Provincializing Europe: Postcolonial Thought and Historical Difference*. Princeton, NJ: Princeton University Press.

Chan, Debby Sze Wan, and Pun Ngai. 2020. 'Economic Power of the Politically Powerless in the 2019 Hong Kong Pro-democracy Movement.' *Critical Asian Studies* 52 (1): 33–43.

Chan, Jenny, Mark Selden, and Pun Ngai. 2020. *Dying for an iPhone: Apple, Foxconn and the Lives of China's Workers*. London: Pluto Press.

Chapman, Simon. 1996. 'Civil Disobedience and Tobacco Control: The case of BUGA UP'. *Tobacco Control*, 5: 179–85.

Chasin, Alexandra. 2000. *Selling Out: The Gay and Lesbian Movement Goes to Market*. New York, NY: St. Martin's Press.

Chatterji, Mo. 2021. 'Repairing – Not Recycling – Is the First Step to Tackling Smartphone e-Waste'. *World Economic Forum*. 19 July 2021. Available: www.weforum.org/agenda/2021/07/repair-not-recycle-tackle-ewaste-circular-economy-smartphones (last accessed 24 March 2022).

Chatzidakis, Andreas and Michael S.W. Lee. 2012. 'Anti-Consumption as the Study of Reasons Against'. *Journal of Macromarketing* 33 (3): 190–203.

Chatzidakis, Andreas and Pauline Maclaran. 2020. 'Gendering Consumer Ethics'. *International Journal of Consumer Studies* 44 (4): 316–27.

Chatzidakis, Andreas, Jamie Hakim, Jo Littler, Catherine Rottenberg, and Lynne Segal. 2020. 'From Carewashing to Radical Care: The Discursive Explosions of Care during Covid-19'. *Feminist Media Studies* 20 (6): 889–95.

Cherrier, Helen. 2009. 'Anti-Consumption Discourses and Consumer-Resistant Identities'. *Journal of Business Research* 62 (2): 181–90.

Chouliaraki, Lilie. 2012. 'The Theatricality of Humanitarianism: A Critique of Celebrity Advocacy'. *Communication and Critical/Cultural Studies* 9 (1): 1–21.

Chouliaraki, Lilie. 2013. *The Ironic Spectator: Solidarity in the Age of Post-Humanitarianism*. Cambridge: Polity.

Clark, Danae. 1991. 'Commodity Lesbianism'. *Camera Obscura: Feminism, Culture, and Media Studies* 9 (1–2 (25–26)): 181–201.

Cohan, Daniel. 2020. 'COVID-19 Shutdowns Are Clearing the Air, but Pollution Will Return as Economies Reopen'. *The Conversation* 8 May 2020. Available: http://theconversation.com/covid-19-shutdowns-are-clearing-the-air-but-pollution-will-return-as-economies-reopen-134610 (last accessed 24 March 2022).

Cohen, Lizabeth. 2003. *A Consumers' Republic: The Politics of Mass Consumption in Postwar America*. New York, NY: Vintage Books.

Colli, Francesca. 2020. 'Indirect Consumer Activism and Politics in the Market'. *Social Movement Studies* 19 (3): 249–67.

Connell, R.W. and James W. Messerschmidt. 2005. 'Hegemonic Masculinity: Rethinking the Concept'. *Gender & Society* 19 (6): 829–59.

Constantine, Stephen. 1987. 'The Buy British Campaign of 1931'. *European Journal of Marketing* 21 (4): 44–59.

Coolsaet, Brendan. 2020. *Environmental Justice: Key Issues*. London: Routledge.

Copeland, Lauren and Boulianne, Shelley. 2022. 'Political consumerism: A meta-analysis,' *International Political Science Review*, 3(1): 3–18.

Corey, Amy M. 2019. 'Love is love is love is love: From flaktivism to consumer activism in LGBTQ+ communities', *Queer Studies in Media & Popular Culture*, 4 (2): 117–37.

Couldry, Nick. 2004. 'Theorising Media as Practice', *Social Semiotics* 14 (2): 115–32.

Couldry, Nick. 2012. *Media, Society, World: Social Theory and Digital Media Practice*. Cambridge: Polity Press.

Couldry, Nick. 2015. 'Why Celebrity Studies Needs Social Theory (and Vice Versa)'. *Celebrity Studies* 6 (3): 385–88.

Couldry, Nick and Tim Markham. 2007. 'Celebrity Culture and Public Connection: Bridge or Chasm?' *International Journal of Cultural Studies* 10 (4): 403–21.

Couldry, Nick, Sonia Livingstone, and Tim Markham. 2010. *Media Consumption and Public Engagement: Beyond the Presumption of Attention*. Basingstoke: Palgrave.

Crenshaw, Kimberlé. 2017. *On Intersectionality: Essential Writings*. New York, NY: The New Press.

Cronin, Anne M. (2018) *Public Relations Capitalism: Promotional Culture, Publics and Commercial Democracy*. Basingstoke: Palgrave.

Cuadras-Morató Xavier and Josep Maria Raya. 2015. 'Boycott or Buycott? Internal Politics and Consumer Choices'. *B.E. Journal of Economic Analysis & Policy* 16 (1): 185–218.

Cupples, Julie and Kevin Glynn. 2019. 'The Celebritization of Indigenous Activism: Tame Iti as Media Figure'. *International Journal of Cultural Studies* 22 (6): 770–87.

D'Alisa, Giacomo, Federico Demaria, and Giorgos Kallis (eds). 2015. *Degrowth: A Vocabulary for a New Era*. London: Routledge.

Daily, Lisa A. 2019. '"We Bleed for Female Empowerment": Mediated Ethics, Commodity Feminism, and the Contradictions of Feminist Politics'. *Communication and Critical/Cultural Studies* 16 (2): 140–58.

Dal Gobbo, Alice and Francesca Forno. 2020. 'Shopping for a Sustainable Future: The Promises of a Collectively Planned Consumption'. In Francesca Forno and Richard R. Weiner (eds) *Sustainable Community Movement Organizations: Solidarity Economies and Rhizomatic Practices*, 72–88. London: Routledge.

Daley, Patricia. 2013. 'Rescuing African Bodies: Celebrities, Consumerism and Neoliberal Humanitarianism'. *Review of African Political Economy* 40 (137): 375–93.

Davis, Corey B., Mark Glantz, and David R. Novak. 2016. '"You Can't Run Your SUV on Cute. Let's Go!" Internet Memes as Delegitimizing Discourse'. *Environmental Communication* 10 (1): 62–83.

Day, Amber. 2018. 'Throwing Our Voices: Ventriloquism as New Media Activism'. *Media, Culture & Society* 40 (4): 617–28.

de Grazia, Victoria. 1996. Introduction. In V. de Grazia and E. Furlough (eds) *The Sex of Things: Gender and Consumption in Historical Perspective*, 1–10. Berkeley, CA: University of California Press.

Debord, Guy. [1967] 1994. *Society of the Spectacle*. Translated by D. Nicholson-Smith. New York, NY: Zone Books.

Dekeyser, Thomas. 2019. 'Subvertising: On the Life and Death of Advertising Power'. PhD thesis, University of Southampton.

DeLaure, Marilyn and Moritz Fink (eds) 2017. *Culture Jamming: Activism and the Art of Cultural Resistance*. New York, NY: New York University Press.

Deleuze, Gilles and Félix Guattari. 1987. *A Thousand Plateaux. Capitalism and Schizophrenia*. Minneapolis, MN: University of Minnesota Press.

Della Porta, Donatella and Diani, Mario. 2006. *Social movements: An introduction* (2nd ed.). Oxford: Blackwell.

Denisova, Anastasia. 2021. *Fashion Media and Sustainability: Encouraging Ethical Consumption via Journalists and Influencers*. A CAMRI Policy Brief. London: University of Westminster Press.

Dery, Mark. [1993] 2010. *Culture Jamming: Hacking, Slashing, and Sniping in the Empire of Signs*. Open Magazine pamphlet. Available: https://markdery.com/books/culture-jamming-hacking-slashing-and-sniping-in-the-empire-of-signs-2 (last accessed 22 April 2020).

Dewey, Amanda M. and Dana R. Fisher. 2019. 'Linking Environmental Sustainability and Consumption'. In Frederick F. Wherry and Ian Woodward (eds) *The Oxford Handbook of Consumption*, 576–91. Oxford: Oxford University Press.

Dog Section Press. 2019. *Subvertisers for London*. Available at: www.youtube.com/watch?v=zunPa9rGndg (last accessed 8 May 2020).

Dosekun, Simidele. 2015. For Western Girls Only? *Feminist Media Studies* 15 (6): 960–75.

Dosekun, Simidele. 2020. *Fashioning Postfeminism: Spectacular Femininity and Transnational Culture*. Urbana, IL: University of Illinois Press.

Doudaki, Vaia, Angeliki Boubouka, Lia-Paschalia Spyridou, and Christos Tzalavras. 2016. 'Dependency, (Non)liability and Austerity News Frames of Bailout Greece'. *European Journal of Communication* 31(4): 426–45.

Doyle, Julie. 2011. *Mediating Climate Change*. Farnham: Ashgate.

Doyle, Julie. 2016. 'Celebrity Vegans and the Lifestyling of Ethical Consumption'. *Environmental Communication* 10 (6): 777–90.

Driessens, Olivier. 2013. 'Celebrity Capital: Redefining Celebrity Using Field Theory'. *Theory and Society* 42 (5): 543–60.

Du Bois, W.E.B. 1903. *The Souls of Black Folk*. Chicago, IL: A.C. McClurg Press.

Duchesne, Sophie. 2018. 'Who's Afraid of Banal Nationalism?' *Nations and Nationalism* 24 (4): 841–56.

Duffy, Brooke Erin and Jefferson Pooley. 2019. 'Idols of Promotion: The Triumph of Self-Branding in an Age of Precarity'. *Journal of Communication* 69 (1): 26–48.

Duncombe, Stephen. 2007. *Dream: Re-imagining Progressive Politics in an Age of Fantasy*. New York, NY: The New Press.

Duvall, Spring-Serenity and Nicole Heckemeyer. 2018. '#BlackLivesMatter: Black Celebrity Hashtag Activism and the Discursive Formation of a Social Movement'. *Celebrity Studies* 9 (3): 391–408.

Eden, Sally. 2016. *Environmental Publics*. London: Routledge.

Eden, Sally. 2017. 'Blurring the Boundaries: Prosumption, Circularity and Online Sustainable Consumption through Freecycle'. *Journal of Consumer Culture* 17 (2): 265–85.

Edwards, Lee. 2018. *Understanding Public Relations: Theory, Culture, Society*. London: Sage.

Einstein, Mara. 2016. *Black Ops Advertising: Native Ads, Content Marketing, and the Covert World of the Digital Sell*. New York, NY: OR Books.

Einstein, Mara. Forthcoming. 'From Cause Marketing to Activist Branding: There's no Sitting It Out in the Age of COVID, #BLM, and Assaults on Democracy'. In M.P. McAllister and E. West (eds). *The Routledge Companion to Advertising and Promotional Culture*, 2nd edition. London and New York, NY: Routledge.

Eli, Karin, Catherine Dolan, Tanja Schneider, and Stanley Ulijaszek. 2016. 'Mobile Activism, Material Imaginings, and the Ethics of the Edible: Framing Political Engagement through the Buycott App'. *Geoforum* 74 (August): 63–73.

Ellsworth-Jones, Will. 2012. *Banksy: The Man behind the Wall*. London: Aurum.

Enghel, Florencia and Noske-Turner, Jessica (eds). 2018. *Communication in International Development: Doing Good or Looking Good?* London: Routledge.

European Environment Agency. 2020. 'Europe's Consumption in a Circular Economy: The Benefits of Longer-Lasting Electronics'. Available: www.eea.europa.eu/publications/europe2019s-consumption-in-a-circular/benefits-of-longer-lasting-electronics (last accessed 24 March 2022).

European Parliament News (2021) 'Understanding Covid-19's Impact on Women', 1 March. Available: www.europarl.europa.eu/news/en/headlines/society/20210225STO98702/understanding-the-impact-of-covid-19-on-women-infographics (last accessed 24 March 2022).

Falasca-Zamponi, Simonetta. 1997. *Fascist Spectacle: The Aesthetics of Power in Mussolini's Italy*. Los Angeles, CA: University of California Press.

FAO, 2016. 'Livestock&Climate Change' Available: http://www.fao.org/3/i6345e/i6345e.pdf

Farrar, Margaret E. and Jamie L. Warner. 2008. 'Spectacular Resistance: The Billionaires for Bush and the Art of Political Culture Jamming'. *Polity* 40 (3): 273–96.

Farrell, Nathan (ed.) 2020. *The Political Economy of Celebrity Activism*. Oxon: Routledge.

Fenton, Natalie. 2017. *Digital, Political, Radical*. Cambridge: Polity.

Finchett-Maddock, Lucy and Eleftheria J. Lekakis. (eds) 2020. *Art, Law and Power: Perspectives on Legality and Resistance in Contemporary Aesthetics*. Oxford: Counterpress.

Finnegan, Margaret Mary. 1999. *Selling Suffrage: Consumer Culture and Votes for Women*. New York, NY: Columbia University Press.

Flynn, Cassie, Eri Yamasumi, Stephen Fisher, Dan Snow, Zack Grant, and Martha Kirby. 2021. 'The Peoples' Climate Vote'. Available: www.undp.org/publications/peoples-climate-vote (accessed 30 August 2021).

Fontenelle, Isleide Arruda and Marlei Pozzebon. 2019. 'Jamming the Jamming: Brazilian Protests as an Illustration of a New Politics of Consumption'. *Culture and Organization* 25 (5): 353–67.

Food Standards Agency. 2021. Food and You 2: Wave 1. Available: www.food.gov.uk/research/food-and-you-2/food-and-you-2-wave-1 (accessed 8 November 2021).

Forno Francesca and Luigi Ceccarini. 2006. 'From the Street to the Shops: The Rise of New Forms of Political Actions in Italy'. *South European Society and Politics* 11 (2): 197–222.

Forno, Francesca and Paolo R. Graziano. 2014. 'Sustainable Community Movement Organisations'. *Journal of Consumer Culture* 14 (2): 139–57.

Fouka, Vasiliki, and Hans-Joachim Voth. 2016. 'Reprisals Remembered: German-Greek Conflict and Car Sales during the Euro Crisis'. http://dx.doi.org/10.2139/ssrn.2340625

Fox, Jon E. 2006. 'Consuming the Nation: Holidays, Sports, and the Production of Collective Belonging'. *Ethnic and Racial Studies* 29 (2): 217–36.

Fox, Jon E. and Cynthia Miller-Idriss. 2008. 'Everyday Nationhood'. *Ethnicities* 8 (4): 536–63.

Fozdar, Farida. 2021. 'Migrant and Mainstream Perspectives on Buying National: An Australian Case Study'. *Journal of Consumer Culture* 21 (3): 539–58.

Frank, Dana. 1999. *Buy American: The Untold Story of Economic Nationalism*. Boston, MA: Beacon Press.

Frank, Thomas. 1997. *The Conquest of Cool: Business Culture, Counterculture, and the Rise of Hip Consumerism*. Chicago: The University of Chicago Press.

Franks, Suzanne. 2014. 'Reporting Famine; Changing Nothing'. *British Journalism Review* 25 (3): 61–6.

Fraser, Nancy. 2013. *Fortunes of Feminism: From State-Managed Capitalism to Neoliberal Crisis*. London: Verso.

Friedman, Monroe. 1999. *Consumer Boycotts: Effecting Change through the Marketplace and the Media*. New York: Routledge.

Fuentes, Christian and Niklas Sörum. 2019. 'Agencing Ethical Consumers: Smartphone Apps and the Socio-Material Reconfiguration of Everyday Life'. *Consumption Markets & Culture* 22 (2): 131–56.

Fuqua, Joy V. 2011. 'Brand Pitt: Celebrity Activism and the Make It Right Foundation in Post-Katrina New Orleans'. *Celebrity Studies* 2 (2): 192–208.

Gerth, Karl. 2003. *China Made: Consumer Culture and the Creation of the Nation*. Cambridge, MA: Harvard University Asia Center.

Gibson, Kristina E. and Sarah E. Dempsey. 2015. 'Make Good Choices, Kid: Biopolitics of Children's Bodies and School Lunch Reform in Jamie Oliver's Food Revolution'. *Children's Geographies* 13 (1): 44–58.

Giddens, Anthony. 2009. *The Politics of Climate Change*. Cambridge: Polity.

Gil de Zúñiga, Homero, Lauren Copeland, and Bruce Bimber. 2014. 'Political Consumerism: Civic Engagement and the Social Media Connection'. *New Media & Society* 16 (3): 488–506.

Gill, Rosalind. 2008. 'Commodity Feminism', in W. Donsbach (ed.) *The International Encyclopedia of Communication*, 583-85. Oxford: Blackwell.

Gill, Rosalind. 2016. 'Post-Postfeminism? New Feminist Visibilities in Postfeminist Times'. *Feminist Media Studies* 16 (4): 610–30.

Gill, Rosalind and Christina Scharff (eds). (2011). *New Femininities: Postfeminism, Neoliberalism and Subjectivity*. Basingstoke: Palgrave.

Gilman-Opalsky, Richard. 2013. 'Unjamming the Insurrectionary Imagination: Rescuing Détournement from the Liberal Complacencies of Culture Jamming'. *Theory in Action* 6 (3): 1–34.

Ginder, Whitney and Sang-Eun Byun. 2015. 'Past, Present, and Future of Gay and Lesbian Consumer Research: Critical Review of the Quest for the Queer Dollar'. *Psychology & Marketing* 32 (8): 821–41.

Giraud, Eva Haifa. 2021. *Veganism: Politics, Practice and Theory*. London: Bloomsbury.
Glickman, Lawrence B. 2004. '"Buy for the Sake of the Slave": Abolitionism and the Origins of American Consumer Activism'. *American Quarterly* 56 (4): 889–912.
Glickman, Lawrence B. 2009. *Buying Power: A History of Consumer Activism in America*. Chicago, IL: University of Chicago Press.
Goldman, Robert. 1992. *Reading Ads Socially*. London: Routledge.
Goldman, Robert, Deborah Heath, and Sharon L. Smith. 1991. 'Commodity Feminism'. *Critical Studies in Mass Communication* 8 (3): 333–51.
Goode, J. Paul, David R. Stroup, and Elizaveta Gaufman. 2020. 'Everyday Nationalism in Unsettled Times: In Search of Normality during Pandemic'. *Nationalities Papers* 50 (1): 61–85.
Goodman, Michael K. 2010. 'The Mirror of Consumption: Celebritization, Developmental Consumption and the Shifting Cultural Politics of Fair Trade'. *Geoforum*, 41 (1): 104–16.
Goodman, Michael K., Jo Littler, Dan Brockington, and Maxwell Boykoff. 2016. 'Spectacular Environmentalisms: Media, Knowledge and the Framing of Ecological Politics'. *Environmental Communication* 10 (6): 677–88.
Gotham, Kevin Fox. 2012. 'Make It Right? Brad Pitt, Post-Katrina Rebuilding, and the Spectacularization of Disaster'. In: R. Mukherjee and S. Banet-Weiser (eds) *Commodity Activism: Cultural Resistance in Neoliberal Times*, 97–113. New York: New York University Press.
Greenberg, Cheryl. 2004. 'Political Consumer Action: Some Cautionary Notes from African American History'. In Michele Micheletti, Andreas Follesdal, and Dietlind Stolle (eds) *Politics, Products, and Markets: Exploring Political Consumerism Past and Present*, 63–82. New Brunswick, NJ: Transaction Press.
Greenfeld, Liah. 2001. *The Spirit of Capitalism: Nationalism and Economic Growth*. Cambridge, MA: Harvard University Press.
Greenfield, Patrick. 2017. Apple apologises for slowing down older iPhones with ageing batteries. *The Guardian*, 29 December 2017. Available: www.theguardian.com/technology/2017/dec/29/apple-apologises-for-slowing-older-iphones-battery-performance (last accessed 22 November 2021).
Gudynas, Eduardo. 2011. 'Buen Vivir: Today's Tomorrow'. *Development* 54 (4): 441–47.
Gulam, Joshua. 2020. 'Promoting Peace and Coffee Pods: George Clooney, Nespresso Activist'. In Nathan Farrell (ed.) The *Political Economy of Celebrity Activism*, 85–99. Oxon: Routledge.
Habermas, Jürgen. [1962] 1989. *The Structural Transformation of the Public Sphere: An Inquiry into a Category of Bourgeois Society*. Translated by Thomas Burger with the assistance of Frederick Lawrence. Cambridge: Polity.
Haiven, Max. 2007. 'Privatized Resistance: AdBusters and the Culture of Neoliberalism', *Review of Education, Pedagogy, and Cultural Studies* 29 (1): 85–110.
Hamilton, Clive. 2010. 'Consumerism, Self-Creation and Prospects for a New Ecological Consciousness'. *Journal of Cleaner Production* 18 (6): 571–75.

Hansson, Lena. 2017. 'Promoting Ethical Consumption: The Construction of Smartphone Apps as "Ethical" Choice Prescribers'. In Franck Cochoy, Johan Hagberg, Magdalena Petersson McIntyre, and Niklas Sorum (eds) *Digitalizing Consumption: How Devices Shape Consumer Culture*, 103–21. London and New York: Routledge.

Haqqi, Salman. 2020. *The Dirty Delivery Report*. Available: www.money.co.uk/guides/dirty-delivery-report-2020 (last accessed 24 March 2022).

Harold, Christine. 2004. 'Pranking Rhetoric: "Culture Jamming" as Media Activism'. *Critical Studies in Media Communication* 21 (3): 189–211.

Harold, Christine. 2009. *OurSpace: Resisting the Corporate Control of Culture*, Minneapolis, MN: University of Minnesota Press.

Harrison, Rob, Terry Newholm, and Deirdre Shaw (eds). 2005. *The Ethical Consumer*. London: Sage.

Harrison, Rob. 2022. *The Handbook of Ethical Purchasing*. London and New York: Routledge.

Harrop, Elizabeth. 2021. 'At What Cost? The Impacts of Advertising and Consumerism on Human, Community and Planetary Well-Being'. Bristol: Adfree Cities. Available: https://adfreecities.org.uk/our-reports/at-what-cost (last accessed 24 March 2022)

Hearn, Alison. 2012. 'Brand Me "Activist"'. in R. Mukherjee and S. Banet-Weiser (eds.), *Commodity Activism: Cultural Resistance in Neoliberal Times*. New York, NY: New York University Press. pp. 23–38.

Heath, Joseph, and Potter, Andrew. 2005. *The Rebel Sell: How the Counterculture Became Consumer Culture*. West Sussex: Capstone.

Heldman, Caroline. 2017. *Protest Politics in the Marketplace: Consumer Activism in the Corporate Age*. Ithaca, NY: Cornell University Press.

Henninger, Claudia Elisabeth, Nina Bürklin, and Kirsi Niinimäki. 2019. 'The Clothes Swapping Phenomenon – When Consumers Become Suppliers'. *Journal of Fashion Marketing and Management* 23 (3): 327–44.

Heynen, Robert and Emily van der Meulen. 2021. 'Anti-Trafficking Saviors: Celebrity, Slavery, and Branded Activism'. *Crime, Media, Culture* April, 1–23.

Hilton, Matthew. 2002. 'The Female Consumer and the Politics of Consumption in Twentieth-Century Britain'. *The Historical Journal* 45 (1): 103–28.

Himmelman, Natasha and Danai Mupotsa. 2008. '(Product)Red: (Re)Branding Africa?' *The Journal of Pan African Studies* 2 (6): 1–13.

Hogre (2017) *Subvertising: The Piracy of Outdoor Advertising*. London: Dog Section Press.

Hollows, Joanne. 2003. 'Oliver's Twist: Leisure, Labour and Domestic Masculinity in The Naked Chef'. *International Journal of Cultural Studies* 6 (2): 229–48.

Hollows, Joanne. 2013. 'Spare Rib, Second-Wave Feminism and the Politics of Consumption'. *Feminist Media Studies* 13 (2): 268–87.

Hollows, Joanne. 2022. *Celebrity Chefs, Food Media and the Politics of Eating*. London: Bloomsbury.

Hollows, Joanne, and Steve Jones. 2010. '"At Least He's Doing Something": Moral Entrepreneurship and Individual Responsibility in Jamie's Ministry of Food'. *European Journal of Cultural Studies* 13 (3): 307–22.

Holt, Douglas. 2016. 'Branding in the Age of Social Media.' *Harvard Business Review*, March, 40–50.

hooks, bell. 2000. *Feminism is for Everybody: Passionate Politics*. Cambridge, MA: South End Press.

hooks, bell. 2005. 'The Significance of Feminism'. In S.P. Hier (ed.) *Contemporary Sociological Thought: Themes and Theories*, 233–54. Toronto: Canadian Scholars' Press Inc.

Horton, Kathleen and Paige Street. 2021. 'This Hashtag Is Just My Style: Popular Feminism & Digital Fashion Activism'. *Continuum* 35 (6): 883–96.

Hua, Julietta. 2018. 'The Foxconn Suicides: Human Vitality and Capitalist Consumption'. *Women's Studies in Communication* 41 (4): 320–23.

Huddart Kennedy, Emily, John R. Parkins, and Josée Johnston. 2018. 'Food Activists, Consumer Strategies, and the Democratic Imagination: Insights from Eat-Local Movements'. *Journal of Consumer Culture* 18 (1): 149–68.

Humphery, Kim. 2010. *Excess: Anti-Consumerism in the West*. Cambridge: Polity.

Humphery, Kim, and Tim Jordan. 2018. 'Mobile Moralities: Ethical Consumption in the Digital Realm'. *Journal of Consumer Culture* 18 (4): 520–38.

Iqani, Mehita. 2016. *Consumption, Media and the Global South: Aspiration Contested*. Basingstoke: Palgrave.

Iqani, Mehita. 2020. *Garbage in Popular Culture: Consumption and the Aesthetics of Waste*. Albany, NY: State University of New York Press.

Jackson, Peter. 2016. 'Go Home Jamie: Reframing Consumer Choice'. *Social & Cultural Geography* 17 (6): 753–57.

Jallinoja, Piia, Markus Vinnari, and Mari Niva. 2019. 'Veganism and Plant-Based Eating: Analysis of Interplay between Discursive Strategies and Lifestyle Political Consumerism'. In Magnus Boström, Michele Micheletti, and Peter Oosterveer (eds) *The Oxford Handbook of Political Consumerism*, 157–79. Oxford: Oxford University Press.

Jeffreys, Elaine. 2016. 'Translocal Celebrity Activism: Shark-Protection Campaigns in Mainland China'. *Environmental Communication* 10 (6): 763–76.

Jeffreys, Elaine. 2020. 'Philanthropy, Celebrity and Governance in Mainland China'. In Kevin Latham (ed.) *Routledge Handbook of Chinese Culture and Society*, 313–27. London: Routledge.

Jeppesen, Sandra. 2010. 'Queer Anarchist Autonomous Zones and Publics: Direct Action Vomiting against Homonormative Consumerism'. *Sexualities* 13 (4): 463–78.

Jiménez Gomez, Isidro and Mariola Olcina Alvarado. (2020) 'ConsumeHastaMorir: Seventeen Years of Experimenting with the Legal Side of Subvertising,' in L. Finchett-Maddock and E.J. Lekakis (eds) *Art, Law and Power: Perspectives on Legality and Resistance in Contemporary Aesthetics*, 54–69. Oxford: Counterpress.

Johnson, Guillaume D., Kevin D. Thomas, and Sonya A. Grier. 2017. 'When the Burger Becomes Halal: A Critical Discourse Analysis of Privilege and Marketplace Inclusion'. *Consumption, Markets & Culture* 20 (6): 497–522.

Johnston, Josée. 2008. 'The Citizen-Consumer Hybrid: Ideological Tensions and the Case of Whole Foods Market'. *Theory and Society* 37 (3): 229–70.

Johnston, Josée and Shyon Baumann. 2015. *Foodies: Democracy and Distinction in the Gourmet Foodscape*. 2nd edition. New York and London: Routledge.

Johnston, Josée and Taylor, Judith. 2008. 'Feminist Consumerism and Fat Activists: A Comparative Study of Grassroots Activism and the Dove Real Beauty Campaign'. *Signs: Journal of Women in Culture and Society* 33 (4): 941–66.

Jones, Andrew. 2017. 'Band Aid revisited: humanitarianism, consumption and philanthropy in the 1980s'. *Contemporary British History* 31 (2): 189–209.

Jones, Ellis. 2019. 'Rethinking Greenwashing: Corporate Discourse, Unethical Practice, and the Unmet Potential of Ethical Consumerism'. *Sociological Perspectives* 62 (5): 728–54.

Jordan, Tim. 2020. *The Digital Economy*. Cambridge: Polity.

Kallis, Giorgos. 2018. Degrowth. Newcastle Upon Tyne: Agenda Publishing Limited.

Kampf, Constance E. 2018. 'Connecting Corporate and Consumer Social Responsibility through Social Media Activism'. *Social Media + Society* 4 (1): 1–11.

Kang, Jiyeon. 2012. 'A Volatile Public: The 2009 Whole Foods Boycott on Facebook'. *Journal of Broadcasting & Electronic Media* 56 (4): 562–77.

Kania-Lundholm, Magdalena. 2014. 'Nation in Market Times: Connecting the National and the Commercial. A Research Overview'. *Sociology Compass* 8 (6): 603–13.

Kapoor, Ilan. 2013. *Celebrity Humanitarianism: The Ideology of Global Charity*. London: Routledge.

Katz-Kimchi, Merav and Lucy Atkinson. 2014. 'Popular Climate Science and Painless Consumer Choices: Communicating Climate Change in the Hot Pink Flamingos Exhibit, Monterey Bay Aquarium, California'. *Science Communication* 36 (6): 754–77.

Kaylor, Brian. 2013. 'Earth-a-lujah! The Prophetic Environmental Discourse of Reverent Billy'. *Environmental Communication* 7 (3): 391–408.

Kellner, Douglas. 2016. *American Nightmare: Donald Trump, Media Spectacle, and Authoritarian Populism*. Rotterdam/Boston/Taipei: Sense Publishers.

Kelm, Ole and Marco Dohle. 2018. 'Information, Communication and Political Consumerism: How (Online) Information and (Online) Communication Influence Boycotts and Buycotts'. *New Media & Society* 20 (4): 1523–42.

Khamis, Susie. 2019. 'The Aestheticization of Restraint: The Popular Appeal of De-Cluttering after the Global Financial Crisis'. *Journal of Consumer Culture* 19 (4): 513–31.

Khamis, Susie. 2020. *Branding Diversity: New Advertising and Cultural Strategies*. Oxon: Routledge.

Khamis, Susie, Lawrence Ang, and Raymond Welling. 2017. 'Self-Branding, "Micro-Celebrity" and the Rise of Social Media Influencers'. *Celebrity Studies* 8 (2): 191–208.

Kipp, Amy and Roberta Hawkins. 2019. 'The Responsibilization of "Development Consumers" through Cause-Related Marketing Campaigns'. *Consumption Markets & Culture* 22 (1): 1–16.

Kjær, Katrine Meldgaard. 2019. 'In/Authenticity and Food-Celebrity Relationships in Michael Pollan's In Defence of Food and Jamie Oliver's Jamie's Food Revolution'. *Celebrity Studies* 10 (3): 332–45.

Klein, Naomi. 2005. *No Logo*, 2nd edition, London: Flamingo.

Kleine, Dorothea. 2016. 'Putting Ethical Consumption in Its Place: Geographical Perspectives'. In Deirdre Shaw, Andreas Chatzidakis, and Michal Carrington (eds) *Ethics and Morality in Consumption: Interdisciplinary Perspectives*, 148–69. London and New York: Routledge.

Koffman, Ofra, Shani Orgad and Rosalind Gill. 2015. 'Girl Power and "Selfie Humanitarianism"'. *Continuum* 29 (2): 157–68.

Kothari, Ashish, Federico Demaria, and Alberto Acosta. 2014. 'Buen Vivir, Degrowth and Ecological Swaraj: Alternatives to Sustainable Development and the Green Economy'. *Development* 57 (3): 362–75.

Kothari, Uma. 2014. 'Visual Representations of Development: The Empire Marketing Board Poster Campaign, 1926–1933'. In D. Lewis, D. Rodgers and M. Woolcock (eds) *Popular Representations of Development: Insights from Novels, Films, Television and Social Media*, 151–73. Abingdon: Routledge.

Kozinets, Robert V. 2010. *Netnography. Doing Ethnographic Research Online*. Thousand Oaks, CA: Sage.

Kozinets, Robert V. and Jay M. Handelman 2004. 'Adversaries of Consumption: Consumer Movements, Activism, and Ideology'. *Journal of Consumer Research* 31 (3): 691–704.

Kozinets, Robert V. and Henry Jenkins. 2021. 'Consumer Movements, Brand Activism, and the Participatory Politics of Media: A Conversation'. *Journal of Consumer Culture*, 12 May, 14695405211013992.

Kozinets, Robert V., Jay M. Handelman, and Michael S.W. Lee. 2010. 'Don't Read This; or, Who Cares What the Hell Anti-Consumption Is, Anyways?' *Consumption Markets & Culture* 13 (3): 225–33.

Kraidy, Marwan. 2016. *The Naked Blogger of Cairo: Creative Insurgency in the Arab World*. Cambridge, MA: Harvard University Press.

Kwon, Jungmin. 2019. 'Between Hyorish and Hyorism: A Korean TV Star and Social Media Activism'. *Television & New Media* 20 (3): 241–56.

Labour Behind Label. 2020. 'Report: Boohoo & COVID-19: The People behind the Profit'. Available: https://labourbehindthelabel.org/report-boohoo-covid-19-the-people-behind-the-profit (25 October 2021).

Lang, Chunmin and Ruirui Zhang. 2019. 'Second-Hand Clothing Acquisition: The Motivations and Barriers to Clothing Swaps for Chinese Consumers'. *Sustainable Production and Consumption* 18 (April): 156–64.

Lang, Tim and Gabriel Yiannis. 2005. 'A Brief History of Consumer Activism'. In Rob Harrison, Terry Newholm, and Deirdre Shaw (eds) *The Ethical Consumer*, 39–54. London: Sage.

Lasn, Kalle. 2000. *Culture Jam: How to Reverse American's Suicidal Consumer Binge – and Why We Must*. New York, NY: Quill.

Lasn, Kalle and Greg McLauchlan 2013. 'Occupy Aesthetics'. *Contexts: Sociology for the Public* 9 February. Available: https://contexts.org/articles/occupy-aesthetics (accessed 24 April 2020).

Lau, Dorothy Wai Sim. 2021a. 'Charity, Cantopop Stardom and the Pandemic: Aaron Kwok's Online Concert 2020'. *Celebrity Studies* 12 (4): 689–92.

Lau, Dorothy Wai Sim. 2021b. 'Aamir Khan and Celebrity Humanitarianism in Asia: Towards a Cosmopolitical Persona'. *Celebrity Studies* 12 (2): 234–49.

Ledin, Per and David Machin. 2020. 'Replacing Actual Political Activism with Ethical Shopping: The Case of Oatly'. *Discourse, Context & Media* 34 (April): 100344.

Lee, Francis L.F. 2015. 'Media Communication and the Umbrella Movement: Introduction to the Special Issue'. *Chinese Journal of Communication* 8 (4): 333–37.

Lee, Francis L.F. and Ivy W.Y. Fong. 2021. 'The Construction and Mobilization of Political Consumerism through Digital Media in a Networked Social Movement'. *New Media & Society* October, 14614448211050884.

Lee, Francis L.F., Samson Yuen, Gary Tang, and Edmund W. Cheng. 2019. 'Hong Kong's Summer of Uprising: From Anti-Extradition to Anti-Authoritarian Protests'. *China Review* 19 (4): 1–32.

Leer, Jonatan and Katrine Meldgaard Kjær. 2015. 'Strange Culinary Encounters'. *Food, Culture & Society* 18 (2): 309–27.

Lekakis, Eleftheria J. 2012. 'Will the Fair Trade Revolution Be Marketised? Commodification, Decommodification and the Political Intensity of Consumer Politics'. *Culture & Organization* 18 (5): 345–58.

Lekakis, Eleftheria J. 2013. *Coffee Activism and the Politics of Fair Trade and Ethical Consumption in the Global North: Political Consumerism and Cultural Citizenship*. Basingstoke: Palgrave.

Lekakis, Eleftheria J. 2017a. 'Economic Nationalism and the Cultural Politics of Consumption under Austerity: The Rise of Ethnocentric Consumption in Greece'. *Journal of Consumer Culture* 17 (2): 286–302.

Lekakis, Eleftheria J. 2017b. 'Banal Nationalism and Consumer Activism: The Case of #BoycottGermany,' in M. Skey and M. Antonsich (eds) *Everyday Nationhood: Theorising Culture, Identity and Belonging after Banal Nationalism*, 285–304. Basingstoke: Palgrave.

Lekakis, Eleftheria J. 2017c. 'Culture Jamming and Brandalism for the Environment: The Logic of Appropriation'. *Popular Communication* 15 (4): 311–27.

Lekakis, Eleftheria J. 2018. 'Buying into the Nation: The Politics of Consumption and Nationalism'. In Olga Kravets, Pauline Maclaran, Steve Miles, and Alladi Venkatesh (eds) *The Sage Handbook of Consumer Culture*, 499–515. London: Sage.

Lekakis, Eleftheria J. 2019. 'Political Consumerism and Nationalist European Struggles'. In Magnus Boström, Michele Micheletti, and Peter Oosterveer (eds) *The Oxford Handbook of Political Consumerism*. Oxford: Oxford University Press.

Lekakis, Eleftheria J. 2021. 'Adversaries of Advertising: Anti-Consumerism and Subvertisers' Critique and Practice'. *Social Movement Studies* 20 (6): 740–57.

Lekakis, Eleftheria J. (forthcoming) 'When Advertising Takes a Stand: Market Activism, Gender, and Social Change in Greece'. In M.P. McAllister and E. West (eds) *The Routledge Companion to Advertising and Promotional Culture*, 2nd edition. London and New York: Routledge.

Lekakis, Eleftheria J. and Francesca Forno. 2019. 'Political Consumerism in Southern Europe'. In Magnus Boström, Michele Micheletti and Peter Oosterveer (eds) *The Oxford Handbook of Political Consumerism*, 457–78. Oxford: Oxford University Press.

Lewis, Justin. 2013. *Beyond Consumer Capitalism: Media and the Limits to Imagination*. Cambridge: Polity.

Lewis, Tania. 2008. 'Transforming Citizens? Green Politics and Ethical Consumption on Lifestyle Television'. *Continuum* 22 (2): 227–40.

Lewis, Tania. 2010. 'Branding, Celebritization and the Lifestyle Expert'. *Cultural Studies* 24 (4): 580–98.

Lewis, Tania and Alison Huber. 2015. 'A Revolution in an Eggcup?' *Food, Culture & Society* 18 (2): 289–307.

Lewis, Tania and Potter, Emily (eds) (2011) *Ethical Consumption: A Critical Introduction*. Oxon: Routledge.

Liao, Sara. 2021. 'Wang Hong Fashion Culture and the Postfeminist Time in China'. *Fashion Theory* 25 (5): 663–85.

Lievrouw, Leah. 2011. *Alternative and Activist New Media*. Cambridge: Polity.

Lim, Merlyna, 2018. Roots, Routes, and Routers: Communications and Media of Contemporary Social Movements. *Journalism & Communication Monographs* 20 (2): 92–136.

Littler, Jo. 2005. 'Beyond the Boycott: Anti-Consumerism, Cultural Change and the Limits of Reflexivity'. *Cultural Studies* 19 (2): 227–52.

Littler, Jo. 2008. '"I Feel Your Pain": Cosmopolitan Charity and the Public Fashioning of the Celebrity Soul'. *Social Semiotics* 18 (2): 237–51.

Littler, Jo. 2009. *Radical Consumption*. Berkshire: Open University Press.

Littler, Jo. 2012. 'Good Housekeeping: Green Products and Consumer Activism'. In Roopali Mukherjee and Sarah Banet-Weiser (eds) *Commodity Activism: Cultural Resistance in Neoliberal Times*, 76–96. New York, NY: New York University Press.

Littler, Jo. 2016. 'Cultural Studies and Consumer Culture'. In Deirdre Shaw, Andreas Chatzidakis, and Michal Carrington (eds) *Ethics and Morality in Consumption: Interdisciplinary Perspectives*, 233–47. London: Routledge.

Lorenzini, Jasmine and Matteo Bassoli. 2015. Gender Ideology: The Last Barrier to Women's Participation in Political Consumerism? *International Journal of Comparative Sociology* 56, 460–83.

Lury, Celia. 2011. *Consumer Culture*, 2nd edition. New Brunswick, NJ: Rutgers University Press.

MacCash, Doug. 2019. 'Brad Pitt: "I Feel Fantastic" about Make It Right'. *NOLA.Com* 18 July 2019. Available: www.nola.com/news/article_c28e8b3e-62ed-5e01-8f74-d8980ce92269.html (accessed 27 September 2021).

MacCash, Doug. 2021. 'Brad Pitt's Make It Right Is Back in Court, Suing Its Former Director over Faulty Homes Project'. *NOLA.Com* 6 April 2021. Available: www.nola.com/news/article_8c4e7556-9658-11eb-8584-6f72071c56e4.html (accessed 27 September 2021).

MacGregor, Sherilyn. 2021. 'Making Matter Great Again? Ecofeminism, New Materialism and the Everyday Turn in Environmental Politics'. *Environmental Politics* 30 (1–2): 41–60.

MacKendrick, Nora A. and Lindsey M. Stevens. 2016. '"Taking Back a Little Bit of Control": Managing the Contaminated Body through Consumption'. *Sociological Forum* 31 (2): 310–29.

Madden, Stephanie, Melissa Janoske, Rowena Briones Winkler, and Zach Harpole. 2018. 'Who Loves Consent? Social Media and the Culture Jamming of Victoria's Secret'. *Public Relations Inquiry* 7 (2): 171–86.

magee, kyle. 2016. 'What the F*#k Do You Do That For? "Anti-Advertising Activist" Kyle Magee Explains Himself'. Available: https://democraticmediaplease.net/2016/12/what-the-fk-do-you-do-that-for (last accessed 25 March 2022).

Maniates, Michael F. 2001. 'Individualization: Plant a Tree, Buy a Bike, Save the World?' *Global Environmental Politics* 1 (3): 31–52.

Mansvelt, Juliana, and Paul Robbins. 2011. *Green Consumerism: An A-to-Z Guide*. Thousand Oaks, CA: Sage.

Marshall, P. David. 2010. 'The Promotion and Presentation of the Self: Celebrity as Marker of Presentational Media'. *Celebrity Studies* 1 (1): 35–48.

Marshall, T.H. 1950. *Citizenship and Social Class*, London: Pluto.

Martens, Lydia. 2009. 'Feminism and the Critique of Consumer Culture, 1950–1970'. In Stacy Gillis and Joanne Hollows (eds) *Feminism, Domesticity and Popular Culture*, 33–48. New York, NY: Routledge.

Marwick, Alice E. 2013. *Status Update: Celebrity, Publicity, and Branding in the Social Media Age*. New Haven, CT: Yale University Press.

Matheson, Eleanor, and Donna Sedgwick. 2021. 'Influencers and 21st Century Consumption'. *Contexts* 20 (2): 18–23.

Mattoni, Alice. 2017. 'A Situated Understanding of Digital Technologies in Social Movements. Media Ecology and Media Practice Approaches'. *Social Movement Studies* 16 (4): 494–505.

Maxwell, Richard and Toby Miller. 2012. *Greening the Media*, New York, NY: Oxford University Press.

Maxwell, Richard and Toby Miller. 2020. *How Green is Your Smartphone?* Cambridge: Polity Press.

McGuigan, Jim. 2012. 'The Coolness of Capitalism Today'. *TripleC: Communication, Capitalism & Critique* 20 (2): 425–38.

McKee, Yates. 2016. *Strike Art: Contemporary Art and the Post-Occupy Condition.* New York and London: Verso.

McRobbie, Angela. 1997. 'Bridging the Gap: Feminism, Fashion and Consumption'. *Feminist Review* 55: 73–89.

McRobbie, Angela. 2008. 'Young Women and Consumer Culture', *Cultural Studies* 22 (5), 531–55.

Meissner, Miriam. 2019. 'Against Accumulation: Lifestyle Minimalism, de-Growth and the Present Post-Ecological Condition'. *Journal of Cultural Economy* 12 (3): 185–200.

Mercer, Kobena. 2017. *The Fateful Triangle: Race, Ethnicity, Nation.* Cambridge, MA: Harvard University Press.

Micheletti, Michele. 2003. *Political Virtue and Shopping. Individuals, Consumerism and Collective Action.* London: Palgrave Macmillan.

Micheletti, Michele. 2004. 'Why More Women? Issues of Gender and Political Consumerism', in M. Micheletti, A. Follesdal, D. Stolle (eds.), *Politics, Products and Markets: Exploring Political Consumerism Past and Present.* Brunswick, NJ: Transaction Press. pp. 245–64.

Micheletti, Michele. 2010. *Political Virtue and Shopping: Individuals, Consumerism, and Collective Action.* New York: Palgrave Macmillan.

Micheletti, Michele and Didem Oral. 2019. 'Problematic Political Consumerism: Confusions and Moral Dilemmas in Boycott Activism'. In Magnus Boström, Michele Micheletti, and Peter Oosterveer (eds) *The Oxford Handbook of Political Consumerism*, 698–720. Oxford: Oxford University Press.

Micheletti, Michele and Dietlind Stolle. 2008. 'Fashioning Social Justice through Political Consumerism, Capitalism, and the Internet'. *Cultural Studies* 22 (5): 749–69.

Micheletti, Michele and Dietlind Stolle. 2015. 'Consumer Strategies in Social Movements'. In Donatella della Porta and Mario Diani (eds) *The Oxford Handbook of Social Movements*, 478–93. Oxford: Oxford University Press.

Midgley, Clare. 1996. 'Slave Sugar Boycotts, Female Activism and the Domestic Base of British Anti-Slavery Culture'. *Slavery & Abolition* 17 (3): 137–62.

Mihelj, Sabina. 2011. *Media Nations: Communicating Belonging and Exclusion in the Modern World.* Basingstoke: Palgrave.

Mihelj, Sabina and César Jiménez-Martínez. 2021. 'Digital Nationalism: Understanding the Role of Digital Media in the Rise of "New" Nationalism'. *Nations and Nationalism* 27 (2): 331–46.

Miller, Toby. 2007. *Cultural Citizenship: Cosmopolitanism, Consumerism and Television in a Neoliberal Age.* Philadelphia, PA: Temple University Press.

Milstein, Tema and Alexis Pulos. 2015. 'Culture Jam Pedagogy and Practice: Relocating Culture by Staying on One's Toes: Culture Jam Pedagogy and Practice'. *Communication, Culture & Critique* 8 (3): 395–413.

Minocher, Xerxes. 2019. 'Online Consumer Activism: Challenging Companies with Change.Org'. *New Media & Society* 21 (3): 620–38.

Molander, Susanna, Ingeborg Astrid Kleppe, and Jacob Ostberg. 2019. 'Hero Shots: Involved Fathers Conquering New Discursive Territory in Consumer Culture'. *Consumption Markets & Culture* 22 (4): 430–53.

Montez de Oca, Jeffrey, Sherry Mason, and Sung Ahn. 2020. 'Consuming for the Greater Good: "Woke" Commercials in Sports Media'. *Communication & Sport* August, 2167479520949283.

Morozov, Evgeny. 2014. *To Save Everything Click Here: Technology, Solutionism, and the Urge to Fix Problems That Don't Exist*. Harmondsworth: Penguin.

Morreall, John. (ed.) 1987. *The Philosophy of Laughter and Humor*, Albany, NY: State University of New York Press.

Morris, Carol. 2018. '"Taking the Politics out of Broccoli": Debating (De) Meatification in UK National and Regional Newspaper Coverage of the Meat Free Mondays Campaign'. *Sociologia Ruralis* 58 (2): 433–52.

Moyer, Matthew. 2019. 'Negativland's Mark Hosler embraces uncertainty', *Orlando Weekly*, 16 January. Available: www.orlandoweekly.com/orlando/negativlands-mark-hosler-embraces-uncertainty/Content?oid=23236389 (accessed: 18 May 2020).

Magubane, Zine. 2008. 'The (Product) Red Man's Burden: Charity, Celebrity, and the Contradictions of Coevalness'. *The Journal of Pan African Studies* 2 (6): 1–25.

Mukherjee, Roopali. 2011. 'Bling Fling: Commodity Consumption and the Politics of the "Post-Racial"'. In M.G. Lacy and K.A. Ono (eds) *Critical Rhetorics of Race*, 178–96. New York, NY: New York University Press.

Mukherjee, Roopali. 2012. 'Diamonds (Are from Sierra Leone): Bling and the Promise of Consumer Citizenship'. In R. Mukherjee and S. Banet-Weiser (eds) *Commodity Activism: Cultural Resistance in Neoliberal Times*, 114–33. New York, NY: New York University Press.

Mukherjee, Roopali and Sarah Banet-Weiser (eds) 2012. *Commodity Activism: Cultural Resistance in Neoliberal Times*. New York, NY: New York University Press.

Müller, Tanja R. 2013. 'The Long Shadow of Band Aid Humanitarianism: revisiting the dynamics between famine and celebrity'. *Third World Quarterly* 34 (3): 470–84.

Mupotsa, Danai. 2016. 'Sophie's Special Secret: Public Feeling, Consumption and Celebrity Activism in Post-Apartheid South Africa'. In Lisa Ann Richey (ed.) *Celebrity Humanitarianism and North-South Relations: Politics, Place and Power*, 88–105. London: Routledge.

Murphy, Patrick D. 2021. 'Speaking for the Youth, Speaking for the Planet: Greta Thunberg and the Representational Politics of Eco-Celebrity'. *Popular Communication* 19 (3): 193–206.

Nast, Condé. 2019. 'Where Did Brad Pitt's Make It Right Foundation Go Wrong?' *Architectural Digest*, 18 January 2019. Available: www.architecturaldigest.com/story/brad-pitt-make-it-right-foundation-new-orleans-katrina-lawsuit (accessed 27 September 2021).

Nava, Mica. 1991. 'Consumerism Reconsidered: Buying and Power'. *Cultural Studies* 5 (2): 157–73.

Nelson, Laura C. 2000. *Measured Excess: Status, Gender and Consumer Nationalism in Korea*. New York, NY: Columbia University Press.

Nelson, Michelle R., Mark A. Rademacher, and Hye-Jin Paek. 2007. 'Downshifting Consumer = Upshifting Citizen? An Examination of a Local Freecycle Community'. *The ANNALS of the American Academy of Political and Social Science* 611 (1): 141–56.

NHS. 2018. Health Survey for England 2018. Available: https://digital.nhs.uk/data-and-information/publications/statistical/health-survey-for-england/2018/summary (last accessed 25 March 2022).

Ofcom. 2017. *Children and Parents: Media Use and Attitudes Report*. Available: https://www.ofcom.org.uk/__data/assets/pdf_file/0020/108182/children-parents-media-use-attitudes-2017.pdf (last accessed 6 June 2022).

Ogilvy. 2019. Making Brands Matter for the Generations to Come. Available: www.ogilvy.com/ideas/making-brands-matter-generations-come

Olausson, Ulrika and Ylva Uggla. 2021. 'Celebrities Celebrifying Nature: The Discursive Construction of the Human-Nature Relationship in the "Nature Is Speaking" Campaign'. *Celebrity Studies* 12 (3): 353–70.

Olutola, Sarah R. 2021. 'Nicki Minaj's COVID-19 Vaccine Tweet about Swollen Testicles Signals the Dangers of Celebrity Misinformation and Fandom'. *The Conversation* 20 September 2021. Available: https://theconversation.com/nicki-minajs-covid-19-vaccine-tweet-about-swollen-testicles-signals-the-dangers-of-celebrity-misinformation-and-fandom-168242 (last accessed 25 March 2022).

Othman, Radwa. 2020. 'Art Forms and Aesthetic Ordering in the Egyptian Revolution of 2011'. In L. Finchett-Maddock and E. Lekakis (eds) *Art, Law, Power: Perspectives on Legality and Resistance in Contemporary Aesthetics*, 134–55. Oxford: Counterpress.

Özkırımlı, Umut. 2000. *Theories of Nationalism: A Critical Introduction*, Houndmills, Basingstoke: Palgrave.

Page, Allison. 2017. '"How Many Slaves Work for You?" Race, New Media, and Neoliberal Consumer Activism'. *Journal of Consumer Culture* 17 (1): 46–61.

Pardes, Arielle. 2020. 'Wellness Influencers Sell False Promises as Coronavirus Fears Soar'. *Wired* 3 April. Available: www.wired.com/story/coronavirus-anxieties-soar-wellness-influencers-step-in (accessed 6 December 2021).

Park, Bo Yun. 2019. 'Racialized political consumerism in the United States'. In M. Boström, M. Micheletti and P. Oosterveer (eds) *Oxford Handbook of Political Consumerism*, 681–98. Oxford: Oxford University Press.

Parker, Traci. 2015. 'Southern Retail Campaigns and the Struggle for Black Economic Freedom in the 1950s and 1960s'. In M. Bay and A. Fabian (eds) *Race and Retail: Consumption across the Color Line*, 99–122. New Brunswick, NJ: Rutgers University Press.

Pecot, Fabien, Sofia Vasilopoulou, and Matteo Cavallaro. 2021. 'How Political Ideology Drives Anti-Consumption Manifestations'. *Journal of Business Research* 128 (May): 61–9.

Pelandini-Simányi, Léna. 2014. *Consumption Norms and Everyday Ethics*. Basingstoke: Palgrave.

Peñaloza, Lisa. 1996. 'We're Here, We're Queer, and We're Going Shopping!'. *Journal of Homosexuality*, 31 (1–2): 9–41.

Peñaloza, Lisa and Christopher Chávez. 2016. 'Latinidad and Consumer Culture'. In A.D. Smith, X. Hou, J. Stone, R. Dennis, and P. Rizova (eds) *The Wiley Blackwell Encyclopedia of Race, Ethnicity, and Nationalism*, 1–3. Oxford: John Wiley & Sons.

Peretti, Jonah with Michele Micheletti. 2004. 'The Nike Sweatshop Email: Political Consumerism, Internet, and Culture Jamming', in Michele Micheletti, Andreas Follesdal, and Dietlind Stolle (eds.), *Politics, Products, and Markets: Exploring Political Consumerism Past and Present*. New Brunswick, NJ: Transaction Press. pp. 127–44.

Pezzullo, Phaedra C. 2011. 'Contextualizing Boycotts and Buycotts: The Impure Politics of Consumer-Based Advocacy in an Age of Global Ecological Crises'. *Communication and Critical/Cultural Studies* 8 (2): 124–45.

Philipps, Axel. 2015. 'Defacing Election Posters: A Form of Political Culture Jamming?' *Popular Communication*, 13 (3): 183–201.

Pike, Jo and Peter Kelly. 2014. *The Moral Geographies of Children, Young People and Food: Beyond Jamie's School Dinners*. Basingstoke: Palgrave.

Piper, Nick. 2015. 'Jamie Oliver and Cultural Intermediation'. *Food, Culture & Society* 18 (2): 245–64.

Pitcher, Ben. 2014. *Consuming Race*, London: Routledge.

PlasticsEurope. 2020. 'Plastics – the Facts 2020'. Available: https://plasticseurope.org/knowledge-hub/plastics-the-facts-2020/

Polynczuk-Alenius, Kinga and Mervi Pantti. 2017. 'Branded Solidarity in Fair Trade Communication on Facebook'. *Globalizations* 14 (1): 66–80.

Ponte, Stefano and Lisa Ann Richey. 2011. '(PRODUCT) RED™: How Celebrities Push the Boundaries of "Causumerism"'. *Environment and Planning A: Economy and Space* 43 (9): 2060–75.

Ponte, Stefano and Lisa Ann Richey. 2014. 'Buying into Development? Brand Aid Forms of Cause-Related Marketing'. *Third World Quarterly* 35 (1): 65–87.

Portwood-Stacer, Laura. 2012. 'Anti-Consumption as Tactical Resistance: Anarchists, Subculture and Activist Strategy'. *Journal of Consumer Culture* 12 (1): 87–105.

Proyecto Squatters. 2019. *Manifiesto Contra Publicidad*. Available: www.scribd.com/document/449039749/ManifiestoContraPublicidad2020

Pun, Ngai, Tommy Tse, and Kenneth Ng. 2019. 'Challenging Digital Capitalism: SACOM's Campaigns against Apple and Foxconn as Monopoly Capital'. *Information, Communication & Society* 22 (9): 1253–68.

Qiu, Jack Linchuan. 2016. *Goodbye iSlave: A Manifesto for Digital Abolition*. Urbana, Chicago and Springfield, IL: University of Illinois Press.

Quantis. 2018. 'Measuring Fashion: Environmental Impact of the Global Apparel and Footwear Industries Study'. Available: https://quantis-intl.com/wp-content/uploads/2018/03/measuringfashion_globalimpactstudy_full-report_quantis_cwf_2018a.pdf (last accessed 19 August 2021).

Reed, T.V. 2019. *The Art of Protest: Culture and Activism from the Civil Rights Movement to the Streets of Seattle*, 2nd edition. Minneapolis, MN: University of Minnesota Press.

Reilly, Ian. 2018. *Media Hoaxing: The Yes Men and Utopian Politics*. Blue Ridge Summit, PA: Lexington Books.

Repo, Jemima. 2020. 'Feminist Commodity Activism: The New Political Economy of Feminist Protest'. *International Political Sociology* 14 (2): 215–32.

Richey, Lisa Ann. 2016a. 'Introduction', in Lisa Ann Richey (ed.), *Celebrity Humanitarianism and North-South Relations: Politics, Place and Power*. London: Routledge.

Richey, Lisa Ann. (ed.) 2016b. *Celebrity Humanitarianism and North-South Relations: Politics, Place and Power*, London: Routledge.

Richey, Lisa Ann and Dan Brockington. 2020. 'Celebrity Humanitarianism: Using Tropes of Engagement to Understand North/South Relations'. *Perspectives on Politics* 18 (1): 43–59.

Richey, Lisa Ann and Alexandra Cosima Budabin. 2016. 'Celebritizing Conflict: How Ben Affleck Sells the Congo to Americans'. *Humanity: An International Journal of Human Rights, Humanitarianism, and Development* 7 (1): 27–46.

Richey, Lisa Ann and Stefano Ponte. 2008. 'Better (Red)™ than Dead? Celebrities, Consumption and International Aid'. *Third World Quarterly* 29 (4): 711–29.

Richey, Lisa Ann, and Stefano Ponte. 2011. *Brand Aid: Shopping Well to Save the World*. Minneapolis, MN: University of Minnesota Press.

Richey, Lisa Ann and Stefano Ponte. 2021. 'Humanitarianism and Corporate Branding: The Case of Brand Aid'. In Lilie Chouliaraki and Anne Vestergaard (eds) *Routledge Handbook of Humanitarian Communication*, 266–84. London: Routledge.

Rink, Bradley. 2019. 'Conspicuous Queer Consumption: Emulation and Honour in the Pink Map'. In Deborah Posel and Iliana van Wyk (eds) *Conspicuous Consumption in Africa*, 183–99. Johannesburg: Wits University Press.

Robinson, Nick W. and Gina Castle Bell. 2013. 'Effectiveness of Culture Jamming in Agenda Building: An Analysis of the Yes Men's Bhopal Disaster Prank'. *Southern Communication Journal* 78 (4): 352–68.

Rodan, Debbie and Jane Mummery. 2019. 'Animals Australia and the Challenges of Vegan Stereotyping'. *M/C Journal* 22 (2).

Rohrig, Brian. 2015. 'Smartphones: Smart Chemistry'. *American Chemical Society* May 2015. www.acs.org/content/acs/en/education/resources/highschool/chemmatters/past-issues/archive-2014-2015/smartphones.html

Rojek, Chris. 2001. *Celebrity*. London: Reaktion Books.

Rojek, Chris. 2014. '"Big Citizen" Celanthropy and Its Discontents'. *International Journal of Cultural Studies* 17 (2): 127–41.

Roser-Renouf, Connie, Lucy Atkinson, Edward Maibach, and Anthony Leiserowitz. 2016. 'The Consumer as Climate Activist'. *International Journal of Communication* 10: 4759–83.

Rottenberg, Catherine A. 2014. 'The Rise of Neoliberal Feminism'. *Cultural Studies* 28 (3): 418–37.

Rottenberg, Catherine A. (2018) *The Rise of Neoliberal Feminism*, Oxford: Oxford University Press.

Routledge, Paul. 2012. 'Sensuous Solidarities: Emotion, Politics and Performance in the Clandestine Insurgent Rebel Clown Army'. *Antipode* 44 (2): 428–52.

Rufas, Alix and Christine Hine. 2018. 'Everyday Connections between Online and Offline: Imagining Others and Constructing Community through Local Online Initiatives'. *New Media & Society* 20 (10): 3879–97.

Rumbo, Joseph D. 2002. 'Consumer Resistance in a World of Advertising Clutter: The Case of Adbusters'. *Psychology & Marketing* 19 (2): 127–48.

Sadian, Samuel. 2018. 'Consumer Studies as Critical Social Theory'. *Social Science Information* 57 (2): 273–303.

Sahakian, Marlyne and Harold Wilhite. 2014. 'Making Practice Theory Practicable: Towards More Sustainable Forms of Consumption'. *Journal of Consumer Culture* 14 (1): 25–44.

Sahota, Amarjit. 2014. *Sustainability: How the Cosmetics Industry Is Greening Up*. New York, NY: John Wiley & Sons.

Said, Edward W. 1978. *Orientalism*. London and Henley: Routledge and Kegan Paul.

Salonen, Anna Sofia. 2021. '"If I Could Afford an Avocado Every Day": Income Differences and Ethical Food Consumption in a World of Abundance'. *Journal of Consumer Culture*, October, 14695405211051033.

Sandler, Ronald and Phaedra C. Pezzullo (eds). 2007. *Environmental Justice and Environmentalism: The Social Justice Challenge to the Environmental Movement*. Cambridge, MA: MIT Press.

Sandlin, Jennifer A. 2010. 'Learning to Survive the "Shopocalypse": Reverend Billy's Anti-Consumption "Pedagogy of the Unknown"'. *Critical Studies in Education* 51 (3): 295–311.

Sandlin, Jennifer A. and Peter McLaren (eds) 2010. *Critical Pedagogies of Consumption: Living and Learning in the Shadow of the 'Shopocalypse'*. New York and London: Routledge.

Sandlin, Jennifer A. and Jennifer L. Milam. 2008. '"Mixing Pop (Culture) and Politics": Cultural Resistance, Culture Jamming, and Anti-Consumption Activism as Critical Public Pedagogy'. *Curriculum Inquiry* 38 (3): 323–50.

Santaoja, Minna and Piia Jallinoja. 2021. 'Food out of Its Usual Rut. Carnivalesque Online Veganism as Political Consumerism'. *Geoforum* 126 (November): 59–67.

Sassatelli, Roberta. 2007. *Consumer Culture: History, Theory and Politics*. Los Angeles: Sage.

Scammell, Margaret. 2000. 'The Internet and Civic Engagement: The Age of the Citizen-Consumer'. *Political Communication* 17 (4): 351–55.

Scatamburlo-D'Annibale, Valerie. 2010. 'Beyond the Culture Jam'. In J.A. Sandlin and P. McLaren (eds) *Critical Pedagogies of Consumption: Living and Learning in the Shadow of the 'Shopocalypse'*, 224–36. New York and London: Routledge.

Schippers, Mimi. 2007. 'Recovering the Feminine Other: Masculinity, Femininity, and Gender Hegemony.' *Theory and Society* 36 (1): 85–102.

Scott, Martin. 2015. 'The Role of Celebrities in Mediating Distant Suffering'. *International Journal of Cultural Studies* 18 (4): 449–66.

Sen, Ronojoy. 2016. 'Narendra Modi's Makeover and the Politics of Symbolism'. *Journal of Asian Public Policy* 9 (2): 98–111.

Sender, Katherine. 2004a. Business not Politics: The Making of the Gay Market. New York, NY: Columbia University Press.

Sender, Katherine. 2004b. 'Neither Fish nor Fowl: Feminism, Desire, and the Lesbian Consumer Market'. *The Communication Review* 7 (4): 407–32.

Senft, Theresa M. 2008. *Camgirls: Celebrity and Community in the Age of Social Networks*. New York: Peter Lang Publishing.

Serafini, Paula. 2018. *Performance Action: The Politics of Art Activism*. London: Routledge.

Serafini, Paula, Jessica Holtaway, and Alberto Cossu, (eds). 2018. *artWORK: Art, Labour and Activism*. London: Rowman and Littlefield.

Serazio, Michael. 2013. *Your Ad Here: The Cool Sell of Guerilla Marketing*. New York, NY: New York University Press.

Serazio, Michael. 2017. 'Co-Opting the Culture Jammers: The Guerilla Marketing of Crispin Porter + Bogusky'. In M. DeLaure and M. Fink (eds) *Culture Jamming: Activism and the Art of Cultural Resistance*, 237–53. New York, NY: New York University Press.

Seyfang, Gill, and Jouni Paavola. 2008. 'Inequality and Sustainable Consumption: Bridging the Gaps'. *Local Environment* 13 (8): 669–84.

Shaw, Deirdre, Andreas Chatzidakis, and Michal Carrington. 2016. *Ethics and Morality in Consumption: Interdisciplinary Perspectives*. London: Routledge.

Simon, Bryant. 2011. 'Not Going to Starbucks: Boycotts and the out-Scouring of Politics in the Branded World'. *Journal of Consumer Culture* 11 (2): 145–67.

Skey, Michael. 2009. 'The National in Everyday Life: A Critical Engagement with Michael Billig's Thesis of Banal Nationalism'. *The Sociological Review* 57, 2: 331–46.

Skey, Michael. 2011. *National Belonging and Everyday Life: The Significance of Nationhood in an Uncertain World*. Basingstoke: Palgrave.

Skey Michael and Marco Antonsich (eds). 2017. *Everyday Nationhood: Theorising Culture, Identity and Belonging after Banal Nationalism*. Basingstoke: Palgrave.

Sklair, Leslie. 2002. *Globalization: Capitalism and its Alternatives*, Oxford: Oxford University Press.

Skotnicki, Tad. 2021. *The Sympathetic Consumer: Moral Critique in Capitalist Culture*. Stanford, CA: Stanford University Press.

Slocum, Rachel, Herry Shannon, Kirsten Valentine Cadieux, and Matthew Beckman. 2011. '"Properly, with Love, from Scratch": Jamie Oliver's Food Revolution'. *Radical History Review* 110 (Spring): 178–91.

Smith-Anthony, Adam and John Groom. 2015. 'Brandalism and Subvertising: Hoisting Brands with Their Own Petard?' *Journal of Intellectual Property Law & Practice*, 10 (1): 29–34.

Sobande, Francesca. 2019. 'Woke-Washing: "Intersectional" Femvertising and Branding "Woke" Bravery'. *European Journal of Marketing* 54 (11): 2723–45.

Sobande, Francesca. 2020. '"We're All in This Together": Commodified Notions of Connection, Care and Community in Brand Responses to COVID-19'. *European Journal of Cultural Studies* 23 (6): 1033–37.

Somerville, Ian and Lee Edwards. 2021. 'Researching the Complex, Hybrid, and Liminal Nature of Contemporary Promotional Cultures'. *Media and Communication* 9 (3): 97–100.

Soper, Kate and Frank Trentmann (eds) 2008. *Citizenship and Consumption*, Basingstoke: Palgrave.

Sørensen, Majken Jul. 2016. *Humour in Political Activism: Creative Nonviolent Resistance*, Basingstoke: Palgrave.

Sörum, Niklas. 2020. 'Ethical Consumption Applications as Failed Market Innovations: Exploring Consumer (Non) Acceptance of "Quasi" Market Devices'. *Journal of Cultural Economy* 13 (1): 91–113.

Sörum, Niklas, and Christian Fuentes. 2019. '"Write Something": The Shaping of Ethical Consumption on Facebook'. In Franck Cochoy, Johan Hagberg, Magdalena Petersson McIntyre, and Niklas Sörum (eds) *Digitalizing Consumption*, 146–69. London: Routledge.

Stevenson, Nick. 2003. *Cultural Citizenship: Cosmopolitan Questions*, Berkshire: Open University Press.

Stillerman, Joel. 2015. *The Sociology of Consumption: A Global Approach*. Cambridge: Polity.

Stolle, Dietlind and Michele Micheletti. 2005. 'The Gender Gap Reversed', in B.L. O'Neill and E. Gidengil (eds.), *Gender and Social Capital*. London: Routledge. pp. 45–72.

Stolle, Dietlind and Micheletti, Michele. 2015. *Political Consumerism: Global Responsibility in Action*. New York, NY: Cambridge University Press.

Sun, Weimei and Brian Creech. 2019. 'Celebratory Consumerism on China's Singles' Day: From Grass-Roots Holiday to Commercial Festival'. *Global Media and Communication* 15 (2): 233–48.

Swett, Pamela E. 2014. *Selling Under the Swastika: Advertising and Commercial Culture in Nazi Germany*. Stanford, CA: Stanford University Press.

Szasz, Andrew. 2007. *Shopping Our Way to Safety: How We Changed from Protecting the Environment to Protecting Ourselves*. Minneapolis, MN: University of Minnesota Press.

The Guardian. 2020. 'The Urban Wild: Animals Take to the Streets amid Lockdown – in Pictures', 22 April 2020. Available: www.theguardian.com/world/gallery/2020/apr/22/animals-roaming-streets-coronavirus-lockdown-photos (last accessed 25 March 2022).

Thrall, A. Trevor, Jaime Lollio-Fakhreddine, Jon Berent, Lana Donnelly, Wes Herrin, Zachary Paquette, Rebecca Wenglinski, and Amy Wyatt. 2008. 'Star Power: Celebrity Advocacy and the Evolution of the Public Sphere'. *The International Journal of Press/Politics* 13 (4): 362–85.

Transform Together. 2018. *Creating Sustainable Smartphones: Scaling up Best Practice to Achieve SDG 12*. Available: https://storage.googleapis.com/www.bioregional.com/downloads/Creating-sustainable-smartphones-Scaling-up-best-practice-to-achieve-SDG-12_Transform-Together_2018.pdf (last accessed 25 March 2022).

Treré, Emiliano. 2019. *Hybrid Media Activism: Ecologies, Imaginaries, Algorithms*. Oxon and New York: Routledge.

Treré, Emiliano and Zizheng Yu. 2021. 'The Evolution and Power of Online Consumer Activism: Illustrating the Hybrid Dynamics of "Consumer Video Activism" in China through Two Case Studies'. *Journal of Broadcasting & Electronic Media* https://doi.org/10.1080/08838151.2021.1965143.

Tsai, Wan-Hsiu Sunny, 2012. 'Political Issues in Advertising Polysemy: The Case of Gay Window Advertising'. *Consumption Markets & Culture* 15 (1): 41–62.

Tsai, Wan-Hsiu Sunny, Aya Shata and Shiyun Tian (2021) 'En-Gendering Power and Empowerment in Advertising: A Content Analysis'. *Journal of Current Issues & Research in Advertising* 42 (1): 19–33.

Turner, Graeme. 2006. 'The Mass Production of Celebrity: "Celetoids", Reality TV and the "Demotic Turn".' *International Journal of Cultural Studies* 9 (2): 153–65.

Turner, Graeme. 2010. 'Approaching Celebrity Studies'. *Celebrity Studies* 1 (1): 11–20.

Turner, Graeme. 2013. *Understanding Celebrity*, 2nd edition. London: Sage.

Turow, Joseph. 2017. *The Aisles Have Eyes: How Retailers Track Your Shopping, Strip Your Privacy, and Define Your Power*. New Haven, CT: Yale University Press.

Tyler, Melissa and Sheena Vachhani. 2021. 'Chasing Rainbows? A Recognition-Based Critique of Primark's Precarious Commitment to Inclusion'. *Organization* 28 (2): 247–65.

Uldam, Julie. 2018. 'Social Media Visibility: Challenges to Activism'. *Media, Culture & Society* 40 (1): 41–58.

UNEP. 2010. 'ABC of SCP: Clarifying Concepts on Sustainable Consumption and Production'. www.oneplanetnetwork.org/sites/default/files/10yfp-abc_of_scp-en.pdf.

UNEP. 2021. 'Worldwide Food Waste'. *ThinkEatSave*. 2021. Available: www.unep.org/thinkeatsave/get-informed/worldwide-food-waste (last accessed 25 March 2022).

UNFCCC. 2015. *Paris Agreement*. Available: https://unfccc.int/sites/default/files/english_paris_agreement.pdf (last accessed 6 June 2022).

United Nations Conference on Environment and Development (UNCED). 1992. *Agenda 21*. New York: United Nations. Available: https://sustainabledevelopment.un.org/content/dsd/agenda21/res_agenda21_04.shtml (last accessed 25 March 2022).

Veg, Sebastian. 2017. 'The Rise of "Localism" and Civic Identity in Post-handover Hong Kong: Questioning the Chinese Nation-state'. *The China Quarterly* 230: 323–47.

Verma, Meghna and B.R. Naveen. 2021. 'COVID-19 Impact on Buying Behaviour'. *Vikalpa* 46 (1): 27–40.

Vrikki, Photini. 2020. 'Twitter as a Space of Resistance to Brexit: Stories of Belonging and the Concept of Affective Citizenship in #1DayWithoutUs', in L. Finchett-Maddock and E. Lekakis (eds) *Art, Law, Power: Perspectives on Legality and Resistance in Contemporary Aesthetics*, 258-80. Oxford: Counterpress.

Wallis, Cara and Yongrong Shen. 2018. 'The SK-II #changedestiny Campaign and the Limits of Commodity Activism for Women's Equality in Neo/Non-Liberal China'. *Critical Studies in Media Communication* 35 (4): 376–89.

Wan Chan, D.S. and N. Pun. 2020. 'Economic Power of the Politically Powerless in the 2019 Hong Kong Pro-Democracy Movement'. *Critical Asian Studies*, 52(1): 33–43.

Wang, Jian. 2006. 'The Politics of Goods: A Case Study of Consumer Nationalism and Media Discourse in Contemporary China'. *Asian Journal of Communication* 16 (2): 187–206.

Warin, Megan. 2011. 'Foucault's Progeny: Jamie Oliver and the Art of Governing Obesity'. *Social Theory & Health* 9 (1): 24–40.

Warner, Jamie. 2007. 'Political Culture Jamming: The Dissident Humor of *The Daily Show with John Stewart*'. *Popular Communication* 5 (1): 17–36.

Welch, Dan and Dale Southerton. 2019. 'After Paris: transitions for sustainable consumption'. *Sustainability: Science, Practice and Policy* 15 (1): 31–44.

Werbner, Pnina, Martin Webb, and Kathryn Spellman-Poots (eds). 2014. *The Political Aesthetics of Global Protest: The Arab Spring and Beyond*. Edinburgh: Edinburgh University Press.

Wernick, Andrew. 1991. *Promotional Culture: Advertising, Ideology and Symbolic Expression*. London: Sage.

Wettergren, Åsa. 2009. 'Fun and Laughter: Culture Jamming and the Emotional Regime of Late Capitalism'. *Social Movement Studies* 8 (1): 1–15.

Wheeler, Kathryn. 2012. *Fair Trade and the Citizen-Consumer: Shopping for Justice?* Basingstoke: Palgrave.

Wheeler, Kathryn and Miriam Glucksmann. 2013. 'Economies of Recycling, "Consumption Work" and Divisions of Labour in Sweden and England'. *Sociological Research Online* 18 (1): 114–27.

Whitney, Elizabeth. 2006. 'Capitalizing on Camp: Greed and the Queer Marketplace'. *Text and Performance Quarterly* 26 (1): 36–46.

Wilén, Kristoffer and Tiina Taipale. 2018. 'Strongly Sustainable Consumption and a Case of Mistaken Identity: A Qualitative Study on Environmentally Concerned Individuals'. In Karl Johan Bonnedahl and Pasi Heikkurinen (eds) *Strongly Sustainable Societies: Organising Human Activities on a Hot and Full Earth*, 209–28. London: Routledge.

Williamson, Milly. 2016. *Celebrity: Capitalism and the Making of Fame*. Cambridge: Polity Press.

Willis, Margaret M. and Juliet B. Schor. 2012. 'Does Changing a Light Bulb Lead to Changing the World? Political Action and the Conscious Consumer'. *The ANNALS of the American Academy of Political and Social Science* 644 (1): 160–90.

Wilson, Kalpana. 2011. '"Race", Gender and Neoliberalism: Changing Visual Representations in Development'. *Third World Quarterly* 32 (2): 315–31.

Wong, Hio Tong and Shih-Diing Liu. 2018. 'Cultural Activism during the Hong Kong Umbrella Movement'. *Journal of Creative Communications* 13 (2): 1–9.

Wood, Rachel. 2020. '"What I'm Not Gonna Buy": Algorithmic Culture Jamming and Anti-Consumer Politics on YouTube'. *New Media & Society*, July.

World Health Organization (WHO). 2013. *Marketing of foods high in fat, salt and sugar to children: update 2012-2013*. Available: https://www.euro.who.int/__data/assets/pdf_file/0019/191125/e96859.pdf (last accessed 6 June 2022).

World Health Organization (WHO). 2017. '*Controlling the Global Obesity Epidemic*'. Available: www.who.int/nutrition/topics/obesity/en (accessed 30 September 2021).

Xu, Jian, Glen Donnar, and Vikrant Kishore. 2021. 'Internationalising Celebrity Studies: Turning towards Asia'. *Celebrity Studies* 12 (2): 175–85.

Xu, Jian and Elaine Jeffreys. 2020. 'Celebrity Politics in Covid-19 China: "Celebrities Can't Save the Country"'. *University of Westminster The Contemporary China Centre Blog* (blog). 15 July 2020. http://blog.westminster.ac.uk/contemporarychina/celebrity-politics-in-covid-19-china-celebrities-cant-save-the-country/.

Yang, Mundo, Lisa Villioth, and Jörg Radtke. 2019. 'Foodsharing as the Public Manufacturing of Food Reuse'. In Matthias Korn, Wolfgang Reißmann, Tobias Röhl, and David Sittler (eds) *Infrastructuring Publics: Understanding Infrastructures and Publics as Intertwined*, 113–37. Wiesbaden: Springer.

Yu, Zizheng. 2021. 'An Empirical Study of Consumer Video Activism in China: Protesting against Businesses with Short Videos'. *Chinese Journal of Communication* 14 (3): 297–312.

Yuen, Samson and Sanho Chung. 2018. 'Explaining Localism in Post-Handover Hong Kong: An Eventful Approach'. *China Perspectives* 3: 19–29.

Zanette, Maria Carolina and Eliane Pereira Zamith Brito. 2019. 'Fashionable Subjects and Complicity Resistance: Power, Subjectification, and Bounded Resistance in the Context of Plus-Size Consumers'. *Consumption Markets & Culture* 22 (4): 363–82.

Zorell, Carolin. 2019. *Varieties of Political Consumerism: From Boycotting to Buycotting*. Basingstoke: Palgrave.

INDEX

Page numbers in *italics* refer to figures.

Abidin, Crystal, 30, 123
AbiGhannam, Niveen, 104–105, 112
Absolute Vodka, 75
accountability, 128–131, 138
The Activist (reality TV show), 121–122
Adbusters (media education foundation), 153, 154, 161, 163–164, 169, 170–171
Adbusters (magazine), 31, 33, *49*, 153, 169
AdFree Cities, 3, 32
Advertising Age (magazine), 159
Affleck, Ben, 21, 127–128, 130, 139
AfreWatch, 119–120n19
agency
  celebrities and, 30–31, 40–41
  citizens and, 26–27, 40–41
  debates and approaches to, 8–9, 21, 25, 187
  digital technologies and, 36–37
  market actors and, 28–29, 40–41
  nationalism and, 61–62
  subvertisers and, 31–33, 40–41, 168
Ahmed, Sara, 76, 77, 86
Al-Asaker, Maha, 177
Al-Sisi, Abdel Fattah, 158
Albert, 107
Amazon, 2, 190–191
American Family Association, 93
Amnesty International, 119–120n19
anti-consumerism
  approaches to, 23
  Brandalism and, 151–153, *152*, 157
  critical issues in, 167–168
  in documentaries, 195–196
  future case studies, 178
  holidays and, 2–3
  ideology and, 155–156, 167–168
  key concepts in, 153–155
  key theories of, 155–167, *162–163*
  methodologies and, 169–171
  Resistance is Female (case study), 171–178, *172–173*, *175*
  as response to mass consumerism, 178–180
  society of spectacle and, 163–164, 167, 170, 174
  See also culture jamming; subvertising
anti-consumption, 23, 62–63, 116–117
Apple, 113
asymmetry of publicities, 37
Atkinson, Lucy, 104–105, 110, 112
authenticity, 128–131, 138
Avfall Sverige (Swedish Waste Management and Recycling Association), 112

backlash politics, 57–58, 192
banal cosmopolitanism, 52–53
banal nationalism, 52–54, 58, 61, 62
Band Aid (charity supergroup), 125, 126–127
Banet-Weiser, Sarah, 23–24, 25, 28, 77–78, 81–82, 88, 92, 164
Bangladesh, 2
Bangladesh Accord on Fire and Building Safety, 8
Banksy, 180n1
Barassi, Veronica, 35, 37, 189–190
Barrymore, Drew, 133
Bekatorou, Sofia, 90
Billboard Liberation Front, 154
Billig, Michael, 52, 53, 58, 61

Binkley, Sam, 23, 156, 169
Biodegr'AD, 166–167
Bite Back 2030 (organization), 143–145
Black Friday, 2
Black Lives Matter (BLM) movement, 29, 57–58, 137
BLACKPINK, 30, 135
Bono, 127
Boohoo, 7–8, *7*
Boström, Magnus, 101–102, 106, 117
brands
  Brand Aid, 21
  brand evangelism, 189–191
  branding, 28–29
Brandalism, 151–153, *152*, 157
Branson, Richard, 144
Brigade Anti-Sexiste (Anti-Sexist Brigade), 31–32
Brockington, Dan, 125–126, 128, 129–130, 134, 139
Brown, Keith, 22, 187
Brown, Nicole Marie, 59, 61, 80, 87
Brundtland Commission, 118–119n7
Brunei, 30–31
Budabin, Alexandra Cosima, 127–128, 130, 131–132, 139
buen vivir, 99
B.U.G.A. U.P. (Billboard Utilising Graffitists against Unhealthy Promotions), 154, 166
Bulakh, Tetiana, 53, 55
Butler, Judith, 79–80

Cameron, David, 161
Cammaerts, Bart, 160
campaigns
  Act Now campaign, 17–19, *18*, 100
  #ActForLove campaign, 91–93
  #AdEnough campaign, 144, 145
  Art in Ad Places campaign, 172
  #changedestiny campaign, 82–83, 88
  Girl Up campaign, 88
  #GrabYourWallet campaign, 73
  Keep Fighting (campaign), 172
  #payyourworkers campaign, 7–8, *7*
Cancer Research UK, 144–145
Carbon Footprint Ltd, 119n15
carewashing, 186
case studies
  anti-consumerism and, 169–170, 171–178, *172–173*, *175*
  celebrity advocacy and, 139–145
  environmental consumer activism and, 111, 112–116, 188, 190
  feminist consumer activism and, 88, 89–93
  nationalism and, 64–67, 188
Casseurs de pub, 154
Castelló, Enric, 56, 61, 66
cause-related marketing (CRM), 21, 28
causumerism, 21, 127, 146, 147
celebrification, 123, 139
celebritization, 123, 139, 143
celebrity, concept of, 123–125
celebrity advocacy
  agency and, 21, 187
  celebrity as intermediaries in, 30–31, 121–122, 146–148
  celebrity chef Jamie Oliver (case study), 140–145
  charitainment and, 125–126
  critical issues in, 137–139
  future case studies, 146
  key concepts in, 123–125
  key theories of, 126–137
  methodologies and, 139–140
celebrity humanitarianism, 125–126, 129–130, 134
charitainment, 125–126
Chatzidakis, Andreas, 28, 79, 86, 156
Chen, Gigi, 176
China
  celebrity advocacy in, 135–136

commodity activism in,
    82–83, 88, 92
mass consumerism in, 2
nationalism in, 51, 54
postfeminism in, 77
publicities in, 37
See also Hong Kong
Chopra, Priyanka, 121
citizenship, 6, 48,
    60, 67
civil disobedience, 165–167,
    168, 177
civil rights movement, 55, 58, 59,
    61–62, 166
Clandestine Insurgent Rebel Clown
    Army (CIRCA), 157
Clark, Danae, 83–84
Clean Clothes, 7
climate change, 17–19, *18*, 97, 98.
    See also environmental
    consumer activism
climate crisis, 97
Clooney, George, 21, 30–31,
    130, 139
Coach, 186
Le Collectif des Déboulonneurs,
    164–165, 166
Collins, Phil, 125
colonialism, 127, 147
commercial spectacles, 157–158,
    167–168
commodity activism, 81–82,
    88, 92, 94
conflict minerals, 112
Conservation International, 123
Constantopoulou,
    Zoe, 90
Consume Hasta Morir, 165
consumer activism
    concept and definition
        of, 8, 19
    #ActNow campaign
        and, 17–19, *18*
    agency and, 8–9, 21, 25, 26–33,
        36–37, 40–41, 168, 187
    approaches to, 19–26
    comprehensive approach to, 8–11,
        14–15
    contradictions in, 183
    debates on, 185–188
    impact of, 183–184
    possibilities, limitations, and
        ambiguities of, 191–192

practices of, 3–4, 9
resistance and, 4–8,
    7, 188–191
See also anti-consumerism;
    environmental consumer activism;
    feminist consumer activism;
    media technologies; nationalism
consumer-friendly simplifications,
    131–133, 138, 147
consumer nationalism, 56–57,
    62–63, 66–68
consumer power, 17–19
consumer social responsibility
    (CnSR), 39
consumer solutionism, 14, 17–19,
    29, 38–39, 40, 192
content analysis, 87–88
content marketing, 189
copyright, 165–166
Corbyn, Jeremy,
    161–162, *163*
Coronavirus Global
    Response, 128
corporate social responsibility
    (CSR), 28, 39
Cotton, Fearne, 144
covert advertising, 189
COVID-19 pandemic
    branding and, 28–29
    celebrity advocacy and, 121, 128,
        130, 147
    consumer culture and, 1–2
    impact on environment of,
        98, 190
    impact on society
        of, 192
    labour justice and,
        7–8, *7*
    nationalism and, 46, 51,
        55–56, 67
    women and, 94–95
critical marketing
    studies, 24
critical publicity, 37
crowdcultures, 187
Cullen, Darren, 160
cultural and communication
    studies, 23–24
culture-ideology of consumerism,
    155–156, 178
culture jamming
    concept of, 6–7,
        31–33, 153, 154–155, 179–180

academic debates on, 158–167,
162–163, 177
critical issues in,
167–168
future case studies, 178
ideology and, 156,
167–168
methodologies and,
169–171
Resistance is Female
(case study), 171–178,
172–173, *175*
society of spectacle
and, 157, 158, 163–164,
167, 170
Cyber Monday, 2

Daley, Patricia, 131,
139–140
data reductionism, 189–191
Dawson, Rosario, 133
Debord, Guy, 157
decluttering, 103
decolonialization, 99
DeGeneres, Ellen, 30–31
degrowth, 99
DeLaure, Marilyn, 154,
158, 160
Democratic Republic of Congo
(DRC), 127–128, 130
Dery, Mark, 154, 179
détournement, 157
developmental
consumption, 146
DeVos, Betsy, 171
digital nationalism, 49–50
digital solutionism, 34,
36, 38
digital technologies
celebrity and, 123–124
environmental consumer activism
and, 106–108, 109
nationalism and, 49–50
resistance and, 189
role in consumer
activism of, 9–10, 33–40,
187–188
Dirty Delivery Report, 2
discourse analysis,
110–111, 140
discursive political consumerism,
153, 154
documentaries, 195–196
Dove, 82, 88

Doyle, Julie, 100, 106, 109, 111,
117, 185
Driessens, Olivier, 123, 139
Duchesne, Sophie, 53–54
Duncombe, Stephen,
157–158
Duran Duran, 125
Dusty Rebel, 176
Duvall, Spring-Serenity,
137, 140

e-commerce, 1
e-waste, 3, 97, 113–114,
116–117, 118, 183–184, 190
Eastern Congo Initiative, 127–128,
139–140
ecological swaraj, 99
economic nationalism, 54–56,
62, 67
L'Eglise de la Très Sainte Consommation
(The Church of the Most Holy
Consumption), 154–155
Egypt, 158
environmental consumer activism
Brandalism and, 152
celebrity advocacy and,
30, 123, 124, 129,
133, 137
contradictions in, 183
critical issues in, 108–110,
117–118
debates on, 117
future case studies, 116
key concepts in, 98–100
key debates in, 97–98
methodologies and, 110–112
smartphone consumption
(case study), 112–116,
188, 190
theory of, 101–108
See also green consumerism;
greenwashing; sustainable
consumption
environmental justice
movements, 99
environmental racism, 99
environmentalism, 99
Erenthal, Sara, 175, 176
Ethical Consumer (magazine), 24,
33, 117
ethical consumption, 26
ethical fetishism, 102
ethical spectacles, 157–158,
163, 170

ethnicity
  concept of, 46–47, 50, 53
  consumer activism and, 58–62, 69
  critical issues in, 60–62
  Yellow Economic Circle and, 66
  See also nationalism; race
ethnographic methods
  anti-consumerism and, 170–171
  environmental consumer activism and, 111–112
  feminist consumer activism and, 89
ethnosymbolism, 50
Evans, Hugh, 121–122
Everett, Rupert, 30
everyday nationhood, 52, 53
Extinction Rebellion (XR), 1

Fabien Tipon & Co, 166–167
Fair Play (previously Campaign for a Commercial-Free Childhood), 6
Fairphone, 108, 117
Faith, Paloma, 144
Farrell, Nathan, 129, 139
fascist spectacles, 157–158
Fearnley-Whittingstall, Hugh, 144
feminism, 76–78
feminist consumer activism
  contradictions of, 183
  critical issues in, 73–74, 85–87, 94–95
  future case studies, 93–94
  key concepts in, 74–78
  key theories of, 78–85
  Lacta (case study), 89–93
  methodologies and, 87–89
  See also gender; Resistance is Female
femvertising, 73, 74, 81, 86
Fink, Moritz, 154, 158, 160
Food Standards Agency, 2
foodie politics, 22
Frank, Dana, 54, 61, 70n4

Franta, Connor, 19
freecycle.com, 39
Fridays for Future, 124
Fyssas, Pavlos, 89–90

Gandy, David, 144, 145
Geldof, Bob, 125
gender
  celebrity advocacy and, 134–135, 136, 138–139, 143
  concept of, 74–76
  See also feminist consumer activism; queer activism and theory
Gender Equality Index, 75
Gerth, Karl, 54, 70n5
Gill, Rosalind, 77, 81
Gillette, 74
Gilman-Opalsky, Richard, 158, 164
Glickman, Lawrence, 40–41
Glimpse, 164–165
Global Citizen, 121–122
Global E-waste Monitor 2020 (Forti et al.), 113
Global Fund to Fight Aids, Tuberculosis and Malaria, 127
Global Gender Gap Report (2020), 75
Global Witness, 119–120n19
Goodman, Michael, 30, 107, 132, 137–138
Goodwill Ambassadors, 126
government-organized non-governmental organizations (GONGOs), 135–136
Graft Architects, 130–131
Greece, 45–46, 89–93
green consumerism
  concept of, 100
  celebrity advocacy and, 30, 133
  critical issues in, 109, 117–118
  debates on, 117
  future case studies, 116
  key debates on, 98
  recycling and, 27
  theory of, 101–105
  See also environmental consumer activism; greenwashing
green economy, 98–99
Green, Philip, 73

Greenberg, Cheryl, 61, 63–64
greenhouse gas (GHG) emissions, 97
greenwashing, 29, 99, 152, 186
Gross, Ella, 17
guerilla marketing, 159
Gulam, Joshua, 130, 139

H&M, 84
halal consumption, 51
Hall, Stuart, 47, 53
Handelman, Jay M., 155, 156, 170
Harold, Christine, 169–170, 175
Harrelson, Woody, 133
Harrison, Rob, 24, 27
Harrop, Elizabeth, 3, 190
hate speech, 32–33, 184
health advocacy, 140–145
Hearn, Alison, 4, 133
Hearst, William Randolph, 55
Heckemeyer, Nicole, 137, 140
Heldman, Caroline, 20, 33
heteronormativity, 75
heterosexism, 75
Heynen, Robert, 132, 140
Ho, Denise, 135, 137
Hogre, 165
Hollows, Joanne, 80–81, 88, 143
homonormativity, 75
Hong Kong
   celebrity advocacy in, 137
   nationalism and consumer activism in, 64–67, 188
hooks, bell, 76, 78
Hosler, Mark, 179
Hough, Julianne, 121
Huawei, 113
human rights, 30–31, 51, 90
humour, 160–161, 180.
   See also play
Humphery, Kim, 23, 153, 185

ideology, 155–156, 167–168
incongruity theory, 160–161
incorporation, 158–159, 177

India, 135, 158
indigenous activism, 123
indigenous environmental justice, 99
individualization and individual action, 5–6, 8, 17–19, 25, 26–27, 38–40
influencers, 124, 133, 146
Institute for Women, 171
intensification, 160
Intergovernmental Panel on Climate Change (IPCC), 98
international relations and development studies, 21
interviews, 111–112, 170–171
Iqani, Mehita, 26–27, 101, 133, 136, 190
Islamophobia, 51

Jallinoja, Piia, 37–38, 106, 111
Jamie Oliver Group, 140–141, 142.
   See also Oliver, Jamie
Jenkins, Henry, 39–40
Jigsaw, 41–42n10
John, Elton, 30–31
Johnson, Boris, 144–145
Johnston, Josée, 22, 82, 92, 111
Jones, Andrew, 126–127
Jordan, Tim, 34–35

Kaepernick, Colin, 42n11
Kellogg Company, 93
Khamis, Susie, 28, 103
Khan, Aamir, 135, 140
Klein, Naomi, 31, 153
Klintman, Mikael, 101–102, 106, 117
Koffman, Ofra, 85, 88
Kostopoulos, Zak, 90, 93
Kozinets, Robert V., 155, 156, 170

Labour behind the Label, 7
labour justice, 7–8, *7*
Lacta, 89–93
Lady Gaga, 121, 135
Lasn, Kalle, 159, 168, 169, 170–171, 179

Lau, Dorothy Wai Sim, 135, 140
Lee, Francis, 156, 188
legality and illegality, 158, 165–167, 168, 177
lesbian, gay, bisexual, transgender, and queer (LGBTQ) communities, 75, 83–84, 89–93
Lewis, Tania, 23, 142
Li Yuchun Fans Charity Fund, 136
Lignadis, Dimitris, 90
Lincoln, Abe, Jr, 171, 172, 174, 175, 177
Littler, Jo
  on anti-consumerism, 23, 156, 169, 170, 180
  on celebrity advocacy, 126, 128–129, 130, 131, 135, 139
  on green consumerism, 101, 103, 104
Live Aid (concert), 125
London Olympics (2012), 151
Look to the Stars (website), 125

Maclaran, Pauline, 79, 86
Madonna, 128
magee, kyle, 165–166
Magubane, Zine, 127, 140
Make It Right (MIR), 130–131
Malababa (magazine), 33
manipulative publicity, 37
Mao Dun, 70n5
market actors, 28–29
mass consumerism, 1–3. *See also* consumer activism
Maxwell, Richard, 29, 108, 112–113, 116, 117, 118
May, Theresa, 161–162, *162*
media ecology, 35–37
media technologies
  environmental consumer activism and, 106–108, 118
  role in consumer activism of, 9–10, 33–40, 187–188
  See also digital technologies
Mediakix, 148n6
Meissner, Miriam, 103, 107, 110–111, 185

methodologies
  anti-consumerism and, 169–171
  celebrity advocacy and, 139–140
  environmental consumer activism and, 110–112
  feminist consumer activism and, 87–89
  nationalism and, 62–64
  See also qualitative methods; quantitative methods; *specific methods*
Meulen, Emily van der, 132, 140
Micheletti, Michele, 20, 25, 79
Mihelj, Sabina, 48, 49, 56, 61, 66
Milam, Jennifer L., 163–164
Miller, Toby, 29, 108, 112–113, 116, 117, 118
Ming, Yao, 135, 136
mixed methods, 63–64, 170–171
MIYAVI, 135
modernism, 50
Modi, Narendra, 158
Montgomery, Robert, 160
Morris, Williams, 55
motherhood, 104–105
Mubarak, Hosni, 158
Mukherjee, Roopali, 23–24, 25, 58–59, 81–82, 129, 140
Mupotsa, Danai, 136, 138, 140
Murphy, Patrick D., 132, 137, 140, 185
Mycoski, Blake, 21
MyDavidCameron.com, 161

National Geographic (magazine), 98
national identity, 48
nationalism
  concept of, 48–50, *49*
  agency and, 187
  consumer activism and, 45–46, 54, 57–58, 67–68
  contradictions in, 183
  critical issues in, 60–62
  future case studies, 67–68
  key theories of, 50–60

methodologies and, 62–64
Yellow Economic Circle (case study), 64–67, 188
See also ethnicity; race
native advertising, 189
Ndaba, Sophie, 136, 140
Negativland, 154, 179
Nelson, Laura, 56–57
neo-colonialism, 85
neoliberalism
  anti-consumerism and, 31–32, 167–168
  celebrity advocacy and, 130–131, 134, 141
  feminism and, 76–78, 81–83, 85, 87, 88
  research on, 9
  See also commodity activism; individualization and individual action
Nestlé, 130
Nike, 34, 42n11
non-governmental organizations (NGOs), 135–136
North/South relations, 10, 133–135, 138, 146–147

Oatly, 28
Obesity Health Alliance, 144
obsolescence, 113
Occupy Movement, 159
Office of the United Nations High Commissioner for Human Rights, 166, 168
Ogilvy, 28, 90–93
Oliver, Jamie, 140–145, 147
One World: Together at Home (virtual concert), 121, 135
online shopping, 1
Orientalism, 47

Pain-Capable Unborn Child Protection Act (2017), 171
Paltrow, Gwyneth, 133
parenting, 104–105
Paris Agreement (COP21), 97
Park, Bo Yun, 60, 61
participant observation, 111–112, 170–171
participation, 158, 161–165, 177

patriotism, 52
#payyourworkers campaign, 7–8, *7*
pedagogy, 158, 161–165, 177
Peñaloza, Lisa, 47, 83
Peoples' Climate Vote, 105
People's Summit Rio+20, 99
Peretti, Jonah, 34
performativity, 79–80
Pezzullo, Phaedra, 111, 185
pink economy, 83–84
Pink Map (Rink), 83
#PinkNotGreen, 73
pinkwashing, 29, 75, 87, 186
Pitt, Brad, 130–131
Pittsburgh Courier (newspaper), 55
planned obsolescence, 113
Plato, 160
play, 158, 160–161, 177
political agency, 25
political consumer nationalism, 56
political consumerism, 9, 20, 22, 23–24, 34, 79–80, 87
political culture jamming, 161–163, *162–163*
political science, 20. *See also* political consumerism; politics of consumption
politics of consumption
  concept of, 3
  anti-consumerism and, 157
  approaches to, 20, 23
  consumer activism and, 69
  environmental consumer activism and, 109
  ethnic and racial injustice and, 58
  feminist consumer activism and, 73, 80–85, 86, 88, 95
  media technologies and, 36–37
  See also political consumerism
Ponte, Stefano, 21, 127, 132, 134, 139

populism, 58
Portwood-Stacer, Laura, 156, 180
post-colonialism, 133–135
post-racism, 77
postfeminism, 76–78, 81, 85, 88
practice theory, 10, 39
A Presidential Parody (campaign), 175
Pretty, Porky, and Pissed Off (PPPO), 82
Primark, 29
primordialism, 50
product placement, 189
programmatic advertising, 32, 189
promotional culture
    concept of, 4
    resistance and, 4–8, *7*, 188–191
promotionalism, 4, 5
Proyecto Squatters, 32
Public Ad Campaign, 172
publicities, 37–38

qualitative methods, 63, 87–89, 140. *See also* case studies; ethnographic methods; textual analysis
quantitative methods, 63
queer activism and theory, 75, 83–84, 89–93, 96

race
    black consumerism 58–59
    concept of, 46–48
    celebrity advocacy and, 134–135, 136, 137, 138–139, 143
    consumer activism and, 58–62, 69
    critical issues in, 60–62
    environmental racism and, 99
    feminist consumer activism and, 80, 85
    See also ethnicity; nationalism
racialized political consumerism, 59, 61, 63
rainbowwashing, 75, 87
recycling, 26–27
RED (Product RED), 21, 127, 132, 139–140

'reduce, reuse, recycle' narratives, 26–27
regressive politics, 9
relief theory, 160–161
religion, 51–52
Repo, Jemima, 84, 87, 94
Resistance is Female, 171–178, *172–173*, *175*
resistance practices, 188–189
responsibilities, 38–40. *See also* individualization and individual action
Reverend Billy and the Church of Stop Shopping, 31, 154–155, 163–164, 170–171
rhetorical analysis, 170
rhizome, 169
Richey, Lisa Ann
    on celebrity advocacy, 125–126, 127–128, 129–130, 132, 134, 139
    on North/South relations, 10
    on RED, 21
Rojek, Chris, 123, 131

sabotage, 160
Sainsbury's, 101
Samsung, 113–114
Sandlin, Jennifer A., 163–164
Santaoja, Minna, 37–38, 111
Schiffer, Claudia, 144
Schor, Juliet, 22, 110, 185
Scott, Martin, 124–125, 129
Seilor, Jordan, 160
Sender, Katherine, 83, 89
sexism, 73, 75
Shen, Yongrong, 82–83, 88, 92
Shift, 117
simplified causes, 131–133, 138, 147
Situationist International (Internationale Situationiste, IS), 156–157
Sklair, Leslie, 155–156, 167–168
slacktivism, 83

Sleeping Giants, 33
smartphone consumption, 188, 190
smartphones, 108, 112–116
Sobande, Francesca, 28, 85
social justice, 187
social movements, 25
socially conscious marketing, 28
sociology, 21–22
South Africa, 136
Spare Rib (magazine), 80–81
Special Patrol Group, 155, 161
spectacles, 156–158, 163–164, 167, 170, 174
Starbucks, 30, 57–58, 130
Stonewall, 29
Stop Funding Hate, 33, 184
street stencil advertising, 166–167, 186–187, *186*
subvertisements (subverted advertisements), 154
Subvertisers International, 31, 152, 155
subvertising
  concept of, 6–7, 31–33, 153, 155
  agency and, 187
  Brandalism and, 151–153, *152*
  civil disobedience and, 165–167
  critical issues in, 167–168
  future case studies, 178
  humour and, 180
  ideology and, 167–168
  methodologies and, 169–171
  #payyourworkers campaign and, 7–8, *7*
  Resistance is Female (case study), 171–178, *172–173*, *175*
  society of spectacle and, 157, 167, 170
  See also culture jamming
superiority theory, 160–161
surveys, 110
sustainable consumption
  concept of, 99–100
  celebrity advocacy and, 30

critical issues in, 109–110, 117–118
future case studies, 116
holidays and, 2–3
key debates on, 98
media technologies and, 107–108
theory of, 101–102, 105–106
See also environmental consumer activism
sustainable consumption and production (SCP), 99
sustainable development, 98–100
sustainable development goals (SDGs), 98, 99
symbolic consumer nationalism, 56
Szasz, Andrew, 102–104, 111

Taipale, Tiina, 105, 108, 110, 112
Tangen, Nicolai, 143
Taylor, Judith, 82, 92
Teracube, 117
textual analysis, 87–88, 110–111, 140, 170–171
Theo Chocolate, 127–128
THINX, 84
Thornton, Kate, 144
Thunberg, Greta, 124, 137
trans rights. *See* Resistance is Female
transgender rights, 84
Treré, Emiliano, 35–36, 37, 107
Trump, Donald, 55, 57, 61–62, 73, 158, 174. *See also* Resistance is Female
Trump, Ivanka, 88, 175
Tsai, Wan-Hsiu Sunny, 81, 84, 87–88
Turner, Graeme, 123, 124

U2, 125
La ultraextensión (browser extension), 32–33
United Nations (UN), 17, 75, 98, 99, 126
United Nations Conference on Environment and Development (Rio Earth Summit, 1992), 99, 100, 101

United Nations Environment
    Programme (UNEP), 118n5,
    118n6, 119n13
United Nations
    Foundation, 88
Universal Negro Improvement
    Association, 59
US Agency for International
    Development, 172
Usher, 121

VAX LIVE: The Concert to
    Reunite the World (concert), 121
veganism, 105–106
Vermibus, 160, 166
Victoria's Secret, 170
visual analysis, 88, 170–171

Wallis, Cara, 82–83, 88, 92
Watson, Emma, 30
Wernick, Andrew, 4, 81
Wettergren, Åsa, 161,
    164, 170–171

Wham! 125
white saviour complex,
    133–134
Wilén, Kristoffer, 105, 108,
    110, 112
Willis, Margaret M., 22, 110, 185
wokewashing, 29, 186
Women's March (2017), 172
Woo-sung, Jung, 135
World Health Organization (WHO),
    74, 121, 145
A World (in support of
    Act Now) (app),
    17–19, *18*
World Meteorological Organization
    (WMO), 118n5
World Press Freedom Index, 89

Xiaomi, 113, 114

Yellow Economic Circle,
    64–67, 188
Yes Men, 154, 170

www.ingramcontent.com/pod-product-compliance
Lightning Source LLC
Chambersburg PA
CBHW070920030426
42336CB00014BA/2461